MILO'S EYES

How a Blind Equestrian and Her "Seeing Eye Horse" Rescued Each Other

LISSA BACHNER

Behler
PUBLICATIONS

USA

Behler Publications

Milo's Eyes
A Behler Publications Book

Library of Congress Cataloging-in-Publication Data

Names: Bachner, Lissa, author.
Title: Milo's eyes : how a blind equestrian and her "seeing eye horse" rescued each other / Lissa Bachner.
Description: USA : Behler Publications, [2022] | Summary: "Lissa Bachner was born with a passion for horses and won her first blue ribbon at age 5. However, blindness struck her in her teens, and it threatened to end her passion for riding. It wasn't until Lissa met Milo, a filthy, emaciated, neglected, horse from Germany, that their instant bond cemented their domination in the jumping ring and their deep friendship outside the ring. As Lissa's eyesight worsened, Milo instinctively knew he had to be her eyes and protect her. This inspirational story of Lissa and 'Magic Milo' is one of going from victim to victor"-- Provided by publisher.
Identifiers: LCCN 2021045051 | ISBN 9781941887103 (trade paperback)
Subjects: LCSH: Bachner, Lissa. | Horsemen and horsewomen--United States--Biography. | Blind athletes--United States--Biography. | Blind women--United States--Biography. | Human-animal relationships. | Horses.
Classification: LCC SF336.B23 A3 2022 | DDC 798.40092
   [B]--dc23/eng/20211103
LC record available at https://lccn.loc.gov/2021045051

Table of Contents

For Marcia Castleman

My hero
best friend
and my mom
because I'm the luckiest person
in the world

CHAPTER ONE

Some people spend a lifetime looking for true love. I am one of the lucky few to discover her heart's desire as a child.

I was only four when I was introduced to my first love, Duke. Many years my senior, Duke was considered rather small in stature, even for a pony, and I had to stand on the tips of my toes to give him a soft pat on his neck.

Duke lived at Deerfield Horse Center, an equestrian facility surrounded by the greenest pastures Virginia had to offer. It just so happened that Deerfield was owned and operated by my mother, so there was never any question where my great passion for horses came from.

Riding was in my blood, and for a year I learned basic horsemanship with Duke. The older kids who rode at the barn taught me the proper way to brush Duke and put tack on him. I rode almost every day, and twice a week I had a lesson with one of the riding instructors in Mom's employ.

My tiny chestnut steed was my world, and I assumed Duke would be mine forever. Unfortunately, soon after my fifth birthday, I was shocked to discover Duke was a loaner pony.

"What do you mean we've only been borrowing Duke?" I tearfully asked my mom.

"It means," she said sympathetically, "he isn't ours and it's time for us to give him back to the family he does belong to."

To make matters worse, Duke's owners were moving away and taking "my" pony with them. One day he was there, sharing an apple with me, and the next day he was gone. Thus, not only had I known love before I was able to write my own name, I also knew heartbreak.

Luckily, within a month, the Duke-shaped hole in my heart was filled by Marshmallow. A white pony with a pink nose, Marshmallow was everything little girls dreamed of.

"Best of all," my mom said, then bent down and whispered in my ear, "she's all yours."

"She's mine?" I gasped. "I never have to give her back?"

My mom shook her head and laughed. "Nope. Never."

Marshmallow was the pony I rode on many of my firsts. I was riding her the first time I jumped a fence. She was my partner on my maiden voyage into the show ring, where I was awarded my first blue ribbon. My first tumble was from her back, and I was riding Marshmallow the first time my mom noticed that I was struggling to see.

"We're riding inside today," Kelly, one of the instructors, announced as she walked by the grooming area where I was doing my best to rid my white pony of the green and brown stains that seemed to grow larger and multiply the more I brushed them.

"Here," Kelly said as she sprayed alcohol on a towel and rubbed each stubborn spot with it. Magically the stains vanished.

"Thank you," I smiled.

"You're welcome. You're running late, do you want some help with the saddle?"

"Yes, please," I nodded vigorously.

"You're usually pretty good about being on time," Kelly said, checking to make sure the girth was safely secured to my saddle, "especially on a lesson day."

"It's raining. The school buses are never on time when it rains."

"Well," Kelly said, giving the saddle a light slap, "Marshmallow is all tacked up and ready to go. I'll meet you in the ring in a few seconds. Be careful, it's busy in there today."

I counted six other horse and rider combinations as I rode Marshmallow into the center of the ring. That wasn't too bad, although each rider was on a gigantic horse that could easily trample Marshmallow and me. I glanced over at the spectators' area and was disappointed not to see my mom. She never missed one of my lessons, especially since I had started jumping.

My lessons always began with walking, trotting, and cantering on the flat. For the most part, the other riders granted me the right of way. Only a few times did I have to weave Marshmallow around the other horses or politely call out, "Heads up, please!" if I felt they were, or had the potential to be, in my way.

Now for the fun part. Pleased with my work on the flat, Kelly lowered one of the fences for me, so it stood about a foot off the ground. It was time to start the jumping portion of my lesson.

I hadn't been jumping for long, three months at the most. Despite being terrified the first time, now all I wanted to do was jump.

Following Kelly's instructions, I trotted Marshmallow up to the fence, gave her a squeeze, and braced myself against her neck as she hopped over the pole. We landed safely on the other side, and as I trotted away from the jump, I heard clapping. Smiling, I swiveled in my saddle, eager to discover the source of the applause.

"Hi, Mom!" I beamed, spotting her standing on the side of the ring closest to her office. She was still clapping but stopped to wave at me and then pointed toward the middle of the ring, wordlessly reminding me that I was in the middle of a lesson.

"Good job," Kelly said approvingly when I returned to her side. "Do you think you can jump this one?" She pointed to a red and white striped fence.

"Okay," I said, already squeezing Marshmallow into a brisk trot. As I had before, I guided Marshmallow toward the fence but there was more than one red and white striped fence, and I couldn't tell which one I was supposed to jump.

They look the same. Maybe it doesn't matter which one I jump. Choosing the fence on the right, I gave Marshmallow a good squeeze just as Kelly yelled, "No!"

Her cry of warning was too late, and as I braced myself against Marshmallow's neck, I realized my mistake.

I felt Marshmallow hesitate and then push off with all of her might, throwing me out of the saddle and onto her neck. I clung to her mane for dear life. No one was clapping for me this time.

Kelly and Mom rushed over to help me right myself in the saddle.

"What were you thinking?" Kelly demanded. "That fence was much too big for you. Are you trying to kill yourself? And what about Marshmallow? Did you even think about her? She could have been badly hurt. That fence is over two feet, much too big for either of you."

"I...I'm s...s...sorry." The words fell from my trembling lips in between sobs. "They looked the same."

Kelly took a breath, but my mom stopped her before she could lambaste me again.

"What looked the same?" my mom asked. "These two fences?" She turned around and pointed. I nodded, but now that I was close to them, I could see the fences looked nothing alike. The one I was supposed to jump was a single rail, low to the ground. The fence I had jumped was higher and wider, and decorated with pine brush and flower boxes at each end.

"I..." I paused, confused that I had ever thought the two fences were interchangeable, and terribly embarrassed because everyone in the ring was staring at me. I wondered what I could possibly say that would put me back in Mom and Kelly's good graces. Finally, with my eyes fixed on Marshmallow's mane, I exhaled shakily and for the second time said, "They looked the same."

"Do they look the same to you now?" my mom asked with an unfamiliar bite to her voice. "Do they?" she asked again, this time the urgency in her voice making me squirm in my saddle.

"No," I answered quickly.

Without taking her eyes off me, my mom took six comically large steps backward. I would have laughed had I not been so frightened and dismayed by her actions. She stopped when she was about twenty-five feet from me.

"Can you see me?" she asked.

I nodded while simultaneously mouthing, "Yes."

"Good," she replied.

I relaxed a little, relieved that my answers had been acceptable. I waited quietly for as long as I could bear, no more than thirty seconds, before I timidly asked, "May I take Marshmallow back to her stall?"

I was staring at my mother who had yet to move or say anything. She was so immersed in her thoughts, I had to repeat myself twice.

"What?" she asked, finally acknowledging me. Again, I asked to be excused from the ring and this time she replied, "Yes, but make sure you brush Marshy thoroughly before putting her away."

I did as I was told, choosing to remain with Marshmallow in her stall until my mom found me, nearly an hour later.

"Ready to go?" she asked.

I picked up the brushes I had used to erase the marks left by my small saddle and followed my mother out of the stall.

Something was still bothering her. I could tell by the way her index finger tapped against the car's steering wheel as she drove us home. She said very little and, concerned that she may still be upset with me, I did nothing to disrupt the silence.

We came to an intersection and as the car rolled to a stop, she turned her head and focused her attention on me.

Summoning my courage, I dared to ask my mother, "Are you still mad at me?"

"Mad at you? Why would I be mad at you?"

Did she forget so soon? Loathe to remind her of the incident, I wished I hadn't brought it up. But she was waiting expectantly for an answer and so, cheeks burning, I mumbled, "Because I jumped the wrong fence."

"No," she was quick to comfort me. "I'm not upset with you at all. I never was. You frightened me though, and it concerns me that you couldn't tell those two jumps apart."

"When I got up close to them, I could see the difference," I reminded her. This seemed to trouble her even more and, once again, I found myself wishing I had kept my mouth shut.

"Have you noticed a change in your vision?" she asked.

"Change?" I replied, not fully grasping what she was asking.

"Has your eyesight gotten worse or a little blurry?"

"Oh. I think my eyes are the same as they always are." For good measure, I closed my eyes and pressed my fingers against my lids. They felt the same, at least.

"Hmm," was all my mom had to say.

Home was less than a mile away when the car slowed to a crawl and Mom pointed at something in front of us.

"Look at the deer," she breathed, in awe of the exquisite buck standing in the middle of the road. "There are the babies," she pointed to the woods where three fawns were emerging followed by their mother.

Always eager to witness any form of wildlife, especially deer, my eyes flew to the spot my mom was pointing to.

"Where?" I asked excitedly.

"A little to our left now," she replied. "About fifty feet in front of us."

"I don't see them. Did they go back into the woods?"

"No, they're still in the road," she assured me, "right there." Taking my chin between her fingers, she positioned my head so the family of deer was directly in my line of view. "Now do you see them?"

I shook my head. "No."

Lifting her foot off the brake pedal, she allowed the car to roll forward, stopping every few feet to ask, "Now?" When we were roughly twenty-five feet away, I was able to catch a glimpse of the stag leaping into the thick underbrush.

"I see him!" I yelped triumphantly. "I guess the babies are already across the road with their mommy." I turned toward my own mother for affirmation, but what I saw banished all thoughts of woodland creatures from my mind. My mom, her head bent low, was crying.

Within a week, I was taken to my pediatrician who, in turn, sent me to an ophthalmologist. After a thirty-minute exam, the doctor shook his head and scribbled a number on his prescription pad. It was a referral to another doctor who, like his predecessors, was unable to confirm a diagnosis.

I would see two more specialists before a pediatric ophthalmologist in Washington, DC, diagnosed me as having uveitis, an immune disorder often triggered by a juvenile form of rheumatoid arthritis.

"The good news," the doctor said, smiling at my mom, "is that children tend to outgrow the disease. By the time she's eighteen, the immune disorder will probably be virtually nonexistent."

The word "disease" sent a chill through me. This sounded worse than being stupid or careless. Suddenly, I was abnormal.

I stayed silent while the grown-ups continued to discuss my future as if I weren't in the room.

"Will her vision be restored at that point?" asked my mom. Her question hung awkwardly in the silence that followed.

At last, the doctor replied, "If there's any vision left, hopefully the disease will stop attacking her eyes."

I had not understood everything my mother and the doctor were talking about, but I did understand his last words. I was not normal and might never see again.

The hoped-for quick fix—some eye drops, perhaps an adorable pair of children's glasses—was not to be. Instead, my vision problems would, from this day on, consume our lives. We were sent to a uveitis specialist at the Massachusetts Eye and Ear

Infirmary in Boston who surgically removed the lenses in my eyes. I was given a pair of glasses with lenses so thick and heavy that I couldn't stop them from sliding down my nose.

The first time I wore them, I wept from sheer frustration but stopped when the tears made my eyes burn. I hated my new glasses and threw them against the wall hoping to crack them in half. They were so strong, and I ended up doing more damage to the wall than to the glasses.

"Please don't make me wear these," I begged my mom. I had been home from the hospital for a week and was still refusing to wear the glasses, even though without them the world had been reduced to a blur of color and movement.

"Put your glasses on and you'll be able to see better than you did before," she remarked calmly. Ultimately, I did, and she was right, but at what a cost.

In school, my fellow first-graders bullied and mocked me, dubbing me "the four-eyed freak." Once I'd been surrounded by friends, but overnight they deserted me. It was bad enough that I had been absent during our long search for answers about my vision, but to return so drastically altered was the kiss of death for my six-year-old social status. Now, I ate alone in the cafeteria. I also sat alone in class in a front row seat where the teacher could keep an eye on me. I was never picked as a partner, and whichever child was unlucky enough to be paired with me received sympathetic glances from our classmates.

The only place I could find any peace was in the barn, surrounded by horses. All that was wrong in my world was left behind and forgotten the moment I stepped through the barn door.

Lugging a bag of carrots that weighed more than I did, I would walk down the barn's aisle, stopping at each stall until every horse had been given a kind word and a snack. They never shied away from me; instead, they welcomed me into their stalls, grateful for my attention as well as for the treats I brought them.

Horses remained the only friends in my life as I endured a series of medical procedures until, one day after a painful surgery, I was given a rabbit puppet, whom I named George. From that moment on, George accompanied me everywhere, even into operating rooms. When I awoke in the recovery room, Mom and George would be waiting for me at my bed, both waving at me enthusiastically.

Both of my eyes were affected by the disease, but my left eye was deteriorating at a much faster rate than my right. Eventually, all I could see out of my left eye was light and movement, so whenever my right eye was patched post-surgery, I had no useful vision. On those occasions, my mother would read to me from a book she had treasured since her childhood. It was called *There Was a Horse,* and its faded cover and yellowing paper enhanced the magical stories tucked inside. The author had compiled fairy tales from around the world, all with a common theme — magical steeds that rescued children and could fly or talk or stamp the ground so hard the earth opened up beneath them.

On my thirteenth birthday, the retina in my left eye detached and I was rushed to the Wilmer Eye Institute in Baltimore.

"Years of inflammation and previous surgeries have severely weakened the eye," my doctor told my mom while a nurse prepared me for surgery. "Even if I can reattach the retina, chances are slim that it will hold."

After surgery, I spent the night in the hospital for observation. The doctor checked on me the next morning before releasing me back into the world.

"Remember, it's very important that you stay as still as possible for the next three days," he warned before he left the room.

So, all I have to do for the next three days is sit in front of a TV and sleep? I can do that.

Easier said than done. Hospitals are gigantic Petri dishes for every bacteria, bug, and germ. During my short stay, I picked up a nasty stomach flu and was already violently ill before making it home.

I'll never know whether it was my illness or fate that doomed the surgery, but fail it did. Four days later, I returned to Wilmer, where my doctor peeled the patch off my eye and, pointing toward the examination chair, told me to have a seat.

The first exam after eye surgery is always the worst. Sticky and swollen lids are pried apart and held open, while a still sore and extremely sensitive eye must endure a lengthy exam. Although this exam didn't take long at all, after five minutes, the doctor shook his head and said, "I'm sorry, it didn't hold. There's nothing we can do."

Oddly, what I found most catastrophic was that I'd never again see out of my left eye. It had been useless for quite some time, and I had come to terms with that already. What terrified me was knowing the same disease that had destroyed my left eye was also invading my right eye. Now, at the age of thirteen, I understood that this disease meant more than painful operations, nasty medications, and ugly magnifying glasses. It was a thief that was literally robbing me blind.

It was only natural to conclude that life was not fair. What made it harder was that none of my friends could understand what I was going through. The worst thing they experienced was wearing braces, which I had to wear, too. I had no one to talk to. Alone and afraid, I was struggling through life.

The children within the pages of *There Was a Horse* also experienced the world as an unjust and lonely place. They, too, knew suffering, but with the help of a horse, they survived. So one day, not long after I lost the use of my left eye, I began to wish for a magic horse.

"Like the ones in my book," I would say, after every penny tossed into a wishing well, as I blew out the candles on my birthday cakes, and each time I ended up with the larger half of a wish bone.

After all, I wasn't that different from the heroes in my book. I, too, needed a horse that could join me in battle against the monsters that threatened to darken my future.

Luckily, as I matured, so did the treatment of uveitis. Procedures and medications became more advanced and my right eye, although severely scarred, managed to provide enough vision for me to legally drive.

The disease forced many changes in my life. I was twenty-five when my left eye had to be removed and replaced with a prosthetic. Throughout years of trauma and uncertainty, the one constant, my passion for horses, grew even more fervent. The only question I would ask my doctor after surgery was, "How long until I can ride?" If the answer was two weeks, I was astride a horse in one. A one-week recovery period was often shortened to four days.

If love conquered all, then the sooner I returned to my horses, my faithful friends who always welcomed me, the better.

CHAPTER TWO

"Do you really have to leave? Can't you wait until after midnight?" Sarah urged as she followed me into the bathroom. We'd been best friends for twenty years and had spent many a New Year's Eve together. Neither of us was dating anyone, so we'd decided to go disco bowling at a new, upscale alley.

But as the hours sped by, I became more and more anxious. I glanced at my watch just as the hour hand hit eleven. We both knew that I had another date waiting to ring in 1999 with me — an exciting new male who had traveled thousands of miles to join his life with mine.

"You know I wouldn't leave if I didn't have to," I said, genuinely regretful but firm about keeping my date. "But he's due to arrive around midnight and I really want to be there."

"I'm aware," Sarah sighed. "It's all you've talked about for a week." A rider herself, Sarah had been very tolerant of my incessant ramblings about my new horse. Purchased on nothing more than the recommendation of my trainer, Bob Crandall, I had yet to lay eyes on the animal.

"Did you ask Bob for a better description of him?" Sarah asked. "He was in such a hurry when he called you about the horse, he forgot to tell you what he looks like."

I grinned. "In his defense, Bob was in Germany when he called. I had to wait for more details until he was back in Maryland."

"And?" Sarah asked, taking a sip of champagne.

"I know he's a gelding. I believe Bob told me he turns five this year. He's on the small side, just under sixteen hands, and has a dark brown coat, a black mane and tail, and a white star on his forehead." I paused, trying to remember what else I had been told about him. "Oh, he has a little white on one of his legs, but I can't remember which one."

Swinging my backpack, now full of evening wear, over my shoulder, I teased, "I think you want me to stay here so you'll have somebody to kiss at midnight. Even if it's only a friendly peck on the cheek."

"Not true," Sarah protested. "I just never get to see you anymore, and I thought we could catch up tonight."

I gave her a look that said, *I don't believe you.* "Fine," Sarah muttered, "I need someone to kiss at midnight, even if it's you."

"You could always come with me." Sarah was my only friend who had ever received such an invitation. She appreciated the sanctity of a barn full of horses, and I wouldn't mind her sharing my first meeting with my new horse.

"Are you kidding?" Sarah said, clearly horrified. "It's only ten degrees outside!"

"Oh, believe me," I said, pulling at the layers of clothing I had exchanged for my little red dress, "I know how cold it is." I gave Sarah a hug goodbye and wished her Happy New Year, then fished my car keys out of my pocket and drove off into the darkness.

For as long as I could remember, my life had revolved around horses. I'd sacrificed my summer vacations to accommodate a full riding competition schedule.

Friendships had withered from neglect while I happily spent all my free time at the barn.

As for love, I'd spent my teen years at all-girl schools and hadn't truly started dating until college. Although I learned to overcome my shyness, once I was in a relationship, it didn't take long for my boyfriend to realize that horses came first.

"Which is probably why I am, once again, alone on New Year's Eve," I mumbled as I merged onto the beltway. I was momentarily intimidated by the dark road that stretched ahead.

At least there wasn't any traffic. Most people must have been at New Year's Eve parties, and I soon noticed that my speedometer was nearing eighty. Slowing to a more reasonable speed, I chastised myself for being so reckless. My night vision was, at best, poor, and with only one eye, I probably shouldn't have been driving at all.

You'd think this was your first horse. In fact, over the years I had owned several ponies and horses. I had been ecstatic with each new arrival and devastated every time I outgrew or had to retire one. I had loved them all, though when it was time to say goodbye, I vowed never to love another as much.

In years past, the American Thoroughbred horse had dominated not only the racetrack but also the equestrian show jumping ring. But recently, the world of equestrian competition had bypassed the more fragile thoroughbred in favor of powerful European horses, bred for strength and agility, like the one I was so anxious to meet.

"He's a diamond in the rough," Bob had said persuasively over the phone from Germany three weeks ago. "He could use a lot of TLC, but I felt so much potential when I rode him. I know with some care and training he's going to be a winner."

I had a lot of respect for Bob's opinion. Along with being an excellent rider and trainer, he had a solid reputation as a dealer who could choose the right horse for its new owner. So, when he asked me to trust him, I took a leap of faith and bought the horse sight unseen.

I finally turned into the long driveway that led to the farm. Bob would be here at any moment, and I decided to wait for him in the barn.

Normally, I arrived at the barn by eight in the morning and helped him set up for the day. He had twelve horses under his care. Some belonged to him and others belonged to his clients, but he loved each and every one of them and referred to them as his "babies."

Because I had a fairly flexible schedule working part-time for my stepfather, I was able to pitch in when Bob needed a hand. This generally involved grooming the horses, keeping tack clean and in good repair, and replacing supplies like brushes and shampoo.

I hated to leave the warmth of my car, but it couldn't compare to the prospect of finally laying hands on my new horse. I jumped out of the car and rushed toward the barn, hurtling myself against the sliding door until, after a few shoves, I created an opening just large enough to slide through.

There, I was enveloped in tranquil darkness. It was intoxicating being inside a barn at night, breathing in the scent of fresh hay. Without the distraction of the barn's daytime activities, I could focus on the subtle sounds coming from the stalls. Winter blankets rustled as the occupants lazily moved about in search of hay. I could hear horses scraping against feed tubs, sniffing for leftovers. Others slurped water from buckets. They were creating such an enchanting symphony, I hesitated to disturb them.

During normal business hours, the barn was my second home. Now, as I stood in the darkness, I felt like an intruder as I flicked on the fluorescent lights and heard the pitter-patter of tiny rodent feet scurrying to their hidden holes.

Suddenly, I was grabbed from behind and a male voice boomed, "Hey!"

"Oh my God!" I shrieked, turning around to see a man of medium build and height grinning down at me. Regaining my composure, I laughed, "You're such an ass, Bob." Then I smiled at him and said, "But Happy New Year anyway."

"Same to you, my blossom."

If not for Bob's prematurely graying hair, no one would guess he was in his mid-forties. Not a single wrinkle lined his face, and his powder blue eyes sparkled with youth and mischief. As annoying as he could be sometimes — bossy, officious, moody — we'd become friends in the nine months I'd been training with him.

Now, while others were toasting the New Year, we were in a barn in our down parkas and warm boots, waiting for two horses from Germany. Bob had another client who had purchased a horse, but she had opted out of spending her New Year's Eve in a stable.

Just as the cold began to penetrate my core and numb the tips of my toes, we heard gravel crunching beneath heavy tires and the unmistakable squeal of brakes.

We hurried to the van and walked up the ramp into the dark interior. It was difficult to clearly see the two occupants, so I grabbed one horse's halter while Bob took the other and we carefully led them out.

The horse I was leading was bundled in blankets that stank of urine and sweat. He was skittish and snorted as we walked from the van to the barn. It was clear that he hated the chain around his nose, but I didn't dare take it off. All I could do was try to soothe him by patting him and running my hand down the length of his dirt-encrusted neck.

Don't panic, I'm sure this one isn't mine.

Once inside the barn, the horse continued snorting, only now it sounded like he was hyperventilating. Concerned, I put him in one of the stalls designated for the new horses, expecting that with two fresh buckets of water, some fluffy shavings for bedding, and a few squares of hay, he'd settle down. Usually, a horse will look for some source of food in its stall, but this piteous animal was far too frightened. All he could do was stand by the wall, trembling.

I decided to give him some time to himself and walked to the stall where Bob was removing the other horse's halter. This horse was also travel-worn, but in far better shape than his companion. He wore a new blanket and seemed fairly clean. Yes, he was a tad bug-eyed, but his breathing wasn't coming in short spurts and he certainly wasn't shaking.

When Bob came out of the stall, I blurted, "Please tell me that the train wreck at the other end of the barn isn't mine."

When he responded with a grin, I knew that the train wreck did, in fact, belong to me. Then, becoming serious, he said, "He is not a train wreck. He's just scared, exhausted, and trying to cope with his new surroundings."

"Look, I understand that he's been through a lot in the past week, but this horse," I said, pointing to the one in front of me, "seems pretty calm. The Reillys have never seen him, and they'll never know if we just...switch them."

Bob stared at me, dumbfounded. "Lissa, I can't believe you'd even suggest such a thing. No way would I do that. These two horses are completely different."

I turned away, feeling trapped, embarrassed, and frustrated. What had I gotten myself into?

"Just trust me," Bob called out as I went to check on the horse I was stuck with, hoping he hadn't passed out. As I began to resign myself to the idea that this quivering animal was mine, my nurturing instincts took hold and I decided to try to bond with him. I approached him slowly and spoke to him softly, and, to my relief, he began to calm down.

During the next hour, I brushed away layers of filth from his coat, feeling his thin body tense every time I moved the brush to a new position. Eventually he relaxed, seeming to enjoy the attention, until I moved on to another area. As I removed the grime, I was appalled to see spur rubs and whip marks all over his body. I applied medication to the wounds and whispered to him, "What did they do to you?"

Poor thing. I began to wipe his face with a towel. It was then that I noticed the color of his eyes: burnished mahogany melting into amber, then turning a velvety brown in the center. As I stared into the depths of his eyes, I sensed his fear and distrust. But beneath that, I perceived a glimmer of hope.

With the back of my hand, I gently smoothed the worried creases around his eyes and, this time, he didn't shy away from me. Instead, he lowered his head and I smiled up at him.

"You've been through a lot in a short time, haven't you, boy? I have, too," I said quietly. "I guess that makes us survivors. We do what we have to do to get through. Maybe you are supposed to be my horse, after all.

"I think it's time you had a name." I took a step backward so I could regard all of him. "Hmm," I cupped my chin in the palm of my hand while I attempted to conjure the perfect name. He stood still, never taking his eyes off me.

I began listing some of my favorite literary characters.

"Hamlet?" I asked him. "He was wise beyond his years and, like you, tormented, but in a different way. Maybe not," I vetoed the name.

"Heathcliff?" I mused. "He was a complex character, not unlike yourself."

My new horse looked unimpressed.

"You're right," I agreed. "Besides, that name has already been taken by a cartoon cat."

Suddenly, the name was right before me. I had always been partial to the political satire of the comic strip *Bloom County*, and I especially loved the young star of the series, Milo.

"Milo," I said, trying the name on for size. I allowed it to resonate before saying it again. "Milo," and this time, the horse's ears twitched at the sound of my voice.

"I like it," I said, smiling with satisfaction. "Hello, Milo. You and I have a long road ahead of us, but I promise, no matter what, you will never know cruelty again."

Early the next morning, armed with carrots, apples, and new blankets, I ventured out to visit my new horse, determined to win him over. Only a handful of people were in the barn, allowing Milo and me some quiet time to get acquainted.

I frowned as Milo immediately scooted to the back of his stall when I entered his domain. Disappointed, but not surprised, I knew it would take a while for him to learn to trust me, which was precisely why I brought so many treats. I knew the fastest way to a horse's heart was through his stomach and I suspected that Milo was no exception. I held an apple under his chin and waited.

"It's okay," I urged. "Try a bite."

Milo sniffed and snorted at the apple, but he was too suspicious to sink his teeth into it.

"I guess your former owners weren't big on treats," I observed sadly. "Let's try it this way." I bit off a smaller, less intimidating piece of apple and offered it.

Milo took a few steps toward me and stretched his neck out as far as he could. I didn't dare move as I felt his warm breath on my hand. He stared at me, clearly tempted but still hesitant.

"You'll like it," I tried to sound convincing. He took one step closer to me and his nose disappeared into my cupped hand. His teeth gently scraped against my skin as he took the apple into his mouth.

Milo's eyes closed in ecstasy and pools of white slobber began to form at the corners of his mouth. He chewed slowly, savoring every bite.

"There you go, Milo," I said merrily and bit off another piece of apple. This time, the juicy morsel was slurped up immediately. "Well, aren't you the clever one," I grinned and repeated the routine until the apple was gone.

After Milo devoured a second apple, he cocked his head and looked at me as if to say, "What else do you have for me?"

I left to retrieve a few carrots from the bag I had dropped outside the stall. Again, Milo scooted to the back of it when I walked in.

"We need to work on this," I told him as I coaxed him over to me, proffering the treat.

He took it from me, but this time, instead of standing with him while he chewed, I walked out of the stall. I waited until the crunching stopped and then returned with another carrot. I repeated the exercise until finally, after thirty minutes, Milo was greeting me at the stall door in anticipation of his next snack.

"What's going on in here?" Bob asked, poking his head into the stall.

"We," I said contentedly, giving Milo a pat, "are getting to know each other."

"I told you he was special. You see it now, don't you?"

"Yes," I replied, unable to suppress a smile, "I most certainly do."

"I take it you don't want to swap him out for a different horse anymore?" Bob joked.

"Nope," I blushed while feeding another hunk of carrot to Milo. "I think he's a keeper."

"Wait until you watch him under tack," Bob said excitedly. "In fact, why don't you start getting him ready for me. He'll be the first horse I ride today."

"Okay," I replied, delighted at the prospect of seeing my new horse in action.

As a professional horse trainer, Bob not only rode and trained his clients' horses, he also made most of the decisions concerning their welfare and who would ride them and when. Bob had warned that despite my long experience with horses, it would be a while before I could ride Milo because he was only five and would require much more training than an older horse. Bob promised that once I was riding and competing on Milo, it would be well worth the wait. For now, I would have to be satisfied with being Milo's groom.

Milo was calm as I led him to the nearest grooming area, but when I clipped his halter to one of the stationary ties, he reeled backward, breaking the connection.

"Whoa, Milo, you're okay," I said just before he knocked over a bucket of brushes. The racket startled him and he vaulted forward, almost crushing me. When he realized that he was about to trample me, he came to a shuddering halt in front of me. His expressive eyes had gone from soft and relaxed to frenzied and terrified.

Hearing the commotion, Bob came running around the corner to make sure that I wasn't hurt.

"I'm fine," I assured him, keeping my voice low and calm.

Milo's nostrils flared and his body shook but I made no move to touch him, waiting until his breathing returned to normal. When the worried arc around his eyes began to relax, I reached my hand out to him. After a few snorts, Milo took a deep breath and began to lick my outstretched palm. Only then did I speak to him.

"You're not in any trouble, Milo," I promised. "You're a good boy."

"What was that about?" Bob asked as he walked up to me.

I was so entirely focused on Milo, I had forgotten Bob was there. "He was spooked by the crossties and knocked the bucket over."

Bob looked down at the brushes scattered across the concrete floor. He began picking them up as Milo watched anxiously.

"Okay, Milo, we're going to try this again," I said, reaching for a crosstie. I waited for Bob to step out of the way before slowly bringing the nylon rope as close as I could to Milo's halter and holding it there.

"Good boy," I said and patted his cheek. I reached into my pocket and pulled out a piece of carrot, which Milo happily accepted. While he chewed, I easily snapped the tie onto his halter.

"We'll have to work on that some more," Bob said. "For now, tack him up so we can see how he reacts to being ridden."

I chose a rubber curry comb and ran the brush in small circles all over Milo's body. Horses tend to enjoy being curried, since it not only loosens dirt and hair, but done properly, it also gives them a good back scratch. Milo's upper lip quivered each time I drew the brush down his neck to his withers and across his back.

Bob rejoined us as I was placing the cool metal bit into Milo's mouth. "Ready?" he asked, obviously eager to demonstrate Milo's talents.

"One more second," I replied, adjusting the bridle. "All set," I said, finally satisfied with how it fit Milo's head. I was about to hand Milo's reins over to Bob but changed my mind. Although I wouldn't be riding him, I wanted to be the one to lead Milo to the ring for the first time.

We walked over to the indoor arena where Bob usually rode during the winter, and I continued to hold onto Milo until Bob mounted him and was grasping the reins firmly. Then I moved to the side of the ring where I could have an unobstructed view of Milo's first ride in America.

I was pleasantly surprised to see how relaxed Milo appeared. He carried his head low, his neck swaying back and forth as he walked. Bob allowed Milo to familiarize himself with the ring before he took a firmer hold of the reins and used the tips of his spurs to nudge Milo into a trot.

Milo tensed immediately, his body becoming rigid, his neck stiffening. His once relaxed pace was now erratic, and the more Bob patted his neck, calmly repeating, "Whoa," the more stressed Milo became.

"He seemed fine ten seconds ago," I observed, baffled by Milo's behavior.

"He was fine, until he thought I was going to make him do something," Bob replied, still trying to calm Milo down.

An idea struck me, and I approached them. "Hold on a second."

"What are you doing?" Bob asked, pulling back on the reins and bringing Milo to a halt.

"I think those might be part of the problem." I pointed at Bob's spurs. "There," I said, pulling the spurs off Bob's boots. "See if he's any better without them."

The change in Milo was dramatic, and within minutes, his trot was slow and his pace even.

"How does he feel to you?" I asked. "He looks more settled. Maybe not a hundred percent, but getting there."

"Much improved, you're right," Bob acknowledged. "Before we took the spurs off, he felt like he was holding his breath."

Glancing at the nasty marks on Milo's side, I said, "I don't blame him."

Bob didn't want to push Milo too hard on his first day, so I was treated to an abbreviated example of his walk, trot, and canter.

"Wow!" I exclaimed as Bob cantered a large circle around me.

"I know," Bob replied proudly. "His canter is what originally caught my eye."

Milo's canter was graceful and balanced, which made him appear to be floating across the ground. "It feels amazing," Bob grinned as he brought Milo down to a walk.

"I can only imagine," I said wistfully. I rushed over to take the reins from Bob as he slid off Milo's back.

"I know you can't wait to ride him. Just be patient. Before you know it, he'll be ready for you."

"Okay," I said more agreeably than I felt. I turned away from him to make a fuss over Milo.

Bob saw through my bravado and put a friendly arm around my shoulder. "I warned you that he was a young horse and wasn't ready for you yet."

"Yes, you did. But how would you feel if you bought a really special car, only to be told that you couldn't drive it?"

"I understand how you feel, but if today's ride was any indication, I think Milo is going to prove to be a very fast learner, and you'll be in the driver's seat in no time."

I smiled up at Bob and gave my newly-proclaimed genius horse a pat on the cheek. Before he left us for his next horse, Bob gave me a quick hug. "This will be a journey for all of us," he said. "I can't do it without you. I need you to do all of the groundwork with Milo. His transformation begins with you."

From that moment on, I took my job as Milo's groom very seriously. I brushed him constantly. The muscles in my arm actually grew from my efforts. It took weeks, but one morning a sunbeam cut a path into Milo's stall, and I saw his coat burst into brilliant, glistening waves of light.

"He must have shed all of his dead hair overnight," I said excitedly to Bob, whom I had dragged over to behold Milo's metamorphosis. "Look at him. He's beautiful."

Bob chuckled. "You do good work."

Heartened, I redoubled my grooming efforts. I poured flaxseed oil over Milo's food to further improve his coat and doused his skin with vitamin E to help erase his scars. Not only did they disappear, but I had the softest cuticles in town.

The flaxseed oil was also helping Milo put on some much-needed weight. "I've had to buy two bigger girths for him already," I told Bob one morning while I was tacking Milo up.

I still had not been offered the chance to ride Milo, but the previous week, Bob told me that Milo was close to being ready. Thrilled as I was, I had to admit that I loved watching Bob ride Milo, especially over jumps.

While they were warming up, I thought back to the first time Bob jumped my new horse for me. Milo trotted to the poles — only twelve inches off the ground — then sprang into the air, taking Bob by surprise and almost dislodging him.

I had doubled over with laughter, tears streaming down my face, when I managed to gasp, "Perhaps you should try that again."

Bob righted himself and shot back, "Well, at least you know he can jump high." Bob looked at the one-foot jump. "It felt like he was four feet over that."

"At the very least," I confirmed proudly.

Bob circled back and trotted to the fence, and again Milo reacted as if the jump were on fire. "I'm starting to understand why you don't want me to ride him yet," I joked. Though younger horses have a tendency to "overjump" the fences, Milo jumped higher than any other horse I'd seen.

Bob had to jump the same fence four more times before Milo apparently decided that it wouldn't hurt him. After a month, Milo was still overjumping, but not as high as he was at first.

Later, while I was brushing the saddle marks from Milo's back, I took extra time to rub down his muscles. "You were a good boy today," I told him and reached for my bag of carrots. "I'm so proud of you."

Breaking the carrot in half, I watched him inhale the first piece and then beg for the second. Twisting his neck and pursing his lips, Milo began to nudge me until I gave in and fed him the rest. At that moment, I understood the biggest change in Milo in the past month. He was happy. When we were together, he was relaxed and even playful.

I was suddenly overwhelmed by love for my little horse and threw my arms around him. Instead of pulling away from me, Milo laid his head on my shoulder and, as only a horse can, hugged me back.

CHAPTER THREE

Despite a chilly beginning, spring had finally arrived. Thanks to the extra hours of daylight, I could spend more time at the barn, which meant more time with Milo.

I had gotten a late start on this May morning and was rushing through Milo's extensive, usually calm grooming ritual. Clearly annoyed by my hurried brushing, Milo pinned back his ears and shook his head at me. "Sorry, boy," I said, "I couldn't get out of bed."

When Milo was ready for the saddle, I looked for it on the rack where Bob usually left it, but it was nowhere to be found.

"Bob," I called out, "where's your saddle?"

There was no response, which I thought strange considering he had walked past me and into the tack room two minutes ago.

"Where'd he go?" I murmured to Milo, giving his back a final wipe with a towel.

"Where'd who go?" a voice behind me parroted.

"You disappeared on me," I said, turning to face Bob. "Which saddle do you want to use?"

It was then that I noticed he had a small, flat saddle slung over one arm. "There's no way that saddle is big enough for you," I said. "Did you grab the wrong one?"

"No. This is the right one."

Bob was up to something, but I took the saddle from him anyway. Once it was in my hands, I knew exactly who it belonged to.

"I don't understand," I said. "Why do you want me to put my saddle on Milo?"

"Well, you're welcome to use mine," Bob began, "but I thought you'd be more comfortable riding in your own tack."

"You want me to ride Milo?"

"Yes, isn't that what I just said?"

I looked at Bob and then to Milo who was waiting patiently for me to finish tacking him up. "What if I ruin him? You've put so much time and effort into Milo's training. What if I make a mistake and undo all of it?"

Exasperated, Bob retrieved the saddle and for a moment, I feared that he had changed his mind.

"I have to say," Bob said as he placed a quilted pad and then my saddle on Milo's back, "I thought you'd be more excited than this."

"Oh, no, I'm beyond excited. But I'm also very nervous."

"Well, don't be," Bob ordered. "You're not going to ruin Milo. I've spent so much time with him so you *can* make mistakes. Besides, I'll be with you the whole time. So hurry up and put your hat and chaps on."

That was all the encouragement I needed. I fairly skipped into the tack room where I quickly readied myself to ride.

"How does he feel?" Bob asked once I was on and walking Milo around the ring.

"Different," I replied, searching for the right word. "He's much wider than I thought he would be."

Milo was not a tall horse, but what he lacked in height he made up for in mass. His body, from shoulder to tail, was short and round. One could say Milo was shaped like a barrel, which is exactly what I felt like I was riding.

"He isn't wide," Bob replied defensively.

"Of course, you wouldn't think so," I laughed. "Your legs are twice as long as mine."

"All right," Bob's stern tone was an indication that it was time to get to work. "When you're ready, start trotting. Now...does he still feel wide?"

"No," I said in awe of the graceful animal underneath me. "He's actually very comfortable."

Bob gave me some instructions while Milo and I trotted around the ring, but for the most part he was quiet, allowing me to enjoy the ride.

When Milo began to canter, I finally understood what Bob had been raving about.

"Wow," I gasped as Milo's powerful hind end pushed us into the three-beat pace. His stride was long and fluid, his rhythm unchanging. If I closed my eyes, I could pretend I was flying.

"Well?" Bob asked when I brought Milo back down to a walk. "Was it worth the wait?"

"I can't stop smiling," I told Bob breathlessly.

"I'll take that as a 'yes,'" he grinned.

After Milo had cooled off, I walked him to the wash rack for a sudsy bath and let him stand in the sun to dry. Then I rubbed his entire body with a towel until the little hairs that ran along his back stood on end.

"You know, Milo, as much fun as it is to ride you, I have to admit that this part of the day is my favorite." As Milo's rider, the fear of making a mistake in front of Bob made it impossible for me to completely relax. As his groom, it was just the two of us and I knew exactly what to do to make him glow from head to tail.

In response, Milo rested his chin on my shoulder and closed his eyes.

"One day he's going to answer you," Bob said, walking over to us. "Frankly, I wouldn't be surprised, since he seems to understand everything you tell him."

I smiled, knowing Bob was right.

"By the way, you did a nice job with him today," Bob said warmly as he ran his hand down Milo's sleek neck.

"Thank you," I beamed. Praise from Bob was rare.

We were silent for a moment, then Bob said, "You know, there's a horse show being held here in two weeks."

I nodded. The facility where Bob worked held an annual spring horse show. Signs for it had been posted on every available space and several workers had already begun sprucing up the place.

"How would you feel about entering Milo?" Bob went on. "We couldn't ask for a more convenient location."

"What division were you thinking of riding him in?"

"There's a division meant for less experienced horses that will have smaller jumps and less technical courses. I think that one would suit Milo perfectly."

"Are you sure he's ready?" I asked, taking a protective step closer to Milo. "We've only had him for four months. What if it's too soon, and he gets scared?"

"Trust me," Bob said confidently. "Not only is he ready to start competing, he's also ready to start winning."

I loved the challenge of competing, but I didn't want to do anything to upset the progress we'd made with Milo. I wasn't ready to give Bob a definitive answer. Instead, I said, "You know I trust you, but I need a minute to think."

I returned a now-dry Milo to his stall. When I freed him from his leather halter, he gave his head a shake so vigorous that his ears made a loud thwack as they slapped against each other.

"You're adorable," I said tenderly and fed him a mint. I had recently discovered Milo's love for the red and white striped candy and indulged him often. When he lowered his head to take the treat, I'd whisper in his ear, "I love you, M."

This time when his head was bowed, I asked, "What do you think, Milo? Are you ready to start your career as a show horse? It isn't easy. The days usually begin before the sun is up. When we travel, you'll have to live in a temporary tent stall. There will be a lot of jumps and they only get bigger as you get older. But it's what you were bred to do, and the height of the jumps shouldn't be a problem for you. And, of course, I'll be right there with you at every show."

Milo appeared unmoved by my words as he ran his pink tongue over his lips in search of bits of candy that had escaped from his mouth.

I chose a spot on Milo's shoulder to lean against and, closing my eyes, inhaled deeply. Soap, horse, and sunshine blended together to create a fresh, earthy aroma that I considered Milo's signature scent.

When I opened my eyes, Milo was staring at me. His eyes were large and round and the gold flecks that lined their centers glowed warmly. I leaned forward and rested my forehead against his for a moment.

"Okay," I said and left the stall. On my way out, I found Bob in the tack room.

"You're right," I told him. "I think it's time Milo made his debut in the show ring. Just let me know what you need me to do."

"Great! Before we do anything else, we have to fill out an entry form."

I nodded agreeably and asked, "Does this mean that I can't ride him again until after the show?"

Bob looked surprised by my question. "Of course, you can continue to ride him. I'll ride him a few days a week and I'll be here to help you when you ride him. It'll be business as usual."

As I had warned, Milo's first day of competition began in the dark. "Good morning, Sleepy," I greeted him.

It was barely six o'clock in the morning and I had already been awake for an hour. Milo picked his head up from his bed of hay and shavings but made no effort to rouse himself. I couldn't blame him. It was chilly and the pile of clean hay looked rather inviting.

While I daydreamed about hunkering down in the hay for a quick nap of my own, Milo closed his eyes, and his breathing became slower and deeper. He had fallen back to sleep. I hated to disturb him, but we had much to do that morning and it all required an upright Milo.

"At least you can sleep standing up." Milo regarded me through heavy lids but remained rooted to his spot. "Okay, you leave me no choice. If you don't get up, I'm going to tickle your ears."

Early in our relationship, I had discovered that Milo's ears were extremely ticklish. Using the tip of my index finger, I ran it lightly over the back of Milo's right ear.

With a mighty stretch and a push, Milo was up and looking none too happy about it. If I didn't know better, I would've sworn my horse was glaring at me.

"Here, this will change your tune," I said, holding out a carrot.

Milo accepted my offering and peace was restored.

Knowing the morning would be cold, I had elected to bathe Milo the day before. Considering how much he enjoyed getting dirty, the likelihood of Milo staying clean overnight was slim. However, a close inspection of Milo's legs, neck, and back revealed the odds to be in my favor. A few passes with a brush and Milo's coat was gleaming.

Busy gazing at Milo with prideful satisfaction, I didn't see the woman standing outside the stall door.

"Excuse me," she said, startling my horse and me. "Is this Milo?"

"Yes, may I help you?"

I had no idea who this woman was or what she wanted with Milo until I noticed the step ladder she carried. Cords of brown and black yarn hung from her belt loops, and she wore a pair of scissors on a chain around her neck.

Recognizing the tools of her trade, I smiled at the young woman who had come to braid Milo's mane and then twist and knot each tiny braid until they ran the length of his neck.

She placed the ladder next to Milo, who was quick to shy away from it.

"Does he usually do that?" she asked.

"I don't know that he's ever been so close to a step ladder," I replied.

"Is this his first time being braided?" she asked, her tone plainly stating her irritation.

I nodded, then picked up the ladder and held it out in front of Milo so he could get used to it. When he began to sniff it, presumably to establish if he could eat it, I assumed he no longer considered it scary. Slowly, I set it down next to him and this time he wasn't bothered by it at all.

"I think he'll be all right for you," I said hopefully. "I'll hold on to him though. Just in case."

In less than an hour, thirty perfectly-spaced braids lined Milo's thick neck.

"Aren't you fancy," I said admiringly. Although his formal coiffure was dashing, the tight braids were uncomfortable, and Milo was dying to rub them out.

"Come on, they aren't that bad," I chided, giving his neck a thorough scratch.

Milo leaned into me, obviously enjoying the few moments of relief.

"You'll get used to them," I promised as I continued scratching, and I could tell by the way Milo's lips quivered that he was in heaven. "Five more minutes," I consented, even though my arm was already growing tired.

I heard the loudspeaker hum to life outside and my hand stilled so I could focus on the announcement.

"Sorry, M," I said when the broadcast was over. "We have to cut this short. That was the twenty-minute call for your division."

I led Milo out of the barn. Overnight, his home had been transformed into a horse show facility, and now there were horses, riders, workers, spectators, vendors, dogs, and cars everywhere. I wanted to give Milo a chance to adjust to the sudden change in his surroundings.

"I know I'd be alarmed if I woke up to find strangers had invaded my house and rearranged all the furniture," I told him as we walked through the chaos to the show ring.

Milo looked at the other horses with mild curiosity. I was certain that the commotion would rattle him, but obviously I had underestimated my young horse.

"How is he?" Bob asked when he joined us at the ring. "Oh!" he exclaimed before I could reply. "He looks incredible."

"I know." I smiled and took a moment to admire my horse. "The braids really show off his neck, don't they?" Handing Bob a bottle of water, I said, "It's too bad he doesn't like them."

"He'll get used to them," Bob said, echoing my earlier sentiments bn gulps of water. "I should probably get on. I don't think there are many horses ahead of us." I nodded and held Milo's reins out to Bob. "Thanks for the water," he said, swapping the empty bottle for the reins in my hand.

"Be a good boy," I said to Milo, giving him a kiss for luck.

"Don't worry so much," Bob said as he stepped off the mounting block and into the saddle. "He's going to be great."

"I know," I said to myself, as I watched Bob and Milo head toward the warm-up ring.

Alone, I gathered my things and walked the perimeter of the show ring until I had the optimal view of the course. Occasionally, I glanced toward the ingate where three horses waited for their turn in the ring, but none was Milo. *Where are Bob and Milo?*

Fighting the urge to search for them, I concentrated on the horse currently in the ring. He was handling himself well. His canter was smooth, and his front legs were together and held evenly over each jump. He was undeniably an animal of quality, and I clapped politely when he finished the course and exited the ring. I had been so busy looking for Bob and Milo that I hadn't witnessed all of the rounds, but I assumed this horse was the one to beat.

The ring sat empty for a minute while the other spectators and I waited for the next competitor. When the horse entered the ring, I noticed a lull in the chatter around me.

Although not a large horse, his presence made the ring appear smaller. He took in his surroundings but didn't appear nervous as the other young horses had. His eyes were bright and his ears sloped forward. When he walked past me, his large, golden eye caught mine. *If I said his name out loud, would he acknowledge me with more than a look?* I dared not try even though I was desperate for confirmation that this majestic horse was, in fact, Milo. He had the same white sock and star on his forehead but other than his physical appearance, this horse bore little resemblance to the timid one I had grown to love.

With the slightest urging from Bob, Milo stepped into a canter. The first jump was directly in front of me, and I held my breath as Bob turned the corner and steered Milo toward its center. They met the fence perfectly and in one fluid movement, Milo pushed off over it, arched his back in the air, yanked his knees evenly to his chin, and then glided back down to the ground.

Pride filled my chest, forcing the air from my lungs with a whoosh. Milo was the ideal blend of power and elegance. His form over the fence was excellent and his canter incomparable. Milo jumped the next two fences with the same ease and grace, banishing any doubt that the horse to beat was mine.

No longer nervous, I grew more and more enthusiastic with each fence Bob and Milo completed until they finished the course. Milo and a smiling Bob left the ring accompanied by whistles, whoops, and boisterous applause. While I was undoubtedly the loudest, it was obvious I wasn't their only fan.

The division consisted of three classes, so Bob and Milo returned to the ring two more times. When they exited the ring for the third and final time, I was there to meet them.

Bob dismounted and my overwhelming desire to take Milo from him propelled me forward, but before I could reach them, a swarm of Bob's fellow trainers surrounded him. I couldn't hear what was being said, but Bob was alternately grinning and patting Milo's neck. A few of the professionals gestured toward Milo. One even made an attempt to touch his face, but he deftly sidestepped the unwanted contact.

Recognizing this as my cue, I pushed past Milo's admirers and stretched my empty hand out. "I'll take him, Bob," I said. Milo, heedless of the people standing in front of him, closed the short distance between us, dragging Bob along with him.

"Wasn't he unbelievable?" Bob asked, handing me the reins. The braided leather bumped against my palm and my fingers snapped shut around it like a Venus flytrap. Milo was officially back in my care and I felt complete again.

"You were *both* unbelievable," I corrected Bob. "But, yes, Milo blew every expectation I had out of the water. It was like watching a rock star take the stage." Bob laughed and Milo nuzzled my cheek. "I'll take him back to his stall unless you want me to wait here and see how you did."

"No, he can go back to his stall," Bob said. "Take his tack off and then come back here and check the results."

Bob was even more eager than I was to see where Milo placed in the three classes. Ribbons were always welcome, but at that moment my mind was on Milo and the cool bath and mountain of treats that awaited him in the barn.

Once again behaving like my lovable Milo instead of a serious show horse, he played with my hair with his muzzle while I crouched down to dry his legs with a towel. From my vantage point, I could see a pair of black boots marching toward me. They stopped and I looked up to see Bob, still dressed in his show clothes.

"What happened to you?" he asked.

"What do you mean?"

"I thought you were coming right back to see how Milo did," Bob huffed.

"I was going to," I said, "but I decided Milo's comfort came first, so I gave him a bath and took his braids out and figured I could check on the results later."

"Don't bother," Bob said. "I've already collected Milo's winnings for you."

"And?"

I noticed that Bob's hands were behind his back. Suddenly, they were over his head, holding a stack of blue ribbons. I counted them.

"He won all three?"

Bob held the bunch of ribbons like he would a bouquet of flowers. Handing them to me, he said, "I almost forgot the best one." Then he reached inside his jacket pocket and pulled out a large multicolored ribbon.

"Milo's first champion ribbon!" I cheered, clapping my hands excitedly. I took the ribbon from Bob and held it up for Milo to see. He sniffed it but lost interest when he discovered it wasn't food.

The championship is awarded to the horse that accumulates the most points in a division. By winning all three classes, Milo had earned the championship by a landslide.

"I still can't believe the regal animal you rode today was my little Milo," I said, stacking the ribbons in a neat pile on the ground. "Normally, he's frightened of his own shadow."

"He was definitely nervous when we first walked into the ring," Bob said. "His heart was pounding so hard I could feel it through my boot."

"Really? Milo looked like he didn't have a care in the world, especially when you started jumping. I couldn't believe how confident he seemed to be. I guess your Milo is a better actor than mine."

"*My* Milo?" Bob asked.

"Yes," I smiled. "Your Milo is the fancy horse that I barely recognize. He wins champion ribbons and appears so sure of himself even though he isn't. This," I said, as Milo rubbed his head against my arm, "this shy boy who loves and trusts me more than anyone else, who shares his secrets and fears with me every day…this is my Milo."

"Good grief," said Bob, rolling his eyes. "You're going to give him an identity crisis."

I laughed and snapped a lead to Milo's halter. "I'm taking our star to his stall." Bob walked back to the ring where several horses waited for him.

Though I was exhausted, I wanted to spend more time alone with Milo. In one afternoon, he had become a show horse. Our lives were changing, and as I sat in his stall with him, I wondered what the future had in store for my Milo and me.

CHAPTER FOUR

With the success of Milo's first show behind us, Bob and I agreed that it would be wise to choose four of the nicer, local venues and only compete there for the rest of the season.

"We don't want to waste him by going to a show every week," Bob said. "He has many years of showing ahead of him. We don't need to push him."

Many show horses spend their lives on the road competing every week with little time off. This was not my vision for Milo, and I was pleased and relieved that Bob felt the same way.

Three weeks after Milo's debut, Bob and I drove to Keswick, Virginia. The horses and equipment would meet us there later in the day. This time, Milo's division would include thirty-five horses, some of which were the most impressive I had ever seen. Bob pointed out one that had sold for around $280,000. "That's quite a price tag," I said, wondering when horses had become as expensive as houses.

When it was time for Milo to show again, I assumed my position at the side of the ring and watched as he transformed into a show horse. Milo and Bob completed five classes over two days. By the end of the second day, we were worn out but managed to perk up when the final results were announced.

Bob and Milo were called back to the center of the ring where a champion ribbon was ceremoniously hung on Milo's bridle.

I began decorating my bedroom walls with Milo's winnings. By summer's end, I had run out of space. Rosettes crowning blue, red, and yellow ribbons covered the once-white walls, occasionally accented by the multicolored rosette of a larger champion ribbon. My room, like my life, blossomed with Milo's success.

We stuck to our plan and competed Milo only four times that summer. It became easier to hand Milo to Bob and watch them take over the ring. I had caught the competition bug, and when Milo finished his final show for the year, I was already looking forward to next year's schedule.

Milo could begin showing again starting in December. But in January, Bob would leave for Florida, where he competed every winter. I wasn't sure what Milo and I were going to do then. I supposed that would be a conversation Bob and I would have sooner or later.

"Well, Captain Chunky," I teased Milo one morning in September, "judging by your ever-expanding waistline, you are in dire need of new blankets." The nights were already dipping into the mid-forties, which was considered blanket weather for the horses. I had neatly bagged and stored Milo's blankets from the previous winter, but when I unpacked them and threw them across his back, it was hard to believe the blankets had ever fit him. I lengthened the belly straps three times before admitting they would never reach around him.

Bob happened by Milo's stall, and although used to my frequent conversations with my horse, he stopped to listen to my latest musings. When he saw me struggling with the blankets, he caught my eye and, then smiling, pointed at Milo's well-rounded rump and the blanket that no longer covered it.

"In Milo's defense," I said, patting my horse's hind end, "it's mostly muscle."

"Uh-huh." Bob smirked, then added, "Do you have a second? I want to talk to you about some plans for the coming winter."

"Of course." I stepped out of Milo's stall, taking the blankets with me. Bob'~~ sat on a tack trunk and I sat on one next to it. "If September's early frost is any indication, I'd hazard a guess that it's going to be a long and frigid winter," I said glumly.

"I think you're right," Bob agreed. "Which is why we need to figure out how to get Milo down to Florida this winter."

"You mean take him with you to Wellington?" I asked.

"Yes."

Bob was talking about the Winter Equestrian Festival, or WEF, a circuit of horse shows held in the West Palm Beach suburb of Wellington, Florida, from January to March. WEF is one of the largest and most prestigious competition circuits. It is also one of the most expensive. I had grown up listening to tales of the immense grounds and opulent barns in Wellington, but as much as I longed to see them, I'd never had the opportunity to go there.

"How much would it cost to show Milo in Wellington?" I asked, almost afraid to hear Bob's answer.

"Probably close to twenty thousand."

"I'm sorry, Bob. There's no way I can swing that."

"Maybe I could make it affordable for you," he countered.

"Even if you didn't charge me the full cost of riding and feeding Milo, I'd still have my living expenses down there. Housing alone will run me six grand and that's if I'm lucky enough to find a decent rental for two thousand a month. Don't get me wrong, I would love for you to show Milo in Florida, but it's not in the realm of possibility."

Bob looked as disappointed as I felt. Then he surprised me by saying, "Well, would you consider sending Milo without you?"

"Without me?" I almost laughed. "Are you kidding?"

"It would only be for three months."

"Now you're just talking crazy. Honestly, you of all people should know how attached I am to Milo."

"Okay, okay, I get it." Bob raised his hands as if to ward off my attack. "I guess I'll have to think up some other way to get you both to Wellington."

I had to give him credit for trying, but I couldn't imagine a single scenario that would land Milo and me in Florida. Knowing

Bob, though, I realized he wasn't going to let this go until he'd explored every angle.

"What could you afford to pay?" Bob asked, cutting into my thoughts.

I had managed to save twelve thousand dollars. A good chunk of change, but it wouldn't cover even half of the tab for Milo and me.

"Unfortunately, that's all I have. But if you can make it work, Milo and I will go to Florida with you."

Bob accepted the challenge and within a day, he presented me with a few options, none of which was reasonable. I was kissing my winter in the sun goodbye when Bob said, "I have one more thought, but I don't think you're going to like it, either. It's a lot of work, you'd have to be very organized, and you'd have to deal with the other customers."

"I can handle all of that. Tell me more."

"You would be in charge of all of the office work at the show," Bob explained. "Entries, adds, scratches, and collecting money from the other owners. You'd be working for me and, in return, I'll make it affordable for you and Milo to come to Florida."

I was thoughtful for a moment. What Bob was offering was beyond generous. Even if he really needed an assistant, which I doubted, the pay would never come close to covering Milo's expenses.

"You must really want Milo with you this winter," I grinned. "It's a deal. I'll be your assistant and you will show Milo at Wellington."

The day after Christmas, Bob and I were on a flight to Palm Beach while Milo and the ten other horses in Bob's care were loaded onto a van along with our trunks and equipment.

"It's amazing you found a place to stay," Bob said after we had taken off.

He was right about that. Every detail about Wellington had fallen into place. Everything except housing. Finding a one-bedroom that I could afford had proven impossible. Rental prices during the show season were astronomical, and I feared I would have to call the whole thing off. That is until one of my oldest friends offered to let me stay with her in her Wellington home for a fraction of the going rate. All I had to do was cook an occasional meal, pay a little rent, and the room was mine.

Bob couldn't believe my luck when I told him and, frankly, neither could I.

Our cars were being transported down so Bob had to rent a car when we arrived at Palm Beach International Airport.

"We have time for a tour of the equestrian area if you want to have a look," Bob said as we passed a sign welcoming us to Wellington.

"I would love that." I sat up straighter in my seat so I wouldn't miss any of the sights.

Believing our excursion would begin at the showgrounds, I was surprised when Bob drove into a gated community called Grand Prix Village. I admired the ornate mansions lined up neatly along the road, complete with circular driveways, bronze statues, and tiered fountains. And then I realized they weren't mansions, they were horse barns, and my mouth gaped.

"Do humans live in here, too, or just horses?"

"As far as I know, this area is primarily for horses," Bob said, "although I think some of the properties have living quarters for the grooms and barn managers."

We rounded a corner and passed an immaculate white barn next to a freshly mowed, emerald-green field. The barn doors had been opened wide, revealing grand archways on both ends and an enormous crystal chandelier hanging from the rafters.

"Is that normal for down here?" I asked, gawking at the glittering fixture.

"A lot of these barns are nicer than most people's houses, and I bet this isn't the only one with a chandelier."

"I'm not sure I fit in with this crowd."

My trainer began to whistle *The Beverly Hillbillies* theme song.

I whacked him lightly on the arm. "I'm being serious and you're comparing me to Elly May Clampett? Some friend you are."

Bob snorted with laughter. "Relax, you'll be fine. Besides, between riding, office work, and taking care of Milo, you'll be too busy to worry about making friends."

"Riding?" I asked as we exited Grand Prix Village. I had hoped Bob would let me ride Milo when he wasn't competing, but the way he said it led me to believe I would be doing more than that.

Bob turned right and I saw a simple white sign that announced our arrival at the Winter Equestrian Festival. We slowed down at the gate where a guard in a booth waved us through.

"Of course, you'll be riding," Bob said as we passed four cement buildings containing dozens of permanent horse stalls. "Including Milo, I'm responsible for eleven horses. I won't have time to ride them all. You'll have at least three a day on your list."

This is even better than I imagined. Not only had I made it to Wellington, but I'd get to ride almost every day.

We came upon a parking area with each parking space marked VIP in bright yellow paint.

"Who gets to park there?" I asked.

"Whoever wants to pay for it," Bob answered.

I chuckled, "So, not us."

"No, Elly May, not us," Bob sighed theatrically.

Beyond the parking area stood row upon row of precisely-aligned blue and white striped tents. Large and sturdy, each tent housed thirty temporary horse stalls. I lost count after the thirtieth tent.

"There must be thousands of stalls here," I marveled. "Do they expect all of them to be filled?"

"Believe me," Bob said, slowing down as the paved road gave way to dirt, "the management wouldn't go to the trouble of setting up so many tents if they didn't need them."

We bumped along the uneven road and soon noticed a change in the scenery.

Here, the tents were arranged in clusters, not rows. Weeds grew around them, and I was dismayed to see a murky canal behind a cluster where Bob came to a rolling stop and said, "I think this is where we're stabled."

"How far are we from the show rings?" I asked irritably. "And are there alligators in that water?"

"I've heard rumors about alligators showing up in the tents, but I've never seen one myself," Bob shrugged.

"I hope you're joking."

"I'm being serious, but I wouldn't worry about it. The gators in the canals aren't very big. As for the show rings, they're a little bit of a trek from here. I'll show you," he said, turning the car around and heading down the road we came in on.

When we were almost back at the guard booth, Bob hung a right and I was treated to a view of the horse show unlike any I had seen before.

"Holy crap," was all I could mutter.

I counted at least five rings, and I knew there were more that I couldn't see. Each ring had been painstakingly watered, dragged, and raked, and, although empty now, would soon be filled with elaborate jumps depicting everything from whales to wishing wells. Some of the rings were numbered while more prestigious ones had names.

"This is the Grand Hunter," Bob said as we drove by a large oval-shaped grass ring.

"The Tower." Bob nodded his head in the direction of a gigantic structure that overlooked this ring and I understood how it came to be named.

Bob showed me the Grand Prix ring where the Olympians competed, and smaller rings meant for kids and their ponies. The grounds seemed to go on and on in every direction. Though the show was not up and running yet, people were busy working everywhere I looked.

"This place is massive," I said. "How am I ever going to learn my way around?"

"Don't worry," Bob chuckled. "You'll have plenty of opportunity to figure it out. When the horses get here, your first job is to ride every single one around the show."

"That actually sounds like fun to me."

"Just wait. Soon this place will be so packed full of horses and people, it will take you all day to walk from one end of the show to the other."

I hoped Bob was exaggerating, but a few days later, I realized he wasn't. Riding each horse around the show grounds turned out to be a bigger chore than I anticipated.

Sometimes I felt like a salmon swimming upstream as I threaded my mount through an onslaught of horses, people, and the occasional golf cart. Each horse I rode found something new to spook at. For Milo, it was the flags of the competing nations that surrounded the Grand Prix ring, especially when a strong breeze made them flutter and snap. He didn't buck and spin as some of the other horses did when frightened. Instead, Milo stopped and stared at the brightly colored fabric waving in the wind. Unable to convince him to move, I was forced to wait until he understood the flags were not a threat. Only then would he start walking again.

"The goal is to make a good impression on these people," I scolded him. "Holding your head in the air like a giraffe, transfixed by the sight of the flags, is not how we do that."

Thankfully, by our third pass Milo hardly glanced in the direction of the Grand Prix ring.

Between his busy schedule of riding, teaching, and socializing, Bob was constantly on the go, but usually I would see him in the morning. On such occasions, he would give me my daily instructions in person. Otherwise, he would write them on the white board that hung in our tent, along with the list of horses I was to ride that day. I was always happy to oblige, though when Milo's name appeared on the list, I was overjoyed.

I had thought once the competition began, I would be riding less. In fact, as Bob grew busier at the show rings, I was given more horses to ride. True to his prediction, it wasn't long before I was finding my way around the grounds like a pro.

Our only day off was Monday and for the first couple of weeks, I slept in and tended to sore muscles. On Tuesdays, Bob worked the horses that were showing that week, while I rode the ones that had the week off.

Competition started each Wednesday and continued through Sunday. Milo showed on Wednesdays and Thursdays, though Bob, still careful not to do too much with him, competed Milo only every other week.

During his first week in the show ring, I learned that it would take more than a pretty horse and eight well executed jumps to win blue ribbons.

Milo and Bob had completed three excellent rounds the first day of competition and two more the second day. The pair had received high scores but not the winning ones.

"Third and fourth place out of about fifty horses is a big deal," Bob said after the judges had pinned the class. "You should be ecstatic."

"I am," I assured him. "I am so proud of both of you, especially Milo. I'm used to winning, but I understand it's different in Wellington. The top horse needs to stand out more."

"It's only the first week," Bob reminded me. "Milo will shine, I'm sure of it. But first he needs more time and experience in the show ring."

Milo was such a fast learner that by his fourth week of competing, he was first in one class and second in another. Bob and I stared in awe at the ribbons that hung on both sides of Milo's bridle.

"You're a star again, Milo," I told him later that afternoon. I'd bathed him and unbraided his mane the minute we returned to our tent, and now he was grazing. "Not that you aren't always a star to me."

Milo pulled at the bits of weedy grass, ignoring me completely.

I watched the waning sunlight play across Milo's back, illuminating the pointed tips of three cowlicks that marred his otherwise flawless coat. I loved those swirly clumps of hair that grew in every direction. My favorite—usually hidden by his forelock—was directly above the star centered on his forehead.

At some point in our second month in Wellington, I realized Milo's name was appearing on my ride list with more frequency. It wasn't long before Bob was riding Milo only on the days he showed him.

"You can do whatever you want," Bob had instructed, "as long as you don't ride Milo in a ring. He spends enough time there and I don't want him to become bored with it. Take him out, show him the sights."

Which I did, happily. Back in Maryland, I rode Milo at least four times a week, but always under Bob's watchful eye. Developing a feel for a horse is a challenge, especially when you have limited time and space, and someone is constantly telling you what to do and how to do it. Now, free of limitations and scrutiny, I didn't have to pay attention to how I held myself in the saddle. My focus could be on Milo alone.

Beyond the horse show property, we explored large tracts of undeveloped land. Some days, Milo and I walked along the canal keeping an eye out for alligators sunbathing on its banks. Other days, I let Milo choose our direction and pace. Bob never allowed me to do much more than canter in circles, but unsupervised I would let Milo take us wherever he wanted to go, whether by galloping across a field or cantering through a flock of pink and white birds.

Each outing was a unique experience for us and by the time we returned to the tent, I had learned something new about Milo.

It could be something funny, such as Milo's love of cantering in mud puddles, making a mess of us both; or something serious, such as the way he protected our left side, as though he knew I couldn't see out of that eye. Milo sidestepped countless holes and low hanging branches that could have injured one or both of us. I knew all of his weaknesses and was quick to protect him, but I never imagined that he would know mine and do the same for me.

Sometimes when we returned — sweaty, filthy, and tired, but exhilarated — Bob would be waiting for us. Once Milo and I stayed out longer than I had intended and as we raced back to the stalls, I imagined Bob was going to be none too pleased with me.

"I'm sorry," I blurted, jumping off Milo and leading him into the tent.

"Is Milo okay? Does he still have all four of his shoes on?" Bob asked.

I did a quick check of Milo's hooves. "Yes."

"All right then. This time I'll let it slide, but from now on try to remember you're on one of the top horses in the country. Don't be gone for more than an hour or I'll have to send in the cavalry."

"What do you mean, I'm on one of the top horses in the country?" Horses are nationally ranked in each division (Milo's was First Year Green Hunter), based on the amount of points they earn at each show. "Exactly where is Milo?"

"Your mud-splattered trail horse is sitting tenth in the nation in his division," he announced.

"He's tenth? How? I know he's been placing consistently, but tenth in the country? I mean, that's amazing."

I looked at Bob and then Milo in disbelief. I never imagined my courageous little horse could overcome his fears and climb the ranks to celebrity status.

"Thank you," I said earnestly.

"You should be thanking Milo, too."

"No, I wasn't thanking you for being tenth. I was thanking you for Milo. I have this extraordinary horse in my life because of you. Thank you for him and for making all of this possible. Being here is a dream come true."

I could tell by his blush that my unexpected gratitude had made him uncomfortable. Regardless of his comfort level, I was glad that he knew how much I appreciated him. After all, without Bob, there wouldn't be Milo.

CHAPTER FIVE

The Wellington horse show circuit gave new meaning to the adage, "The show must go on." I watched as Bob and Milo competed during a torrential downpour, including wind that knocked over the jumps. On other days, both horse and rider sweated through hundred-plus degree heat. By the end of each day, the three of us were beat, drenched in sweat, rain, or both.

"Are you feeling okay?" I asked Bob at the end of a particularly grueling day.

Now that he could finally sit on something other than a horse, Bob had slumped in one of the director's chairs in front of our tent and removed his riding helmet, revealing flushed cheeks and a red nose. He had a habit of turning crimson when he overexerted himself.

I dampened a washcloth and handed it to him. After wiping it across his face and down his neck, he wrung it out and groaned, "I feel the way this looks."

"Don't we all," I commiserated as I wiped my own brow. I cringed as a bolt of familiar pain worked its way across my head and settled above my right eye.

"Your head still hurts?" Bob guessed, noticing my discomfort.

For the past week, I had been plagued by the same irritating headache. I'd attributed it to the heat since the pain was worse when the sun was out in full force.

Talking about it didn't help, plus I wasn't in the mood to listen to lectures about taking better care of myself.

"It's much improved," I fibbed.

"That's good, because you were looking pretty grim earlier this afternoon," Bob replied, frowning, "when your face turned a particularly unbecoming shade of green."

"I'm pretty sure it was just a mild case of overheating," I said, pushing myself up from my chair.

"Where are you off to now?"

I selected a few of the more appetizing carrots from a bag. "I'm going to check on Milo. He's due for another carrot."

"Of course, you are," Bob laughed. "After all, it's been a whole twenty minutes since the last time you checked on him."

Milo was waiting for me at the front of his stall.

"You look perkier," I told him, observing with amusement the mixture of hay and shavings that peppered his back and sides. Apparently, after his bath he had settled down on the floor of his stall for a well-deserved nap.

Milo chewed his carrot while, one by one, I plucked the shavings out of his thick mane.

"I bet you're ready to go home." Milo had already finished his first carrot and was looking for a second. I missed the peace and quiet of the barn in Maryland and I was sure Milo did as well. Our rented paddock in Wellington was small and offered little shade and hardly any grass. It couldn't compare to the lush, rolling hills that Milo enjoyed back home. "If it's any consolation, I'm ready to say goodbye to this place, too, at least for now."

Wellington had been fantastic, but I was anxious to resume my life in Maryland with my family and friends. Or so I thought.

It seemed as though I had been gone forever, but, finally, I was homeward bound. From my window seat, I had a glimpse of Baltimore as the plane prepared to land. To my surprise, I felt disconnected from the familiar view below rather than comforted by the idea of being home. As the plane hit the runway with a thud, my thoughts scattered into a million pieces. By the time I unbuckled my seatbelt, I was asking myself, *Do I really want to resume a life that was so easy to put on hold?*

I was returning to an empty house where I lived alone. Soon, I'd fall back into my routine of going to the barn, going to work, and going home to eat and sleep. I had chosen to live in Columbia, Maryland, because of its location near the barn, my job, and my mother. On the other hand, though convenient, Columbia was geared toward families with children. When I felt the need to seek out my fellow singles, I had to drive an hour to Bethesda where most of my friends lived.

I was still preoccupied with thoughts about my future when I reached the congested baggage claim area. I had to scan my surroundings several times before I found my mother standing by one of the carousels. I rushed toward her and let her strong hug squeeze the discontent out of me — at least, temporarily.

On the way home, Mom informed me that, for my welcome home dinner the following night, we'd be eating at my favorite Chinese restaurant. The prospect of dinner with my mother and stepfather and the best vegetable moo shu in Maryland already had me in a better mood.

Once we arrived at my townhouse and had transferred my bags from the car to the kitchen, Mom glanced around my darkened house. "Are you sure you'll be okay?"

"I'll be fine," I muttered, watching dust motes floating through the air.

Dinner the next night with my mom and my stepfather, Howard, was not the normal relaxing, lighthearted family event I was expecting. While my parents silently stared at me from across the table, I knew that the moment of reckoning was at hand after my three-month hiatus in Florida.

Nervously, I twirled one of my chopsticks while perusing the laminated pages of my menu. I already knew what I was going to order, but I needed something else to look at besides my dinner companions.

"Don't you usually need glasses to read the menu here?" my mom observed.

The chopstick stilled in my hand while I considered her question. I was pleased I had momentarily distracted her from the interrogation I sensed was coming, although my mom's remark did give me pause.

That's odd, I thought. I hadn't noticed any improvement in my sight. If anything, lately I had struggled more than usual with my distance vision. I hadn't wanted to worry my mom, so I kept it to myself. Most likely, my prescription needed a little tweaking, so I made a mental note to see my eye doctor sooner rather than later.

Howard interrupted my musings by coming straight to the point. "So, tell us, was your winter in Wellington successful?"

My stepfather rarely showed any interest in Milo and although the question appeared innocent, I had my doubts. Cautiously, I replied, "He did just fine."

"Was there any interest in him?" Howard asked.

And there it was. The real reason the three of us were having dinner together.

Now aware of our conversation's topic, I needed time to figure out how I could safely circumvent any questions involving the sale of my precious Milo. I stabbed at a dumpling and crammed the entire greasy ball of dough into my mouth. It was chew or choke, which gave me a minute or two before I had to come up with a suitable answer.

To be fair, Howard wasn't being cruel or even insensitive. Before my mom bought Milo for me, we'd all agreed the purchase could potentially be a good investment. How could I have known then that Milo and I would share a bond that transcended any amount of money.

Thankfully, the topic of selling Milo didn't come up again for almost a year. By then, his value had tripled due to his early success in the ring. So when we began discussing the prospect of competing in Wellington, naturally Howard had asked, "Would Milo have a better chance of selling in Florida than he does in Maryland?"

It was the perfect time to let my mom and Howard know that my intentions had changed and selling Milo was no longer part of my plan. On the other hand, they had both been on the fence about me going to Wellington at all.

"You won't be generating any income while you're away. Are you sure that's a good idea?" Howard had asked.

In order for Florida to happen, I needed their support. So, to Howard's inquiry regarding Milo's salability, I had replied, "Absolutely. The Wellington circuit is home to the top equestrians in the country. I'm sure Milo will spark the interest of many."

My mom and Howard were staring at me expectantly as I swallowed the last bit of dumpling and still had no idea what to say.

In the end, honesty won out. "I can't sell Milo. I don't think he would survive without me, and I know I couldn't without him." I needed to take several deep breaths in order to calm the emotional riptide inside of me. "I know he's just a horse to you, but for the past year I've dedicated my life to Milo. I healed his wounds, I gave him confidence, and he trusts me. I can't betray that trust by selling him to the highest bidder. He's my world. I can't sell Milo now, and maybe not ever."

I could think of a dozen or more reasons why Milo and I couldn't part ways, but my composure was rapidly falling to pieces. Deciding it was in my best interest to remain quiet, I readied myself for the worst. *Who would yell at me first? Mom or Howard?*

My mother cleared her throat and asked, "Milo means that much to you?"

"Yes," I replied, as though guilty of a crime.

"All right," she said, "then don't sell him."

Stunned, I was sure I hadn't heard her correctly. "What?"

The servers had begun to put more food on the table and my mom, now more interested in dinner than me, said, "He's your horse. If you don't want to sell him, don't."

Incredulous, I stared at my mom who was too engrossed in her Peking duck to notice. Then, suddenly ravenous myself, I said, "Okay, I won't," putting the subject of selling Milo to rest.

Per usual, I had eaten too much and, on the drive back to my house, I felt a little sick to my stomach.

"Do you have any plans for the next few days?" my mom asked unaware of my discomfort. "You'll have your freedom back tomorrow when the transport from Florida drops your car off, and I'm sure you and Bob are planning on giving Milo a break after he gets home."

Milo would be back in Maryland in two days. I would, of course, see him as soon as he arrived, but my mom had assumed correctly. I wouldn't begin riding him for another week. I wanted to give him plenty of time to rest and reacclimate. Since we wouldn't compete again for another month, I had to decide whether Bob or I would show Milo.

What's wrong with me? I berated myself. *Why is this even a question?* For the past year, all I had wanted was for Bob to hand over Milo's reins and say, "It's your turn now." So, when he had casually pulled me aside before we left Wellington and said, "If you want to start showing Milo when we get home, I think you're both ready," I was overjoyed.

I had dashed off to Milo's stall for a private celebration, but halted when I saw the mountain of ribbons neatly stacked by his door.

Suddenly, I didn't feel like rejoicing. Instead, my shoulders sagged under the weight of those ribbons. I realized I felt intimidated by my own horse's achievements. I was afraid that if I were the one to show him, I couldn't deliver the spectacular results Bob and Milo had produced together.

Now, sitting in the back seat of my stepfather's car, fighting back nausea, I again asked myself, *Can I ever fill Bob's boots on Milo? Or should I stay on the sidelines and allow them to continue their winning streak? Was I being selfless, or simply a coward?*

Luckily, there was time before I had to make a decision.

"I don't have any plans," I told my mom. "My dance card is wide open." I considered calling a few friends and arranging a girls' night out, but Sarah was out of town and, without her, girls' night lost its appeal.

"I'm sure you'll think of something," my mom said as I got out of the car.

Lamely, I decided my time would be best spent by creating a list of every household chore I had neglected since Milo entered my life. I walked around my townhouse taking inventory of each project that begged for my attention, and dove right in. By the time the last light bulb was changed and each smoke detector had been tested, I was ready for Milo to be home.

"You're wearing a path in the cement," Bob teased, watching me pace up and down the barn's aisle while we waited for a trailer full of horses, including Milo, to arrive.

"What time did the van driver call you?" I asked Bob without breaking stride.

Sighing, Bob replied, "He called me at seven this morning to let me know that he and the horses were an hour out."

The morning was chilly and my hands were nestled in the pockets of my down vest. I extracted my left hand and glanced down at my watch. My brows knit together in a frown as I stared at my wrist. *I've never had a problem reading this watch before.* Numbers blurred and folded into each other while the delicate gold hands all but disappeared. *Why am I having a problem now?*

"What's the matter?" Bob asked, noticing my frown. "Did your watch stop?"

"No, my eye can't seem to decide if it wants to be near sighted or far sighted. What time do you have?"

"Five past eight. Should I be worried about you?"

"No," I replied, touched by my friend's show of concern. "I'm sure it's nothing."

"If you say so," Bob said, but he obviously wasn't convinced. "I'm still planning on giving the horses a couple of days off before putting them back to work. Why don't you use that time to get checked out by your eye doctor? If you're going to show Milo, you need to have at least one working eye."

"I promise, I'll go see my doctor. Probably not this week though," I said stubbornly. "Plus, I haven't decided if I'm going to show Milo or not."

"Of course, you are," Bob scoffed. "It's all you talked about for the first year you owned him. I'll make sure that you have loads of practice time. I'll ride him once a week and you can have as many lessons as it takes for you to feel comfortable."

"Definitely maybe," I replied.

Thankfully, my eye and my show career were all but forgotten when we heard the rumbling of a semi-truck pulling into the driveway.

Bob's boot camp, as I referred to my daily lesson, began a week later and was every bit as challenging as it was exhilarating. The more time I spent in the saddle, the more confidence I gained.

"Well?" Bob asked after two weeks of boot camp, "are you comfortable enough on Milo to show him?"

"I definitely have a better feel for him, but I'd like one more lesson before I make up my mind. Is it okay if I let you know after my lesson on Thursday?"

But early Thursday, we were hit by a violent thunderstorm and Bob called me to reschedule.

"What are you going to do now that you have a whole day to yourself?" I asked him.

Bob was always playing catch-up with business projects, so I wasn't surprised when he replied, "Paperwork, I guess. What about you?"

I stared at my reflection in the bathroom mirror. "I think," I said while I examined my face, "I'm going to get a makeover."

The mall was close by, and as I drove, I realized that my vision had changed again. Everything seemed fine until I needed to check my speed. The numbers on the speedometer were too fuzzy for me to read, and I was relieved that I'd remembered to make an appointment with my ophthalmologist. *It's okay*, I told myself. *I'm sure this is nothing more than a contact lens issue.*

As much as I wanted this theory to be true, deep down I knew it wasn't, and that something else was going on with my eye. But I didn't want to think about it. As was my M.O., I just wanted to keep busy and not face the truth.

Once I got to the mall, I found a makeup counter that featured my favorite brand of cosmetics. The friendly, young makeup artist showed me to a chair and went to work on my face. When I saw her reach for the eyeliner and mascara, I began to wiggle free of the chair. "Thanks, but I think that's enough for now."

"Oh, no," she protested, "it won't look right if I don't finish. It will only take me a few minutes, I promise."

Reluctantly, I slid back into the chair and tried not to cringe as she pulled the hair away from my face. She tilted my chin to the left and to the right, and then let out a tiny "Hmm."

Cringing, I dreaded what I knew was coming next. "Look," I told her, "I know that my eyes are uneven—"

At that exact moment, her eyeliner pencil clicked against my fake eye. Shocked, she dropped the pencil, then hastily covered up her embarrassment by diving for it. This time when I leapt from the chair, she did not try to stop me.

Mortified, I fled down the hall, wanting to put as much distance as possible between myself and the makeup counter. All interest in shopping was gone. But then, as I found myself walking past the pet store, something stopped me. In the front window sat a tiny black and tan Miniature Pinscher with huge, soulful eyes.

Unable to resist, I walked into the store and asked one of the clerks if I could see the Min Pin in the window. She led me to a roped-off area and had me wait while she went to fetch the puppy.

What are you doing? I had almost convinced myself that the last thing I needed was a dog when the clerk walked in with the pint-size puppy and placed him in my lap. I stared down at him, he stared back, and the yearning that shone in his eyes told me I was a goner.

Yes, I knew the risks of buying a dog from a mall pet store. I suspected he was from a puppy mill, and that his certification papers probably had been forged. But when he made himself comfortable in my lap and fell asleep, everything I knew about mall pet stores became irrelevant. All that mattered was this puppy and what I was going to name him.

"Ike? Radar? Bandit?" I watched my new puppy's reaction to the names I was trying out. We were sitting on my kitchen floor, surrounded by plush dog toys, puppy food, and treats. I rubbed his plump, pink belly until his eyes began to close.

"Spike?" I asked him. One eye popped open. "Spike," I tried again and this time his head tilted to one side. "Okay," I said, "I think you have a name."

My phone rang and Spike jumped up in surprise. I was laughing as I answered, "Hello?"

My mom's voice greeted me. "You're in a good mood."

"I am. I found a new roommate."

"Really?" She made no attempt to hide her surprise. "Who is she?"

"Oh, it's a he," I teased.

"A he?"

"Yes," I rubbed Spike's velvety ears. "He weighs about three pounds and is only five weeks old."

"You got a dog!" I could hear the excitement in her voice as I told her all about Spike. "I'm coming over to meet him tomorrow," she announced, "and then we can go out to dinner in Baltimore."

"Super," I said, before hanging up. "You're going to meet Grandma tomorrow," I informed Spike as I carried him up to bed.

Our ladies-only dinner turned out to be a wonderful evening full of easy conversation and fresh seafood. We both felt fortified and contented as we headed back home.

Staring out the window, I noticed something odd about the lights. "Mom, do you happen to see a rainbow when you look at the street lights?"

"What?" she asked sharply.

"I'll take that as a 'no,'" I said slowly.

"You're seeing rainbows?"

"Only when I look at the lights," I said. "It isn't even a full-size rainbow. It's more of a halo full of colors. It's actually kind of pretty."

"How long has this been going on?"

"This is the first time I've noticed it," I said, trying to sound reassuring.

"Okay," my mom replied, taking a deep breath. "Other than rainbows, how is your vision?"

I knew this question was coming and I had dreaded it. "Well…" I hedged.

That was all she needed to hear. "Oh, you have got to be kidding me. Why haven't you said something? What are you thinking? Don't you know by now that your vision is not something to screw around with?" Her questions came at me rapid-fire, and I stumbled trying to answer.

"Never mind," she cut me off. Rummaging in her purse, she pulled out her cell phone. "Here," she pushed the phone into my hands. "Call Henry."

Dr. Henry Jordan was my ophthalmologist. After twenty years under his care, he had become more than my eye doctor. Henry was my friend. Now, when Henry answered his phone, I had to force my voice to remain steady as I greeted him.

He didn't bother with pleasantries. "What's wrong?" he asked.

I described the rainbow halos and the changes in my vision. When I was finished, he only asked how long I had been seeing the colorful halos.

"You need to be in my office first thing in the morning," he said, leaving no room for argument. "It sounds like you have a severe case of glaucoma."

I knew from experience that "first thing" meant 9:00 a.m., and it also meant that Henry was worried. Before he hung up, he assured me that we had many treatment options. We just needed to pick one and start right away.

"That's good," I said, hoping those treatments wouldn't involve surgery. It was bad enough that I would have to cancel tomorrow's lesson with Milo; an operation would mean more time away from him.

"What did he say?" my mom asked after I had hung up.

"He thinks that my eye pressure is too high," I replied, purposefully avoiding the word "glaucoma."

"Oh," Mom breathed a sigh of relief. "Your eye pressure has been a little high in the past and went down with medicine. Did he say he would call something in for you?"

I remembered years ago when Henry had mentioned glaucoma to me, but back then my vision hadn't changed, and I hadn't seen rainbows. Something was definitely different this time. I knew it and, from the tone of Henry's voice, so did he.

"Actually," I said quietly, not wanting to scare my mom, "Henry wants to see me first thing tomorrow."

"What were his exact words?" she demanded.

"He suspects I have a severe case of glaucoma," I admitted, adding quickly, "but he said we have treatment options and not to worry."

Is that what he said? Or is that what I wanted him to say? I couldn't think straight, but at this point I'd have said anything to take the panic out of my mom's voice and stifle the despair that was building in mine.

"I'll be fine," I said reassuringly. "It's like you said, Henry will prescribe some medication and my pressure will go back to normal." I smiled and waved my hand as though the problem were nothing more than a pesky fly.

I could see that my mother wasn't buying my act. We had stopped at a red light, and she turned to me and asked, "Do you really believe that?"

I held her stare, wondering if I could look her in the eye and lie.

"No," I confessed. "I don't."

We were silent for the rest of the drive. When we pulled up in front of my house, I didn't spring from the car. I stayed in the passenger seat, staring out the windshield.

"What are you thinking?" my mom asked, taking my hand.

I turned to her. "Since I can remember, doctors have been telling me that I could lose my vision, but I never believed them. I knew my eye was stronger than they said it was, and it could survive whatever was threatening it."

"And now?" she asked, squeezing my hand.

"This time…" I paused, trying to think of the best way to describe my feelings. "It's starting to feel like more than I can handle."

My mom dropped my hand and reached across the car's middle console to hug me. When she let go of me, I could see that she was in tears.

"I'll be okay," I promised. "Henry will fix me. He always does."

CHAPTER SIX

Immune disorders, such as mine, invade the bodies of children. They wreak havoc, forever altering the lives of their hosts.

When I was old enough to understand medical research, I began to gather as much information about uveitis as I could. In my early teens, I came across an article, which confirmed my pediatric ophthalmologist's prediction years before, and showed it to Henry.

"This," I said, giving a copy of the article a shake, "claims that uveitis can be outgrown."

Henry didn't bother to look at it before replying, "That's true. In many cases, the juvenile form of the disorder will go into remission, often permanently."

"I assume that's not the case with my eye?" I asked dubiously.

"Actually," Henry said, "I wouldn't be surprised if you outgrow the disease. Or at least force it into remission through treatment."

Thereafter, I had been mindful of my doctor's appointments, medications, and even my diet. Whatever it took to stay ten steps ahead of the disease, so that one day it would grow tired of chasing me and give up. It had already wrapped its tentacles around my left eye, and I vowed that it would not do the same to my right one.

At the age of eighteen, when I was no longer considered a juvenile, I believed the disease would respect my adult status and vacate the premises.

When that didn't happen, I asked Henry if he stood by the claim he had made five years earlier. "Or have you changed your mind? Am I going to be dealing with this for the rest of my life?"

"Give it time," Henry had counseled me. "The disease is not going to let go of its hold on you that easily. In the meantime, we have to keep fighting."

My right eye survived another ten years of inflammatory flares, surgeries, and steroid injections before Henry revisited the possibility of remission. This was during my last checkup, a little over four months ago. My eye had been in good shape then.

"In fact," Henry had said as he flipped through my extensive file, "your eye has been stable for the better part of a year."

"What does that mean?"

"It means," Henry said as he double checked his notes, "that we may be out of the woods."

"Really? You're saying I've finally outgrown the uveitis?"

"I think it's a definite possibility," Henry corrected me.

That was nice to hear, but deep down I feared my eye problems were not over. Having lived with something for such a long time, I presumed I would notice its absence, but I didn't feel any different.

As it turned out, I was right to question my supposed remission. For here I sat four months later, along with a dozen of Henry's other patients, most of them complaining about the flimsy, paper sunglasses that guarded their slowly dilating pupils from the bright lights.

My mom sat in the chair next to me, arbitrarily flipping through the pages of a well-worn issue of *People* magazine. She caught me watching her and smiled.

"In all of the years that we've been coming here," she said, "I think this is the first time I've seen you look worried."

"I'm more aggravated than anything else," I replied. "I don't know why my eye has to have such lousy timing. It's as if it knew I was looking forward to my lesson on Milo today." I didn't bother to mention the months I had ignored warnings that my vision was deteriorating. The knot in my stomach tightened like a noose as I wondered how much damage could have been avoided had I made an appointment with Henry the minute I noticed a change in my sight.

"I take it back," I said. "I am a little worried."

Under normal circumstances, my appointments with Henry began with a preliminary screening performed by a technician. Today, however, I was allowed to skip the basic screening and was escorted directly to one of Henry's examination rooms.

"I now understand what people mean when they claim to be sitting on pins and needles," I told my mom. We had been waiting for five minutes and I could hear Henry's muffled voice through the walls. He was, I assumed, talking to another patient. *Wrap it up, Henry*, I thought anxiously.

The door to the room next to mine opened and before I had time to hope I was next, Henry was walking into my room.

"Let's see what's going on," he said, bypassing a greeting altogether. Henry tilted my head back and I felt several cool drops of liquid flood my eye. He used a tool called a slit lamp to take my eye pressure. After he measured it the first time and groaned unhappily, my heart sank. I didn't think it could sink any further until he rechecked his measurements and again made the unpleasant sound that sent my heart into a tailspin.

"How bad?" my mom asked from her chair in the corner of the room.

"Not good," Henry replied. "Her eye pressure is thirty-three."

"What is it usually?" I asked.

Henry glanced over my file.

"During the past three years, your eye pressure has fluctuated, but it has never gone above twenty."

"Where should it be?" my mother asked.

"Generally, anywhere from six to twelve is acceptable," Henry replied, turning down the lights. "At this point, we're definitely dealing with glaucoma."

As the light in the room dimmed, so, too, did the strain on my eye.

Ever observant, Henry asked, "Have you noticed any sensitivity to light?"

"Maybe a little," I replied. "Although it's hard to say for sure since my eye has never reacted well to bright light."

"Unfortunately, you may experience an increase in your discomfort, especially in sunlight," Henry warned.

A light at the end of the room blinked on, illuminating the eye chart below it.

I began with the large E and read each line of letters until they were no longer recognizable.

Once again consulting my file, Henry said, "You've lost two lines. This isn't good."

"I'm 20/60?" I asked, knowing that with my contact lens, I had been seeing 20/40 consistently for more than a year.

"Yes," Henry confirmed. "You aren't driving, are you?"

"No," I croaked, dangerously close to tears.

"Good," Henry said. "You aren't legally able to right now."

"And the roads are safe again," I said, masking my pain with humor.

"Will her vision return once we lower the pressure?" my mom asked.

Handing me a prescription, Henry replied, "If we can bring the pressure down soon, then yes, I'd expect her vision to be restored."

I nodded, too overwhelmed by my current circumstances to manage more than that.

"Have that filled right away," Henry said, pointing to the piece of paper clutched in my hand. "One drop in your eye, four times a day."

With some effort, I managed to reply, "Okay."

"I want to see you in a week," Henry ordered. "By then, the medicine will have started to lower the pressure."

Before we left, Henry gave me a hug and told me to try not to worry. I almost laughed but suddenly it seemed I had forgotten how.

We stopped at the pharmacy near my house and filled the prescription. I had already administered not one but two drops to my right eye when my mom pulled up to my front door.

"Call me if you need anything," she said huskily. We had said very little on the ride home and I now noticed the roughness of her tone.

"I will." I could feel her eyes on me as I walked into the house and shut the door behind me. It was a little while before I heard her drive away.

After five days of house arrest, with no place to go and no way to get there, I was going stir crazy, missing Milo more than I thought possible.

Henry had been correct about my eye's intolerance to light. I could be driven back inside by a sunny day, and I was beginning to feel like a vampire. At least I had Spike to keep me sane. He was excellent company and happy to take the majority of our walks after sundown.

I was vigilant about my medicine. Like clockwork, four times a day, I squeezed a drop into my eye.

I spoke to Bob every day. Either he would call to check on me or I would call him to check on Milo. I ached to see my horse and it killed me that I had left him without telling him why, or where I was.

"I hope he doesn't think I've abandoned him," I said to Bob during one of our phone calls.

"He doesn't think that," Bob assured me. I could practically hear him rolling his eyes. "Besides, your appointment is in a few days and, fingers crossed, you'll be back riding in no time."

I wanted to share Bob's optimism, but the migraine headaches that were becoming an everyday occurrence stopped me from doing so. The next day my migraine was so severe I could hardly lift the phone to my ear, but, somehow, I managed to call Henry and let him know what was happening.

"I don't want to wait until next week to see you. Can you be in my office by nine tomorrow morning?" he asked.

"Isn't tomorrow Saturday?"

"Yes."

"You don't mind coming in on your day off?"

"How bad are your headaches?" Henry answered my question with one of his own.

"Bad," I replied. "If they get worse, I'll take my eye out."

"Then, yes, I think I can spare a Saturday if it prevents you from self-mutilation."

My mom and I followed Henry through the empty waiting area and into an exam room. It didn't take long for Henry to discover the source of my headaches.

"The medicine isn't working," he said after taking my eye pressure. "Your pressure is closing in on forty. I don't blame you for wanting to take your own eye out. It must be excruciatingly painful."

After I gave up on the eye chart, Henry continued to be the bearer of bad news. "You've lost another line of vision," he said.

There were so many questions that needed to be asked but all I could think of was, "Am I going blind?"

I heard my mom's quick intake of breath.

"No one said anything about going blind." Henry was adamant. "But we do need to treat the glaucoma more aggressively. Fortunately, we still have some options."

Henry went over the alternative routes we could take that he thought were most likely to work. He suggested we try an oral medication that had proven successful in cases similar to mine. "It has a tendency to be hard on the stomach, which is why, although it's effective, it isn't widely prescribed," Henry clarified before moving on to surgical alternatives, of which there were two. Actually, they were two variations of the "not terribly invasive surgery" theme. "That is, if we can find a glaucoma specialist who is willing to operate under these circumstances," Henry added.

I stared at Henry blankly. "What circumstances?"

"You only have one eye," my mom answered for Henry.

"Exactly," Henry concurred. "No doctor wants to operate on a patient who has only one eye. Especially when the eye being operated on is as fragile as yours. This is why we need to exhaust all of our other options before we go down that path."

Henry insisted I begin taking the medicine immediately. While we waited for the pharmacist, my mom managed to talk me into moving in with her. "At least until you're driving again," she reasoned.

I could feel my independence slipping through my fingers, but as much as I hated to agree with her, I knew my mom was right.

"Fine," I sighed defeatedly.

"We'll stop by your place, and you can pack a bag for yourself and Spike."

I went into my house to gather my things. Henry had prescribed a week's worth of medication. That didn't seem long enough for it to have an effect, but at the rate my eye was worsening, that was all the time I had.

I packed enough clothing and essentials for a week, poured Spike's food into a container, and met my mom in the kitchen, where she was on the floor playing with the puppy.

"That was fast," she said, looking disapprovingly at my small bag. "Are you sure you have everything you need?"

"It isn't hard to pack when you don't go anywhere." I said. "All I need are pajamas and sweatpants."

"And fuzzy socks?"

"Of course," I smiled. "I never go anywhere without those."

Not ten minutes after I had moved into my temporary dwelling at my mom's house, my head began to pound. The area directly above my right eye felt like it would burst. It was all I could do to crawl into the bathroom and lay my cheek against the cold tile floor.

Thirty minutes later, I hadn't moved when Mom found me lying there. I was so worn out I barely twitched as she screamed my name. She helped me into bed, brought a cold compress for my face, and, most importantly, turned out the lights.

My headaches became more frequent and intense while the glaucoma continued to ravage my eye. I didn't need to wait the full week to know that the new pill was not working.

Henry prescribed three more medications, all of which failed, before he admitted our only option left was surgery.

Right before Halloween, my mom and I were sent to a glaucoma specialist, Dr. Sullivan, who, despite the huge risk, agreed to operate on my eye. The surgery would involve inserting a microscopic tube shunt into my eye to drain its excess fluid into my bloodstream.

"That sounds incredibly complicated," I said. "How long will the procedure take?"

"The surgery itself is fairly common," Dr. Sullivan replied. "It usually takes up to an hour from start to finish. In your case, it will probably be closer to two." Considered a priority, my surgery was scheduled for the next day.

Dr. Sullivan's office was in Washington, DC, an hour from my mom's house. I hadn't spoken with Bob in a couple of days, so I used the drive time to catch up on my favorite subject, Milo.

"I hope you're calling with good news," Bob said.

"I wish."

"No better? Not even a little bit? With all of the medication you've been on, not one of them worked?"

"It's worse. I'm having surgery tomorrow."

"But I thought your eye wasn't strong enough for surgery." Bob sounded alarmed.

I started to explain the procedure to Bob but when I began describing the tube's insertion into my eye, he asked me to stop. It was the opportunity to turn the conversation toward happier topics.

"What's Milo been up to?" I asked.

"Up to? I know you have a hard time believing this, but Milo is a horse. He eats, walks around in his paddock, and sleeps."

"Very funny."

"He's fine," Bob said. "I've hired a new groom who absolutely dotes on him. Not as much as you do, but it's close. He thinks Milo is very special."

"I don't have to meet this man to know I like him," I laughed. "Please let him know he has excellent taste. How has Milo been for you?"

"Perfect, of course. Although I've been going easy on him since he won't be entering any horse shows until you return."

There was a painful lull in the conversation, and I could practically hear Bob wishing to take his words back.

"I'm sorry," he said. "I know you were looking forward to showing him."

"I never did make up my mind about that. I guess it doesn't matter anymore."

"You would have decided to show him."

"How do you know?"

"Because in the years that I've known you, I've never seen you look as happy as you do when you're riding Milo."

I held the phone away from my face so he couldn't hear my tortured breathing. "I miss him, Bob," I whispered.

"I know you do. But you'll be back on him soon."

"I hope so."

Traffic was terrible and it took us two hours to get home. All I wanted was to crawl into bed, but there were other things I had to do first.

I considered myself an expert when it came to having an operation. After more than sixty surgeries over a period of twenty-three years, I knew exactly what to do pre- and post-op. Like the one I would have in the morning, most of my procedures began before 8:00 a.m. To save time, I always planned my outfit the night before. Loose fitting clothes that are easy to put on are key. I usually dress in sweatpants and slippers with a hard sole. Eye procedures, of any kind, call for a shirt with buttons. The last thing I want to do after surgery is pull something tight over my sore and bandaged eye. Inevitably, before surgery, I'll be asked to slip into a backless hospital gown. Under that particularly drafty ensemble, I'll be sporting a pair of boy shorts. They help keep the chill away, and the operating table is simply no place for a thong.

I got into bed early that night but couldn't sleep. Images of my eye imploding during surgery kept me tossing all night. Around the same time as the sun was rising, I gave up and got out of bed. I was fully dressed and ready to get this day over with even before my alarm began to beep.

Spike was still in bed, snoring. "Sorry, little guy," I apologized as I picked him up and carried him downstairs. By the time I had fed and walked him, my mother and Howard were ready to drive me to the surgery center. I gave Spike a quick kiss and promised him that I would be back in a few hours.

We arrived on time, and I was whisked out of the waiting area and into a changing room. My surgical gown and cap in place, I was helped into a hospital bed and instructed to say goodbye to my family. My mom and Howard were not allowed to accompany me into the sterile pre-op room, so I gave them both a hug, and while we all knew there was a good chance my eye wouldn't survive the surgery, I promised them everything would be fine.

I woke up, cotton-mouthed and confused. Wherever I was, it was very dark. I licked my lips in hope of promoting some moisture, but even my tongue was dry.

"Are you awake?" my mom asked, setting something heavy on the bed.

My throat felt like sandpaper, but I managed a raspy, "Uh-huh." The thing on the bed whined and placed a tiny paw on my hand.

"Hi, Spikers," I said in my new voice. The fog in my head began to lift and I gasped, remembering the surgery. My hand shot to my eye and met with thick cotton padding and lots of tape.

"My eye?" My heart pounded as I asked the question.

Pulling my probing fingers away from my face, my mom gave my hand a squeeze, and I didn't have to see her to know she was smiling when she said, "Your eye is fine. The surgery was successful."

"There weren't any problems?" I asked, unable to believe something had finally gone right. I heard the unmistakable pop and hiss of a soda can and gratefully accepted the ginger ale my mom pressed into my hand. Parched as I was, I sipped it slowly, savoring its cold, bubbly sweetness.

"Not a single one," Mom replied. "I think your eye is much stronger than we give it credit for."

"Maybe," I yawned and let my head relax against the pillows. Within seconds, I fell back to sleep.

My post-op activities were so limited, the only exercise I got was walking from my bed to the bathroom. My eye was still covered by a patch except for the daily changing of my bandage, expertly executed by my mother. She also had the challenging task of pulling my swollen and sticky lids apart in order to squeeze antibiotics into my eye.

"When is my follow-up appointment with Dr. Sullivan?" I asked while she taped a fresh bandage over my eye.

"You're not on lockdown for too much longer. Your appointment is Tuesday."

"Oh, good. What day is today?" I asked, not surprised I had lost track of time.

"It's Friday afternoon. You only need to hang in there for four more days."

The appointment went surprisingly well, and Dr. Sullivan deemed my surgery a success. "Of course, we won't know how much of your vision will be restored until your eye is completely recovered. However, the implant looks good, and there's no sign of infection."

But until I was allowed to put a contact lens in my eye, I was still at my mother's mercy.

Much of my time was spent creating lists in my head of all the things I was going to do once I had my vision back. Naturally, Milo was at the top of each and every list. I was planning on practically living in his stall with him in order to make up for lost time.

I couldn't wait to feel alive again. To read, take a walk in the sunlight, or drive. All of the things that I had taken for granted. *No more. I will treasure each word on the page. I will cherish every sunbeam that reaches out to me. I will delight in the freedom to go anywhere, anytime.*

As for Milo, the more I thought of him, the less patient I was. I had even started to pester my mother about taking me to the barn.

"I just want to pat him and give him some treats. He won't come near my face, I promise."

Mom sounded skeptical. "He always has his head on your shoulder or is resting it on top of your head. The last time I saw you together, he was licking your face like a dog," she reminded me. It took one more day of pleading and negotiating for her to give a little.

"If Henry says it's okay, I'll take you to the barn after tomorrow's appointment," she sighed.

My appointment with Henry couldn't come soon enough. *Have I ever been this excited for a doctor's appointment? Not lately.*

My luck was changing. I could feel it. Tomorrow I would see Henry and we would celebrate the success of my surgery. My mom would take me to Milo and I would feel whole again. The light at the end of the tunnel was in clear view.

CHAPTER SEVEN

As predicted, my luck did change but not in the way I had hoped. My eye, Henry explained, was rejecting the tube shunt.

"How can you tell?" I asked suspiciously.

"I can see it," Henry replied. "The implant is rooting through your eye and we need to remove it before it causes any permanent damage."

"Hold on," I said, leaning back in the examination chair. "You want me to have another operation to undo the one I just had? This is ridiculous, Henry. Why isn't anything working?"

"I don't know," Henry admitted. "I agree, it is ridiculous. Even for your eye, which has never played by the rules. If it helps, this is a much easier and less risky procedure than the last one. I'll even do it myself."

"When?" asked my mom.

"The sooner the better," Henry answered. "My office will call the hospital and see what's available this week."

"I can't have surgery this week," I mumbled.

"Why not?" my mom asked.

"Because I don't want to," I snapped.

"I get that," Mom said sympathetically. "But it doesn't sound like you have a choice."

There was nothing I could do. The decision had been made and whether I wanted it or not, I was having another operation.

"What then?" I asked Henry. "I'll still have glaucoma once the tube comes out."

"I've been trying to decide what the next step should be," he replied.

"Do we have many options left?" my mom asked.

"Honestly, no," Henry sighed. "There's a doctor in DC, Charles Garter, I'd like you to talk to. He's been working on a relatively new procedure to lower eye pressure."

"Another surgery?" I groaned.

"This would be a laser surgery," Henry explained. "You have tiny cilia in the back of your eye that are responsible for creating the intraocular fluid that is causing your glaucoma. The laser cauterizes the cilia and thereby reduces the production of fluid. You don't have to have anesthesia and your eye will be completely numb. You won't feel a thing."

Two days later, Henry removed the tube shunt from my eye. After a speedy recovery, my mom made an appointment for me to see Dr. Garter.

Seated in an exam room in his office, I watched the door swing open and a large, albeit blurry, figure bustle into the room.

"Hello, I'm Dr. Garter," the figure introduced himself, then paused for a moment as though expecting applause.

He had to settle for a mechanical "hello" from my mom and the merest nod of the head from me.

"I've consulted with Dr. Jordan about your case and we both agree that my laser surgery is the only hope you have of saving your vision. Now, I'm happy to consult with you today and you can go back home and decide what you want to do. However, I'm sure you're aware that we are running short on time and options."

His words hung over the room like an ominous, black cloud. Eventually, I cleared my throat and asked, "If I do have the surgery today, will my vision go back to what it was?"

"I promise," Dr. Garter covered his heart with his hand, "you will get it all back." He paused and amended his statement. "There's a chance that you may lose one or two lines on the eye chart. That's the worst-case scenario and, you have to admit, that's better than no vision at all."

"Mom?" I leaned forward in my chair. "What do you think?"

My mother crossed the room to where I was sitting and laid her hand on mine. "I can't tell you what to do and at the same time, I don't know if there's anything else to do."

I looked around the room, hating the way objects were distorted to the point of being unrecognizable. Over time, the building pressure in my eye had also caused colors to lose their intensity, making the world around me appear bland and uninspiring.

Can I continue to live like this? If my vision gets worse until it's completely gone, do I want to live at all? If I do nothing, I will lose my vision over time. If I have the surgery and it works, I will walk out of here with my vision restored. If I have the surgery and something goes wrong, I could lose my vision today. According to this guy, the surgery is foolproof, but I don't believe that for a second.

It was a classic case of damned if you do, damned if you don't. I kept weighing my options but couldn't reach a decision, until I thought of Milo and pictured him trotting toward me.

This surgery was my only hope of riding Milo again.

"I'll have the surgery today," I said shakily.

Within seconds of my announcement, the small room came alive with movement. Between dropping numbing medication into my eye and sterilizing the room with alcohol pads, the nurse, Jackie, was in constant motion.

Dr. Garter readied the laser and, as I heard it hum to life, I naïvely asked, "Is this the same machine used for Lasik surgery?"

"Oh, no," he scoffed. "This laser has to reach the back of your eye. It's much, much more powerful."

Next, I heard the thwack of latex gloves as the doctor pulled them over his hands. Jackie hovered nearby, her sickly-sweet, floral perfume giving her away. When Dr. Garter gave the command to "lay her flat," Jackie pushed a button that lowered the back of my chair until I was parallel to the floor.

My heart began to race painfully, and I forced myself to take deep, slow breaths. Something cold and wet was applied to the area around my eye. Iodine, I gathered, from the sharp smell.

Gloved fingers pulled downward on my lower lid and Dr. Garter warned, "This may sting a bit, but you need to hold very still."

The initial pain of the needle piercing my lower lid intensified as the anesthetic was pushed through the syringe. Unable to stop myself, I began to whimper. I heard my mother's chair scrape backward as she prepared to rush to my side.

"Please stay seated," Jackie ordered as she blocked my mother's path. "We must keep the area around the patient sterile." A few tense seconds passed as my mom reluctantly returned to her seat.

"Ready for the next one?" Dr. Gartner asked as he pulled my upper lid into position. "The first injection should be taking effect, so this one won't hurt as much."

It was worse. We were only ten minutes into the procedure and, so far, the doctor had been wrong about everything. Somehow, I made it through the next two shots, though not without several well-placed expletives that caused Jackie to cluck her tongue disapprovingly.

Finally, the injections were over, and Dr. Garter and Jackie gathered the used needles and prepared to leave the room. "We'll give you some time to get numb," he said, returning my chair to an upright position and closing the door behind him.

"Are you sure you want to go through with this?" my mom asked as soon as they were gone.

"The worst part is over," I reminded her. "It will be smooth sailing once the anesthetic kicks in."

Fifteen minutes later the duo returned to check on what should've been a completely desensitized eye.

"Can you feel this?" Dr. Garter asked, rubbing a Q-tip across my eyelid. The soft cotton tickled as it brushed against my lashes.

"Yes," I replied.

"Are you sure?" he asked, once again dragging the cotton tip over my lid.

Dr. Garter grunted, obviously aggravated, when I confirmed that my eye was still sensitive to touch. "I'll give you a few more minutes," he said, his voice now holding a hint of impatience.

I shouldn't have, but I took advantage of the doctor's absence to perform tests of my own on my eye.

"Numb yet?" my mom asked hopefully.

"No, and I'm getting worried." I let the tissue I had been sweeping back and forth across my face drop to my lap.

"Are you sure that this isn't all in your head?" Dr. Garter asked me after a third pass at my eye with a cotton swab.

"My eye is closed," I pointed out. "How would I know when you're touching it if I couldn't feel anything?"

He ignored my logic and tapped the lower corner of my eye with the swab.

"Do the injection sites still burn?" Dr. Garter asked.

"No," I returned. "The area you just touched feels more tingly than anything else."

"Good, that means we can start there and by the time I'm ready to move on, the rest of your eye will be tingly."

"You're going to start lasering before my entire eye is numb?" I squeaked.

"Of course not," the doctor replied. "You said yourself it was getting tingly. That means the medication is working and by the time I begin to laser, your entire eye will be tingly."

He moved around the room, adjusting lights and positioning equipment. As if on cue, Jackie returned to the room and gently eased my head into place so my chin sat squarely on the chin rest. Another quick flick of a switch and I was briefly mesmerized by a barrage of red lights.

"Here we go," Dr Garter announced, and the laser began making a ticking sound much like a clock. I pressed my head against the head rest and held my breath. The ticking stopped and a beam of red light shot into my eye.

I wasn't numb. When the laser's fiery beam touched my eye, I felt every lick of its blistering heat. I was screaming and only vaguely aware of a pair of hands holding my head in place. Jackie's long nails dug into my scalp, but that was nothing compared to the sensation of having my eye set on fire.

"You must hold still and keep your eye open," she hissed at me.

Abruptly, the beam of light vanished and Jackie released her hold on my head. I leaned over, panting like a dog. Jackie squatted down next to me. "Goodness, it wasn't all that bad, was it?" she asked as if she were speaking to a petulant child.

My stomach heaved once, then twice, and I threw up all over Jackie.

"What the fuck just happened?" My mom's voice was deadly and this time when she got up, nobody dared stop her.

The doctor stumbled over his words before he replied, "I don't understand. She shouldn't have felt anything. She was numb. She said so herself."

"No, I didn't," I managed to say between each labored breath. "Never said that."

"She couldn't have felt anything," Dr. Garter repeated defensively.

His weak argument only served to enrage my mother further.

"Asshole," she fairly spat at him. "Generally, when people are screaming in pain, it means they are feeling everything. Or did they not teach you that in medical school?"

Furious as she was, her touch on my arm was gentle. "We're leaving," she announced.

The doctor swiveled in his chair to face her. "We are in the middle of a procedure! You can't leave."

"If you think for one second that I'm going to allow you to put my daughter through that..." my mom paused searching for the right word, "that torture again, you've lost your mind."

"Then she'll know who to thank when she is learning to read Braille and walking with a white cane," he retorted nastily.

Dr. Garter had my full attention now and he knew it. "That's right," he said smugly. "If you walk out that door, you'll assuredly be blind within weeks. Now I don't know why you think you can feel this laser. Maybe you're not as numb as we would like you to be. But I have six more passes to do with my laser and, young lady, I promise you'll be thanking me when you can see again."

I needed a few minutes to think. When I had made up my mind, I sat up straight in my chair. I wiped the tears from my cheeks and wordlessly placed my chin back on the rest.

"Put the speculum on her," Dr. Garter ordered Jackie, who was still brushing the contents of my stomach from her clothing. I didn't know what he was talking about, but I found out all too soon. Jackie abruptly attached a wire contraption to my lids to hold them apart, making it impossible for me to close my eye.

My mom sat back in her chair and the room was again quiet. Until the laser began to tick, tick, tick.

By the third pass of the laser, I was wishing for an instantaneous death. I tried to think of Milo, Mom, Spike, anything that brought joy to my life, but the red-hot laser sliced into my eye again and again until I thought my head would explode.

By the fourth round, I had screamed myself hoarse and during the fifth, much to everyone's relief, I lost consciousness.

I had to be carried to the car and I don't remember anything about the drive home. I slept for twenty-four hours and awoke to the sound of my mother speaking softly to someone on the phone. I dragged myself into a sitting position and was hit immediately by a wall of nausea. I steadied myself in time to hear my mom say, "Thanks, Henry. We'll see you this week."

"What did Henry say?" I asked in a hoarse whisper. Heat radiated from my eye, and I knew it must be swollen. I was incredibly grateful for the cold compress my mom placed in my hands, and instantly sank back into the pillows and laid the cloth over my eye.

"He explained why your eye didn't get numb. According to Henry, the countless surgeries and inflammation your eye has endured over the years have created an enormous amount of scar tissue. When medication is injected into scar, or dead, tissue, it isn't absorbed. Dr. Garter never took this into consideration."

I was only mildly surprised that Dr. Garter had failed to recognize uveitis as my primary disease. When he looked at me, he saw nothing more than another glaucoma patient.

"Henry couldn't believe you went through with the surgery and survived it," my mom added. "He was very upset."

I winced, remembering one of the more gruesome moments of the procedure, then gently shook the memory away. "If it works and my vision returns, it will all have been worth it."

CHAPTER EIGHT

My head rested against the passenger window of my mom's car. I hadn't moved in a long time or made a sound. The only proof of life were the smoky rings my breath left on the glass.

My mother, having given up on conversation, pressed down on the accelerator, eager to put as many miles as possible between Henry's office and us.

In the last few hours, my life had changed so drastically, it was hard to believe that I was the same person. *Was I really?* I didn't feel the same. Frankly, I was trying my best not to feel anything at all.

That morning, I woke up early, beating my alarm clock by an hour. Had it been any other day, I would have remained in bed until the insufferable beeping forced me to get up. However, today was exactly one week since the laser surgery, and I had an appointment with Henry to find out if it had been successful.

"I have a good feeling about this," I told my mom as we pulled out of the driveway.

"Is your vision better today?" she asked optimistically.

"I'm still on contact lens restriction," I reminded her. "It's hard to tell without the contact but I definitely feel better." Two days after the surgery, my eye was still red and inflamed but the headaches that had plagued me for months had, mercifully, subsided.

More signs of improvement followed. My eye no longer felt tight, as if it had outgrown the socket. Nor did it appear to be bulging in the center.

It seemed to me that my eye was making a full recovery. I was so close to resuming my old life, I could practically feel Milo's reins in my hands and the scrape of his teeth against my palm as I fed him his favorite peppermint candies. I had spent an hour looking for my car keys and finally found them in my suitcase. Now they sat on top of my dresser, waiting for the moment I was told I could drive again.

Henry's waiting room had been full of people. I couldn't see them well, but I could hear them talking quietly to one another. My mom helped me to a chair and once I was safely seated, she returned to the front desk to check me in.

I was thinking about Milo and how I hadn't seen him for two-and-a-half months. Distractedly, I ran my palm along my thigh where the once-hard muscles had grown soft and weak from not riding. It would take some time to build them, as well as my stamina, back up.

My name was called, generating objections from the other patients who had arrived long before I had.

"Here we go," my mom said, taking my hand and pulling me to my feet, which had suddenly become very heavy.

Mom gave my hand a light tug and when I didn't fall in line behind her, she turned around to face me.

"What's the matter?" she asked.

"What if the surgery didn't work?"

"I seem to recall that a little over an hour ago, you were positive the surgery had been successful," she replied, giving my hand a supportive squeeze.

"I know," I said miserably. "But what if I'm wrong?"

"Then, we deal with it," she said encouragingly. "Just like we always do."

"If you say so," I agreed half-heartedly and followed her into the examination room.

"What is it?" my mom and I asked in unison the moment the technician was finished measuring my pressure.

"Three," the tech responded as if it were just another number and not my salvation.

"Are you sure?" my mom asked.

"Yes," he said a little insulted. "I checked it twice."

Tears of relief rolled down my cheeks and I started gulping in air as if I had been holding my breath for months.

Unsure of what he should do or say, the technician slipped out of the room after mumbling something about the doctor seeing me shortly.

We were all smiles when Henry arrived.

"You heard the good news?" my mom asked cheerfully.

"I heard the news," Henry answered gravely.

If his reply didn't say it all, then his tone did.

"I don't understand," I said. "Is there a problem?"

"Let me take a look and then I'll answer all of your questions," Henry said, pulling his chair closer to mine. "I promise I'll be quick."

True to his word, Henry performed a much-abbreviated version of his usual exam.

"So, this is what has happened," Henry said when he was finished. "The laser surgery worked but we didn't get the results we wanted."

"That clarifies nothing," I said angrily, my patience at an end. "My pressure has dropped down to three and my eye doesn't feel like it's going to jump out of my head anymore. Despite my eye being set on fire, it sounds to me like the surgery was a success."

"I know," Henry said gently," but that's the problem. Your pressure is now too low."

"What?" I shouted. "How does that happen?"

Henry took a few seconds to consider the best way to reply. "There's a balance of pressure that your eye must maintain. Like a balloon. If there's too much pressure, it will pop."

"And if there's too little, it'll deflate," I finished for him.

"Maybe we should take her pressure again," my mom suggested. "Perhaps the technician was off."

Henry shook his head, moving forward to check me further. He lifted my lid and looked at my eye. "I can tell by looking at the eye that the tech was correct. If anything, I would guess the pressure is even lower than three."

"How can you tell?" I asked.

"Close your eyes," Henry said. "Now run your finger over your lid."

I did as I was told, lightly rubbing my finger over the delicate skin.

"It doesn't feel round anymore, does it?" Henry observed.

"Not really," I mumbled dismally. Behind my lid, my eye was small and flat. "What do we do now?" I groaned. "Do I have to start all over with different medication?"

"No," Henry said. "Glaucoma is a fairly common affliction. As you well know, there are several medications that treat it. Low pressure, on the other hand, is extremely rare and there's no treatment."

"There has to be!" I demanded. "There's medication for everything."

"Not for this." Henry sounded so forlorn, I almost felt sorry for him.

"What caused this to happen, Henry?" My mom's voice was tremulous. I wanted to get up and hug her, but I couldn't move.

"It was the laser surgery," I said. "I should have run the minute Dr. Garter started promising he would save my vision."

"I don't know about that," Henry said. "I do think that Dr. Garter treated your eye as if it were healthy. Which, of course, it isn't. Plus, he could have been distracted because you were screaming in pain. Whatever the case, he was too aggressive with the laser and destroyed too much of the ciliary body. Your pressure is going to continue to drop until it's zero."

I was seething as Henry told my mom and me that the surgery had not only failed to cure the glaucoma, it would also blind me.

Dr. Garter and his beloved laser had ruined my life.

"I still don't know how you managed to withstand that laser when your eye wasn't numb," Henry was saying as I clenched my fists so tightly that my nails dug into the palms of my hands. "It sounds to me like mistakes were made from start to finish."

"Mistakes?" I echoed, my voice shrill, my rage gaining momentum. "Dr. Garter promised he'd get my vision back. Then he shot a beam of fire into my eye, which wasn't numb because he was sloppy, and now you're telling me he blinded me? I think that goes far beyond a 'mistake!'"

I stared at Henry, daring him to answer but also knowing there was nothing he could do or say to end this nightmare. I felt badly for lashing out at him. At the same time, all I wanted to do was keep screaming and never stop.

"Can we go home now? I just want to go home," I snarled. I stood and turned toward Henry, who had also risen from his seat. Putting his arms around me, the man who had fought for my vision for the past twenty-three years hugged me tightly, and I began to cry.

I don't remember leaving Henry's office or walking through the parking lot alongside my mom in the pouring rain.

I tried to make sense of what was happening, but there was a tornado inside me that was spinning so fast, it was making me sick.

Eventually, I realized that the steady sounds of the other cars had diminished, and the only wet smack of tires cutting through puddles was our own. We must have gotten off the highway, but that couldn't be right, since we had a good ten miles to go before the exit for home.

I straightened in my seat searching for something recognizable in the blurred objects flying by. Giving up, I turned to my mom and asked, "Where are we going?"

She didn't answer right away, and I was about to repeat the question when, at last, she replied, "Right now I can think of only one thing that can help you. That's where we're going. To get help."

"I can't be helped right now."

"Trust me."

"Please, Mom, I really just want to go home."

We pulled off onto another road. The car slowed and I tried one more time to make my mom see reason.

"Please don't do this to me," I said, willing each word to penetrate her resolve. "I know you mean well, but I just found out that I'm going blind. It's too new for me to talk about and I'm too unstable to be talked to. I'm close to falling apart and I'd like to do so in private."

For a second, I thought my mom was going to turn the car around. Instead, she reached for my hand and held it.

"If I could trade places with you, I would. I'd do anything for you. I'll take you home and you can hide in your room for as long as you want. However, we're going to make a stop first because I know there is at least one thing left in this world that will make you happy, even today."

"Happy? I don't think I'll ever be happy again. How could I be when I've lost everything that's important to me. Freedom, friends—" I stopped abruptly, unable to finish my thought.

I was wrong. One thing that was slipping through my fingers wasn't lost to me yet.

"We're going to the barn. You're taking me to see Milo," I said, in awe of my mother for knowing even before I did that Milo was the key to saving my sanity.

Weekdays were quiet at the barn and I was grateful that the only person there, besides us, was Bob. Mom must have called him at some point to tell him about our unexpected visit. Bob had always seen me as strong and independent. Now, as my mother guided me along a path I had walked hundreds of times, I worried that Bob would see me as weak and helpless.

"Hello," he said as we drew closer. His voice was more formal than usual. My brain scrambled for something to say that would lighten the mood. Nothing came to mind, and I decided it was probably best to stare at the ground and say nothing at all.

My mom's hand fell away from my elbow as she hugged Bob and gave him a quick update about my prognosis. I felt naked without her hand on my arm, and I took a small step closer to her. Noticing what I had done, she returned her hand to its spot above my elbow, and I immediately felt safe again.

"Well, it's nice to see you again. It's been a very long time," Bob said, pretending to be offended, "and when you finally do come to the barn, it's not to visit me, it's to see Milo."

I was relieved that Bob had started to relax. His humor, cheeky and familiar, was so welcome that I actually managed half a smile. Encouraged by my response, Bob proceeded to tell me that I looked truly awful.

"It hasn't been my best day," I shrugged.

I was about to ask him a question, but I didn't make it past the first word before a neigh, guttural at first and then explosively high-pitched, interrupted our conversation.

"That didn't take long," Bob chuckled. "I believe Milo knows you're here."

"You think so?" This time my smile was effortless. I untangled myself from my mom's hold and, without assistance, covered the short distance to Milo's stall. The door squealed as I closed it behind me. Milo quieted down the moment I joined him.

The sound of a horse walking slowly down the aisle, its aluminum-clad hooves ringing out as they met the concrete floor, caught my attention. Standing on tiptoes, I looked between the dusty steel bars on Milo's door. I was barely able to make out the large, round hindquarters of a horse. My mother was on one side, Bob on the other. They were heading for the indoor riding ring, where my mom was going to watch Bob ride one of his horses.

Grateful for the private time with Milo, I found him patiently waiting for me in the rear corner of his stall. The wind and rain continued to drum against the barn's metal roof, but inside Milo's sanctuary, it was warm and dry.

I reached my hand out to him, expecting him to at least check for a treat, but he ignored my outstretched palm.

"What's the matter, M?" I asked quietly and moved closer to him. "Did you forget me already?"

Milo tossed his head and snorted a few times, chastising me in his own way for my extended absence.

"I'm sorry, Milo," I said sincerely. "I know I was gone for a long time. It was hard for me, too, but I didn't have a choice."

Sighing heavily, Milo took a single step that brought him within my grasp. I reached for him and felt a sense of relief as soon as I wrapped my arms around his neck. He lowered his head until his chin rested on my shoulder, and we stayed like that for a long time.

After more than two months, I was, at last, precisely where I needed to be. I began to cry. A flood of tears streamed down my face and onto Milo, leaving dark, wet tracks in his coat.

"I missed you so much," I wept, overwhelmed by emotions I had been holding back until now.

Milo waited for me to stop sobbing then ran his soft muzzle through my hair and down my cheek.

Without any warning, he stuck out his giant tongue and painted my face with saliva and bits of chewed hay that stubbornly stuck to my cheeks, regardless of how many swipes I made at them with my sleeve.

"Yuck!" I yelped at Milo, who stared at me innocently. "Oh, you think you're funny, do you?" I tried to sound indignant, but my laughter gave me away.

It felt so good to laugh. I couldn't remember the last time I had found anything funny.

"What am I going to do without you, M?" I asked before I could stop myself. I blanched, wishing I could take the words back, but they hung in the air demanding to be acknowledged.

Sagging against Milo's shoulder, I contemplated what arrangements had to be made before I went blind. According to Henry, there was no way of knowing exactly when it would happen. I just knew it was coming.

Although my future was a giant question mark, Milo's needn't be.

Realistically, why would I own a horse if I couldn't ride or take care of him? Certainly, keeping Milo so I could occasionally pet him when someone had time to drive me to the barn was out of the question. Milo was a show horse, born and bred to compete, even if it wasn't with me.

As if knowing the wretched path my thoughts had taken, Milo turned his head until we were looking at each other, eye to eye. His was so close to mine, I could see each luminescent fleck of gold within its dark center.

"I remember the first time I saw you," I murmured. "You looked like life had already chewed you up and spit you out."

Smiling wistfully, I ran the back of my hand down his cheek. "But then I looked into those eyes of yours, and I saw fire. I knew you had plenty of life still in you. It was hiding, but it was there."

Milo's seal-brown ears twitched at the sound of my voice. "You're a fighter, M," I told him fondly. "You remind me of the magic horses in my book of fairy tales. They were always rescuing their humans from one terrible fate or another." Nudging me gently, Milo rubbed his nose against my cheek. "I know you would save me if you could."

He raised his head and I braced myself, ready to run at the first sight of his tongue.

Crooking his neck, Milo set his mouth so close to my ear, I half expected him to tell me a secret. What he did instead was even more amazing.

Milo took a deep breath and exhaled slowly, and the stream of warm air caressed the side of my face. He did it a few more times before I understood why.

Horses are incredibly affectionate animals, especially with each other. Nuzzling, hugging, and even biting are ways in which they communicate love. When a mother wants to calm her foal, she'll blow slowly and rhythmically into her baby's nose.

Just as Milo was doing to me now.

Oddly enough, there was something soothing about it. When I spoke to Milo again, my voice was more composed.

"I promise you, I won't give up yet," I said solemnly. "If there is a way for me to get my vision back, I'll find it. And if I can't, I'll still find my way back to you, somehow."

The barn door scraped across the concrete floor, signaling the end of my visit. My mom and Bob were discussing their favorite Baltimore restaurants, their voices light and cheerful. I was glad my mother had found a momentary reprieve from this devastating day.

Milo's ears perked forward, his attention divided between the noise in the aisle and me. I scratched him under his chin and was once again his sole focus.

Something told me it would be a long time before I would see him again. "I love you, M," I said tenderly.

"Ready to go?" my mom asked gently.

"Yes."

Milo stood next to me and I held his face in my hands, our unwelcome separation already beginning to tear at me.

"I'll be back, Milo," I whispered, giving him one last hug. "As soon as I can."

CHAPTER NINE

My promise to Milo drove me to do everything I could think of to raise my eye pressure and save my vision. At least once every hour throughout the day, I would hold my breath, pinch my nostrils together, and force the air through my sinuses. This succeeded in clearing my ears. but didn't stop my eye from deflating.

Twice a day, I drank the thick, red pulp of a medicinal plant called bloodroot, which is known to increase eye pressure. It had no effect on my eye, but it did cause terrible stomach cramps. and I stopped taking it after three or four days.

I even tried meditation a few times. I remembered being told that stress could raise eye pressure, so I meditated on all the things in my life that caused me angst. Despite the abundance of material I had for this disturbing ritual, the only thing it raised was my blood pressure.

Mostly, I waited for Henry to call to tell me he had found a way to reverse the damage done by the laser surgery. When a week passed, I began to panic and called him.

"Have you found anything that will raise my pressure?" I asked him expectantly.

"I told you when you were in my office, there isn't a single medication for low pressure."

"I know that's what you said. I thought you might be looking for another way to bring my pressure back up. There has to be something that causes eye pressure to rise."

I thought my argument was reasonable. Over the years, no matter what problem my eye was having, Henry had managed to solve it.

"I'm sorry, I know this is hard to accept. There's nothing I, or anyone else, can do to help you," Henry said soberly. "I wish I could do more, you know I do. But short of a miracle, you need to prepare yourself for a complete loss of vision."

The next day, I called Henry again.

"I heard on TV that certain cold medicines may elevate eye pressure. Should I start trying different ones?" I had just listened to a commercial for a cold medicine that ended with the warning, "Do not take this if you have glaucoma."

"It's a good thought," Henry said, "but it won't bring your pressure up. I understand where you're coming from, but only take cold medicine if you have a cold. It isn't going to help your eye."

Too distressed to listen to Henry explain why, I told him I had to go and ended the phone call abruptly.

My heart began to pound, and the world tilted, throwing me off balance. Henry couldn't save me, and my eye wasn't magically healing itself. I was really going to go blind. For a long time, I stood very still and stared accusingly at the phone, wishing I hadn't called Henry today. *How did I let this happen? I promised Milo I wouldn't give up, but I don't know what else to do.*

Out of ideas and hope, I retreated to my bedroom and stayed there for five days. I barely ate, I didn't sleep, and I hardly noticed Spike. Every now and then my mom checked on me to make sure I was alive or to tell me there was food on the table. Other than that, she left me alone to come to terms with what was happening to my life.

Most of my time was spent staring at the white wall across from my bed. I stared at it until my brain went numb, then kept staring so it stayed numb. That was the only way to avoid the pain of my grief, anger, and fear, and to keep myself from going crazy while I waited to go blind.

On the fifth day, there was a knock on my door and before I could answer, my mom entered the room and sat on the bed beside me. Spike's stubby tail wagged happily as she greeted him with a gentle pat on his round head.

"How are you doing?" she asked, stroking my cheek with the back of her hand.

I flinched and turned my face away from her. I didn't want to feel anything. Not even the sympathetic touch of someone who loved me.

My mother resumed petting Spike while she waited for my answer. If I described the waves of panic that were crushing me, she might want to talk about them. I was in no mood for conversation. In fact, since I had shut myself in my room, I only spoke when spoken to.

"I guess I'm as okay as I can be," I answered dully.

"I know you are. But just so you know, you don't have to be strong for me. You can scream, or cry, or go back to staring at the wall if the mood strikes you."

"Okay. Is that what you came in here to tell me?"

"No. There are a few things I'd like to talk to you about."

"I'm listening," I said warily.

"There are decisions that have to be made and I can't make them without you. Your townhouse has four flights of stairs," she said matter-of-factly, "and I don't think it's safe for you to go back there. I'd like to put it up for sale."

Until she mentioned it, I hadn't even thought about my house. It was just one more thing I was losing, and it didn't matter to me anymore.

"That's fine," I said, "do whatever you need to do. But where will I live? I can't live with you and Howard forever."

"For right now, you're welcome to live with us. And when you can live on your own, we'll find a place that works better for you," she promised.

"My car should be sold, too," I said flatly. "I won't be needing it and I could use the money to help pay Milo's bills."

"Howard took your car to his dealership a few days ago. He thinks it'll sell quickly. But whatever you get for your car, it isn't going to cover Milo's expenses for very long."

Those words jolted me out of my stupor and awakened my instinct to protect Milo.

"Would you have me sell him, too?" I growled fiercely. "Get rid of the house and the car, I really don't care. Just don't make me sell Milo. I know it's extravagant to keep paying for him. But if we sell him now, it will destroy me."

"Slow down a second." Mom touched my arm, but I pulled away. "I never said anything about selling Milo. I wouldn't do that to you. However, it is a lot of money to pay every month for a horse that you aren't riding. I spoke with Bob yesterday and he agreed with me."

I felt betrayed. "You spoke to Bob about Milo?" I asked accusingly.

"You weren't answering your phone and he was getting worried about you. He called me yesterday to make sure you were okay and to discuss Milo's immediate future. He knows selling Milo isn't an option, but what do you think about leasing him?"

The thought of my mother and Bob planning Milo's future without me was infuriating. "I don't know," I scowled. "Does Bob have someone in mind?"

"Apparently he has a young student who has ridden Milo a few times and she loves him. She has a pony now but wants a horse. Bob told me her name, but I can't remember it."

I knew the girl in question must be Wendy, a teenager who had started riding with Bob the year before. I liked Wendy and her mom, and had the situation been different, I would have admitted that Wendy was a good match for Milo.

Instead, I was gnashing my teeth as I signed the one-year lease agreement that Bob faxed to my mom, temporarily waiving my rights as Milo's owner. I had a sinking feeling that this was just the first step toward losing him. My hand trembled, causing the piece of paper in it to shake.

Taking the lease from me and setting it aside, my mom hugged me.

"Milo isn't going anywhere, he's still your horse. The lease fee will give you some income and a much-needed reprieve from his bills for a year."

"Then what do we do? I'll be completely blind by then."

"I don't know, I can't look that far into the future. Besides, a lot can change in a year. For now, Milo will stay in Bob's care, and you can visit him whenever you want."

The lease contract was finalized and later that day Howard came home and gently told me that my car had been sold. Last on my "Things I Never Thought I'd Have to Do" list was pack up my house and get it ready to be sold.

While my mom was on kitchen duty, dividing my utensils and dishes into "keep" and "give away" boxes, Spike and I were in my bedroom walk-in closet, surrounded by mounds of shirts, jeans, dresses, sweaters, and shoes.

Tossing them into the appropriate box was easy, until I dug into a new pile and my hand landed on the fine wool of a riding coat. These beautifully tailored jackets were part of the specialty attire worn in the show ring that I often referred to as my "costume." I was joking, but there was something about the buff-colored breeches, tall black boots, and fitted jacket that kick-started my adrenalin every time I put them on.

I'd forgotten that my show clothes would be in my bedroom closet. I gnawed on my bottom lip wishing I could decide their fate as easily as I had the rest of my wardrobe. *These clothes are part of me. I can't just give them away.*

I reached for the box of items I planned on storing but stopped myself before I could grab it. *I'm going to have to get rid of them eventually. I might as well get rid of them now.*

My hand, still hovering in the air, changed course and I grasped the edge of the box destined for Goodwill and dragged it closer to me. *Don't think about it. Start with the jacket and keep going until it's all gone.*

On autopilot, I started chucking jackets, breeches, boots, and show shirts into the box. I didn't stop until it was filled and the only item that remained was a new, black jacket.

I'd loved this jacket the moment I saw it hanging in Hadfield's Saddlery, an equestrian boutique in Wellington known for extraordinary leather work and fine apparel. Simple, yet elegant, I dared not try it on. I didn't have to look at the tag to know it was beyond my budget. Returning to the shop before I left Florida, I was overjoyed to find the jacket had been put on sale. I bought it and was planning on wearing it when I showed Milo for the first time.

"What do you think?" I asked Spike who was napping on the floor. The sales tags still dangled from the sleeve and made a soft swishing sound when I picked up the jacket and showed it to him. "Oh, well," I whispered and gently laid the jacket on top of the other clothes in the box.

"You're not getting rid of all your show clothes, are you?" my mom asked, joining me in the closet.

"What else would I do with them? I don't need them anymore."

"Even if that's true, I know how much you love these clothes," she said, opening the box and rifling through it. "You've had some of them since you were a teenager. At least keep a few things. What about this one? It's never been worn."

She held up the black jacket and I took it from her. Folding it neatly, I returned it to the box, which I then taped shut.

"Mom, it doesn't matter whether or not I've worn something, what matters is that I'll never wear it again."

"It doesn't feel right to me but they're your things, so do what you want," she said unhappily.

It took us the rest of the day to finish packing my belongings into boxes. I brought a suitcase full of clothes to my mom's house and the rest was sent to storage or donated to Goodwill.

Bob called me the day after Thanksgiving to tell me that he and the horses would be heading to Florida at the end of the month.

"Wendy will have fun showing Milo in Wellington, he was so good there last year." My voice cracked with emotion.

"I'm sure she will," Bob said kindly. "You should come see us if you're in Florida this winter. Your parents' house is only forty-five minutes from the horse show."

"I don't know, it might be too hard for me," I replied truthfully. "I really thought I'd be the one showing Milo in Wellington this year."

"Just so you know," Bob said, "it won't be the same without you."

I wished him safe travels and asked him to let me know when the horses arrived in Florida.

That night, I sat in bed thinking about Milo. I missed him more than ever. It seemed that while everyone else's life was moving forward, mine was being leased, sold, or packed into boxes.

Bob surprised me by remembering to call with a Milo report. All of the horses had made it to Wellington in good health and Milo, especially, was enjoying the Florida sunshine.

"Was that Bob I heard you talking to?" my mom asked a little later. "How's Milo?"

"It sounds like he's happy to be back in Florida," I said, sitting down at the kitchen table.

I was making a rare appearance beyond my bedroom. Lately, as my vision worsened, the house had become a giant obstacle course. I had fallen several times, slammed into door frames, and once tripped over a mystery object I suspected was my mom's cat. It was getting scary for me to walk around the house. It was much easier and safer to stay put in my bedroom.

"What brings you to the kitchen?" my mom asked, taking a seat next to me.

"Actually, I was wondering if we could spend the winter in Florida."

"I'll take you wherever you want, but why Florida? Because Milo's there?"

"Yes, I like the idea of being closer to him, even if I can't see him. But that's only part of it. I'm losing my sight much faster than

I thought I would," I said bluntly. "Every morning, I wake up and stare at the same three things. That's how I measure how much I lost while I slept."

"What do you look at?" my mother wanted to know.

"The back of my hand, the doorknob on my bathroom door, and the clock. But two days ago, I wasn't able to see the clock anymore. I don't have much time before I'm completely in the dark. Everything here is cold and gray. I want to be in Florida where it's warm and the colors are bright. I don't want the last thing I see to be a patch of dirty snow."

After some thought, Mom got up from the table, placed her hand on my shoulder, and asked, "When would you like to leave?"

Five days later, we were walking through the Baltimore airport to get on our flight to Florida. Like a child, I clung to my mom's arm, fearful that we would become separated.

Airports bring out the worst behavior in people.

Glued as I was to my mom, my left side was still a moving target for the throngs of passengers racing to get to their gates. They banged their suitcases against me and stepped on me so many times that my left ankle and foot were throbbing.

"People are incredibly rude," I griped. By the time we reached Security, I was so frazzled I almost let Spike go through the x-ray machine. Luckily, my mom snatched his carrier off the conveyer belt just in time.

Our cab pulled up in front of the house my parents had bought several years ago. Mom helped me out of the car, and I stood there drinking in my surroundings like a prisoner starved for a taste of nature. A light breeze boosted the vibrant, tropical hues to life as the palm trees swayed back and forth. I took a deep breath and felt myself relax. How I loved it here.

"Are you actually smiling?" my mom asked incredulously. She took me by the arm to guide me the short distance from the car to the house.

Reluctantly, I followed her inside. "It's so pretty here," I said. "How could anyone not smile?"

Letting go of me long enough to retrieve her house key, she asked, "How much can you see?"

"It's a lot like living in a kaleidoscope. One that's very out of focus."

When I called out to Spike, a little blob of black and tan came bounding up to me. The three of us walked into the house and I heard the door shut behind us. Then, without warning, everything went black.

I gasped, alarmed, and began to wildly wave my hands as if to beat back the darkness. *This can't be it*, I thought desperately. *Does sight get turned off in an instant? I'm not ready. I need more time.* But the darkness persisted, and it felt like a black hole was sucking everything into it, including me.

Then, with a click, the lights came on. "Are you okay?" my mom asked, aghast at what must have been a look of terror on my face.

I took a deep breath to steady myself. "I'm fine," I said weakly. "I wasn't expecting it to be so dark. I thought I'd gone blind."

"Oh God, I'm so sorry. I should have warned you that the hurricane shutters are still on all the windows and doors, and they block out the light."

I sat on the couch with Spike, still shaken, while Mom opened up the house. As she pushed back the dense accordion doors one by one, the sun began pouring in and the house came back to life.

Once my equilibrium was restored, I began to explore my temporary home. I wandered into the bedroom I always used during my visits. I'd spent many long weekends and vacations in this house, so the layout was familiar. This factor had played a large part in my decision to head here for the winter. If I had to learn to navigate through life primarily by memory, I wanted it to be as easy as possible.

Fortunately, there was only one staircase. The second floor was dedicated to the master bedroom, so I had no reason to go up there. I had learned the hard way that stairs could be dangerous. On two separate occasions, I'd missed a step and found myself sprawled on the floor, angry, bruised, and humiliated. No need to tempt Fate any further.

Our arrival in Florida had exhausted both my mom and me, and we went to bed early. As I slept, Milo appeared in a dream. I could see his eyes clearly, but this Milo looked different. Gone was the fire that transformed the center of his eyes from brown to gold. In my dream he stared at me through dull, lifeless eyes. I reached for him, but he turned away from me.

"I'm sorry!" I cried. "I tried but no one could help me. I can't do it on my own, Milo." I pleaded with him to come back, but he didn't turn around.

I had the same dream a few times. It always ended with Milo walking away from me and, each time I woke from it, I was overcome with guilt and shame.

Over the next month my sight continued to slip away from me. Colors lost their brilliance, then faded completely. Soon my surroundings were reduced to a thick haze of light and dark that rippled with movement.

One night in February, I woke up and couldn't go back to sleep. I sat up in bed and switched on the table lamp, but nothing happened. *That's weird, the lightbulb must be out.*

As I was having this thought, alarm bells started ringing in my head. Then I heard other sounds but not in my head. Rustling was coming from the kitchen, and outside my window, birds were chirping to greet the new day. My body went cold with the realization that it wasn't night, it was morning.

Frantically, I turned the lamp on and off, on and off. It went click-click-click-click, but no light pierced the darkness.

Please, let the bulb be dead. I could hear the low hum of electricity and placed my hand on the base of the lamp where the sound was coming from. I moved my hand upwards until I felt the delicate shape of the glass bulb. It was warm to the touch.

The lamp was working perfectly. My eye was not. I looked to my left and then my right, giving my eye every chance to see something. It didn't. While I was sleeping, my ability to see light had vanished, leaving me completely sightless.

I was beginning to hyperventilate when I heard my mom ask from the other side of the door, "Are you awake?"

"Yes," I replied, forcing myself to breathe normally and wishing I could spare my mom the pain I was about to inflict on her.

The door creaked open and I felt her sit on the bed by my side. I hung my head and in a low voice told her what I sensed she already knew.

"It's gone. It's all gone."

Embracing me, she whispered, "I'm sorry." She clung to me, rocking us both back and forth. "I'm so sorry."

I stayed in her arms for a moment, allowing her to comfort me.

"It's okay, Mom," I said, before pulling away as a rising swell of emotions threatened to overwhelm me. I had to stop it. Picturing a white wall, I started staring at it to shut out the world and make myself go numb.

CHAPTER TEN

I went into seclusion in my bedroom fortress, turning off my cell phone and sleeping a lot. My mom, the only person allowed to see me, checked on me often. I managed to eat a little and use the bathroom. Occasionally, Mom reported a phone call, but I would shake my head, not caring who had phoned or for what reason.

Each day another layer of misery, thick and heavy, piled onto the ones already weighing me down. I sank further into myself under their weight, desperate for a reprieve from the darkness that closed in on me, making me claustrophobic. I felt imprisoned by the pitch-black walls of a coffin, and no matter where I went, there was no escape.

After five days of fighting the darkness, I gave up and let it overtake me. Time and space ceased to exist, and like a bug under a glass, I was trapped inside my head. It didn't matter where my physical body was; I didn't wish to be attached to it anymore, and I stopped eating and wouldn't get out of bed. I learned to exist on memories and imagination. The life outside my mind was filled with loss and pain. In my catatonic state, I was finally free. Sometimes I would hear my mom calling me from far away, but I was too lost to answer her.

I wasn't aware that five more days went by. My body was beginning to shut down, and I didn't even know it. And then, I woke up. One minute I was aware of nothing and the next, something powerful was shoving me back to reality.

It was the feel and sound of someone next to me, quietly weeping.

"Mom." My voice was hoarse and barely audible. "Mom," I croaked again. I stretched out an emaciated arm and patted the bed around me.

The crying suddenly stopped, and my probing hand was gripped by my mother's damp one.

"Are you awake?" she asked, squeezing my hand. "Are you back with me?"

Having no idea that I'd been unresponsive for days, I replied, "Yes, Mom, I'm here. Where else would I be?"

Tempting as it was, for my mom's sake, I did not allow myself to be sucked back into oblivion, though I still struggled with bouts of claustrophobia. My sleep patterns were thrown off as well, and there were days I slept more than Spike did.

I was jolted out of a deep sleep one afternoon in early March by the sound of someone knocking impatiently on my bedroom door. I had to clear my throat twice before I managed, "Come in."

My mom rarely knocked, and Howard wasn't in town. I had no idea who was going to enter my room.

The door flew open, and a familiar voice squealed the greeting my best friend and I reserved for each other: "Hello, Schweetie!"

For lack of a better hiding place, I yanked the sheets over my head.

I'd seen Sarah a handful of times since deserting her on New Year's Eve two years ago, the night Milo entered my life. I couldn't remember the last time we had been together, but I knew it was several months ago.

To be fair, it wasn't Sarah's fault. Of all my friends, she was the only one who continued to call me every day, even though I never answered or returned her calls.

"What are you doing here?" I asked, my voice muffled by the covers.

"What are you doing under the covers?" Sarah countered.

"Hiding."

"Which is why I'm here. You've been in hiding for a really long time."

"What do you expect me to do? The entire world hides from me now. Why can't I hide from it?"

"I'm right here. Just because you can't see me doesn't mean I'm hiding from you," Sarah corrected me.

I was running out of air and excuses. Pulling the covers away from my face, I said, "I'm sorry I didn't call you back."

"It's okay." Sarah sighed and flopped down on the bed alongside me. "I totally understand why you weren't in the mood to talk."

The two of us had spent our entire friendship rescuing each other. From bullies to boyfriends, Sarah and I had always protected one another. But this time was different. I couldn't protect myself anymore, let alone her. And she certainly couldn't rescue me, not this time.

"You're right. I most definitely have not been in the mood to talk. Still, l feel bad that you came all the way down here to check on me."

"What do you mean?" Sarah feigned innocence. "It's freezing in Maryland and I had some vacation time. Florida is so nice this time of year and—"

"You spoke to my mother," I guessed, cutting her off.

"And I spoke to your mother. Look, you weren't answering my phone calls. Of course, I'm going to worry. So, I called your mom. The last time I spoke to her, she told me…" Sarah paused searching for the right words, "she told me you had given up. You stopped coming out of your room, you weren't eating or talking. I've known you and your family most of my life, and I've never heard your mom as frightened as she was on the phone. So, I told her I'd be down as soon as possible."

"I know I'm upsetting her, but I don't have the will to do anything about it. My mom's right. I did give up."

"Don't be ridiculous. You're the toughest person I know. You can try to convince yourself otherwise, but I know you. Somehow, you'll get through this." Sarah's voice, usually so full of laughter, was uncommonly fierce, and I almost smiled at her fervent resolve to resurrect the person I used to be.

"Okay, enough about me," I said. "Tell me what you've been up to."

"Nice deflection." Sarah sat up and I heard her sniffing the air. "I promise I'll fill you in on all the boring details of my life. But first, and please know what I'm about to say comes from a place of love...you need to shower."

"That bad?" I frowned.

"There's a Cheerio in your hair," Sarah said, plucking the cereal from my grimy tangles.

While Sarah unpacked her things in the guest room adjacent to mine, I showered, washed my hair, and then, for the first time in a week, changed my clothes. My exceptional memory made it possible for me to move about the bedroom and bathroom with little difficulty. As long as my things such as clothing, towels, and toothbrush were put back in the same place, all I had to do to find them was picture where they were.

"You're clean!" my mom cheered when I shuffled into the kitchen.

"Much better," Sarah confirmed.

Embarrassed that I had neglected my personal hygiene for so long, I took a seat at the kitchen table and simply said, "Thanks."

As promised, for the next hour Sarah entertained my mom and me with stories about her work, disastrous dates, and family gatherings. We listened intently, desperate to hear about anyone's life other than our own. After we were sufficiently caught up, Sarah moved on to a different subject.

"Have you been to see Milo lately?"

"I haven't seen Milo since October," I admitted.

"What? It's March. You haven't been out to Wellington yet?"

"No. I thought about it when we first got down here, but I was losing my vision so quickly and now it's too late. I'm not ready to be seen like this. Not even by Milo. I've talked with Bob a few times. He said Milo is doing fine."

"I doubt Milo cares that you can't see anymore," Sarah reasoned. "I'm sure he misses you and I know you miss him."

"I miss him all the time. But I'll never ride him again, and it would be unbearable to visit him right now." I left the kitchen without another word, holding my palms out in front of me to feel the way back to my room.

Thankfully, Sarah didn't follow me. I didn't want to explain my real reason for avoiding Milo: I knew the next time I visited him would be the last. Owning Milo had become pointless. Once the lease was up, I planned to tell Bob to sell him.

I was sitting up in bed when Sarah walked into my room and announced herself by saying, "Knock, knock."

"Come in," I murmured unnecessarily since Sarah was already padding across the room to the chair I often sat in while listening to an audio book.

The chair's overstuffed cushion made a whooshing sound when Sarah sat down, but other than that, we were both silent and still.

I broke the silence by asking a question that had been bothering me.

"Sar, what do I look like?"

"What do you mean? You know what you look like."

"No, I don't," I insisted. "You have no idea how easy it is to forget the simplest things like color or shape when you can't see anymore. Anyway, I want to know what I look like now. Not the last time I saw myself in the mirror clearly. That was about ten months ago, and I know I've changed drastically since then."

I could feel Sarah studying me for what seemed like several minutes.

Uncomfortable, I had to remind myself that I'd asked for this and, at least, I'd get a truthful and detailed answer.

"You're an unhealthy version of your old self," Sarah began. "You're very pale and your hair is longer, but it isn't at all shiny like it used to be. You are so thin that if I didn't know the reason behind it, I'd be jealous."

I smiled weakly, appreciating her attempt at humor.

"You used to have this inner sparkle that drew other people to you, but all I see now is sorrow and pain."

"You know what?" My voice wobbled as I fought back tears. "Life got so hard so fast. It feels like everything was taken from me and I don't have anything to live for."

"What about me? We've been friends for most of our lives and you don't think I'm something to live for? How about your mom? Or Milo? Don't you think they're worth living for?"

Sarah was breathing hard, and I felt terrible for upsetting her.

"Of course, you all are. But, like you said, I'm not the same person anymore. I can't be the friend to you that I once was. My mom is more like my babysitter at this point. As for Milo, I'll never be able to ride or take care of him like I used to. So, you see, I don't have much of a purpose anymore. I really don't know what or who I am, and I don't think it matters."

Sarah got up from the chair and moved to the bed to sit beside me. She hugged me tightly and whispered, "I understand that you're scared and that's why you stay hidden, but the people and animals that love you still need you whether you can see us or not."

Pulling away, I finally told her what had been preying on my mind. "I'm terrified. I don't leave my room, much less the house, because I don't want to hear the whispers, and I don't want to feel the rejection."

"Is that why you don't want to see Milo? You're afraid that because you can't ride or take care of him, he won't love you anymore?"

I hadn't allowed myself to think or talk about Milo this much in a long time. My heart felt like it had been ripped out of my chest, stepped on, and then shoved back into my body. I was beyond words and Sarah wisely accepted my silence as her answer.

"But that's nuts," she said. "If Milo were blind, would you stop loving him?"

I shook my head briskly from side to side until I was able to speak. "No, never. But I'm a person and Milo is a horse. He isn't capable of understanding what's happening. He probably doesn't even remember me."

It hurt to say this, and Sarah must have seen that I was close to falling apart because her voice grew quiet. "I think he would not only remember you, but he probably needs you as much as you need him right now. You may not want to admit it, but deep down you know I'm right."

She hugged me again and, this time, I didn't pull away. Sarah let me cry on her shoulder until her shirt was soaked and I was a sniffling mess.

"I didn't mean to upset you," Sarah said as she got up. "Will you be all right?"

"I think so," I said, wiping my face with my sleeve.

"Good, because I'm pooped. We'll talk more in the morning."

We were both exhausted but, before she could make it out of the room, I called to her.

"What?" she yawned.

"I'm really glad you're here."

The next morning, after Sarah woke me up with orders to get dressed, I was ready to retract my statement.

"Go away, please," I said, rolling over.

"Come on," Sarah groaned as she dragged me out of the bed by my arm.

"Fine, I'm up."

"Good. Now get dressed and wear something other than pajamas. No sweatpants, either."

"Why not?"

Sarah took my hand and placed a travel mug full of coffee in it. "We're going on a road trip."

I almost dropped the mug. "That sounds like a horrible idea."

"Like it or not, we're going to Wellington. You need to spend some time with Milo."

"I know you mean well, but this isn't the kind of thing you can decide for me. I meant what I said yesterday. I need to protect myself and Milo. I don't know how he's going to react, but I know for a fact he's not going to be the same because I'm not the same. I have nothing left to give that isn't saturated in grief and anger. Milo will feel my suffering. I can't hide this much pain from him."

Sarah was quiet while she decided what to do next.

"I'm putting your clothes in the bathroom. I suggest you put them on because we're leaving in ten minutes whether you're dressed or not."

After forty minutes of driving and little conversation, I was so anxious I couldn't sit still.

"We're almost there." Sarah sounded exasperated. "Quit fidgeting."

"Have you always been this bossy? I don't know if I love this side of you."

Finally, the car stopped. Neither of us made a move to get out of it.

"Are you okay?" Sarah asked.

"I don't know," I replied, sliding my hand over the door until I found the metal handle and gave it a tug. "I guess we'll find out."

Sarah held my arm and led me into the barn where I took comfort in the familiar smells of hay, grain, and horse. I heard a few voices but none that I recognized.

"Where is everyone?" I asked.

Sarah steered me around something and said, "Bob is the only one meeting us here. He wanted you to have a peaceful visit with Milo, so he shooed everyone out of the barn."

"Hello," a soft-spoken voice said behind me.

"Tom?" I asked.

Bob's barn manager, Tom, took my hand and gave me an awkward hug. "How are you?"

I had grown to resent that question, but Tom was just being polite, so I smiled and said, "I'm fine, thank you."

"That's good to hear," he said warmly. "Bob asked us to clear out of the barn, but I hope it's all right that I stayed. I wanted to say hello. Do you need me to show you where Milo is?"

"That would be great," Sarah was quick to reply. "Lead the way."

As we moved down the aisle, I wondered if Bob had sent everyone out on a trail ride. I thought of the long trail rides Milo and I had enjoyed in Wellington, and I hoped Wendy was taking him for walks along the canals.

We stopped and I heard the clang of a stall door being unlocked. Something on the other side of the door made a sudden movement and I jumped back, bumping against Sarah who tightened her hold on my arm.

As the door swung open, a whoosh of air fanned my face and I heard a tiny bit of rustling.

I had hoped Milo would acknowledge my presence with his usual happy nicker or friendly grunt, but I heard neither. The near silence prompted me to ask, "Is Milo in there?"

"Yes," Sarah answered. "He's watching you."

Tom placed his hand on my shoulder, taking over as my guide. Together we stepped into Milo's stall. Tom took another step urging me forward, but I refused to move.

"What's the matter?" Sarah asked.

"I'd like to do this alone," I explained. "You don't have to worry about me, it isn't as if I can get lost in a stall and Milo won't do anything to hurt me."

"If you're sure you'll be okay," Sarah said. "Yell if you need me. I'll be nearby."

I waited until I heard Sarah and Tom walking back to the barn's entrance before I concentrated on Milo.

I imagined him as he was now. Probably hugging the corner in the back of his stall, his dark brown coat recently clipped short.

Most definitely, wood shavings were entwined in his thick, black tail, and the picture my brain conjured was so vivid, my fingers moved as though plucking the paper-thin chips from each dark strand of hair. I wondered what expression he was wearing, and though I flipped through a mental rolodex stocked with images of Milo, I had no way of gauging his reaction to my sudden appearance after my five-month absence.

Still standing where Tom had left me, I timidly called out, "Milo," but it sounded more like a question than a name.

Milo shifted his weight causing the hay underneath his feet to crackle, and for a second, I thought the air around me moved, signaling his approach. Catching my breath, I held it and waited but nothing happened.

I exhaled slowly and despite feeling like an uninvited guest, I took another step into the stall. I felt the pull of an invisible tether drawing me closer to Milo, and I took two more steps toward him. With each one, my heartbeat grew stronger and faster.

After a few more steps, I could hear Milo breathing. I held my hands out, reaching for him, but Milo found me first, brushing my palms with his nose as he sniffed my hands in search of a treat.

"Hi, M," I said and this time there was no question in my tone, only love.

Milo's chin scraped against my cheek as he draped his head over my shoulder. Then he lowered his head to the small of my back, pushing me against his soft, warm chest.

I was reminded of the last time I had seen him and the promises I had made. Overcome with grief, I fastened my arms around his neck and held him tight, wishing I'd never have to let go. I began to cry.

"I'm sorry I've been gone for so long," I said through my tears. I wanted to tell Milo we'd be together again soon, and I would take care of him, just as I always had. I wanted to tell him I hadn't given up and there was still a chance my vision would come back. I wanted to tell him I could re-write our future.

Instead, I let go of his neck and moved to his side, where I could run my hands up his neck and past his ear until I found the irregular swirl of white hair high on his forehead.

Milo's star, insulated by his thick forelock, was always the warmest spot on his head. I held my hand over it and felt the heat against my palm.

"I failed you," I said shakily. "All my vision is gone and my life is over. After your lease is up, I won't be able to afford to keep you, and I refuse to continue leasing you year after year to whomever will pay for you. I know you wouldn't like that, and I don't want that for you. I'm sorry, Milo, you are my horse of a lifetime, but I have to let you go. I have to say goodbye."

There was more I wanted to say. I wanted to tell Milo how proud he had made me and how much I loved him and would always love him. But I was having trouble breathing past the pain in my chest, and I was forced to lean against Milo for support.

Nestled in the crook of his neck, I wept silently. Racked with pain and guilt, I didn't realize Milo had moved his head closer to mine, until his warm breath tickled my ear. Milo was breathing deeply, slowly. When he exhaled, air sweetened by hay and grain mixed with molasses washed over my face. The next time he inhaled, I imitated him, my breathing becoming an extension of his. As we exhaled together, our breaths intermingled. We continued to breathe in unison, I closed my eyes, and I began to calm down.

I don't know how long we stayed like this, but by the time I heard stirrings at the opposite end of the barn, I'd drawn enough strength from Milo to stand on my own.

"I have to go, M." I kissed the soft spot on his nose and turned away from the horse that would forever reside in my heart.

Finding my way out of Milo's stall was not as easy as I'd expected.

I had created a mental map of the door's location, but when I tried to re-trace my steps to it, I kept hitting a wall. I had to resort to walking along the stall's perimeter until the pressure of my outstretched fingers caused the unlocked door to swing slightly on its hinges.

I pushed the door with more force and produced an opening large enough to walk through. The door shut behind me but as I turned around to find the bolt that would lock Milo inside, the door flew open. Instinctively, I jumped to my right, clearing the way for the door to swing open to the left.

"What in the—" I managed to yelp before something large and furry brushed my upper arm.

Milo stood by me, with the front half of his body in the aisle and his hind end in his stall.

This was not the first time Milo attempted to follow me out of the barn. Ordinarily, I would have laughed at his willfulness, but today it was cause for alarm. Without being able to see him, I wasn't sure I could get him back into his stall.

"Milo, what are you doing?" I spun around, hooked my right arm over his face just above his nose, flattened my back against his chest, and shoved with all my might to make all twelve hundred pounds of him step backward into his stall. But Milo didn't budge.

While I pondered the best way to handle this predicament, Milo rested his chin on the top of my head.

"This is interesting," I heard a familiar voice say. "Do you need some help?"

"Hi, Bob." I tried turning in the direction of his voice but the weight of Milo's head on top of mine made it impossible to move. "Yes, please, I could use a little help."

"C'mon, Milo, back up," Bob said, grunting with exertion and eventually convincing Milo to return to his stall.

"Is everything okay?" Bob asked as he closed Milo's door. "You look like you've been crying."

With his hand on my shoulder, Bob and I began walking to the front of the barn, while I tried to ignore the sound of Milo's restless movements.

"I don't know what I am anymore. I'm miserable all the time. I'm angry. I'm frustrated. And I just had to say goodbye to Milo. I'm the furthest thing from okay."

Bob slowed our pace so we could talk in private a few minutes longer. "Why did you say goodbye to Milo? Neither one of you is going anywhere. You can come see him every day if you want. I know he'd like that, and he is still your horse."

"Bob, I can't come out here every day. It's not like I can drive, and I'm not going to ask my mom to take three hours out of her day so I can pat Milo. I'm blind and it's a reality I have to face. I'm not going to get better. This is my life now and there's no place for a horse in the dark."

"I understand that you're blind, but what doesn't make sense is your hurry to get rid of Milo. His lease isn't up until the end of May. You keep talking about the things you've lost, but Milo is still in your life. You're the one kicking him out of it."

"The truth is," I said slowly, "I don't know if I can go on like this and, if I decide that I can't, I don't want to have any loose ends. I have to say goodbye to Milo at some point. It may as well be today."

Bob didn't say anything until I was back in Sarah's care, and it was time for me to go. Giving me a friendly hug, he said gruffly, "Promise me you'll call me if things get worse. I'm here for you. All you have to do is ask for help."

"Thank you," I said. "Take care of my boy for me, please."

As Sarah and I drove away from the barn, she asked, "Was it as bad as you thought it would be?"

No answer.

"Are you mad at me for dragging you here?" Sarah probed.

"No, not anymore. I know you meant well."

We drove in silence for a while.

"What are you thinking about?" Sarah asked, startling me. "It's making you smile, whatever it is."

"I was thinking about Milo and how much I love him. I guess that would account for my smile."

"You two definitely have a unique relationship."

"Yes, we do. We belong together. I've felt that way since the very beginning. Milo is such a large part of who I am that I'm afraid when he's sold, I'll lose even more of my identity. I worry for Milo as well. At least I know he's being taken care of as long as he's with Bob. But what happens when Milo belongs to someone else? He's not just another horse to be passed around. I suppose once he's sold, I'll spend the rest of my life thinking about him."

Loaded with grief, I slumped over.

"If it's going to ruin your life, why are you so convinced that selling Milo is a good idea?"

I sank further into the seat, mumbling crossly, "I never said it was a good idea."

It was the worst possible idea, but for months I'd been telling myself and everyone else that Milo no longer had a place in my life.

Was I wrong? Did I give up too easily? Are there other options I should explore?

"Oh my God," I groaned, sitting up and squaring my shoulders.

"What?" Sarah asked.

"I think I've made a mistake. You may have been right about me. I'm not myself. The real me would never let Milo go without a fight. Sight has nothing to do with my feelings for Milo. I don't need to be able to see him or ride him to know that selling him is the last thing I should do."

The car picked up speed as Sarah merged onto I-95. "So, what are you going to do?"

"I'm not sure yet, but I'll figure something out."

"That's the girl I know and love." Sarah thumped me on the arm approvingly. "I should have realized it would take Milo to remind you who you are."

CHAPTER ELEVEN

arah left Florida two days later, but not before saying, "Call me if you need help remembering who you are. I'll be happy to tell you."

For the next three days, I wandered about the house, searching for something to re-awaken the fighter in me the way Sarah and Milo did. I had to tell my mom that I couldn't sell Milo and that I refused to be blind any longer. But I couldn't find the strength. I knew it would continue to elude me if I retreated to my room and again gave in to self-pity and despair. So, I kept moving. On the fourth day, missing Sarah and tired of roaming the house, I sat down in front of the TV to listen to my favorite sitcom. Spike jumped up on the couch and his little feet padded across the leather cushions until he found a spot next to me and lay down.

I was enjoying one of my favorite *Friends* episodes when I heard my mom walk into the room.

"Guess what?" she said. "I just got off the phone with Henry."

"Henry, as in my doctor?"

"Yes, he checks in periodically to see how you are. Today he called to tell me he's in town visiting his father and he wanted to know if he could stop by. I said 'fine' and he's on his way."

"Cool. It'll be great to see him, and I have questions about my eye that I'd like to ask him."

I was pulling a clean T-shirt over my head when the doorbell rang and I heard my mom greet Henry. I used my hands and their voices to guide me to the front hall where they were standing.

"There's my favorite patient!" Henry exclaimed.

"If I'm still your favorite, then you really need to get better patients," I joked.

My mom excused herself and went into the kitchen as Henry took my elbow to lead me into the den.

I pulled away from him saying, "I can take it from here," and sat in my usual spot on the couch. I could hear Henry making himself comfortable in the chair across from me.

"Your mom tells me you've been having a rough time."

Of course, it's been rough. How else could it be?

"It hasn't been easy," I said curtly, annoyed that my mother and Henry had been talking about me.

"I'm sure it hasn't. Do you mind if I take a look?"

"Can you see anything without your equipment?"

"Enough," Henry said, getting up to wash his hands in the kitchen. "I just want to take a quick peek. Do you mind standing up? I think it'll be easier that way."

I obliged and Henry propped my eye open with his forefinger and thumb. Then he had me look left, right, up, and down. "Are you able to see anything?"

"No. Every now and then I see different shades of black, but I'm not sure if it's real or in my head."

At the end of his impromptu exam, Henry confirmed my suspicions. My eye was dying, if not already dead. Henry couldn't be certain what was going on inside my eye, but it had shrunk so much, it could barely hold my lid open. Neither my retina nor my optic nerve could survive for long without any measurable eye pressure.

I still had questions for Henry but decided to wait until after dinner when he and my mom would be a captive audience.

We had pizza that night and, in honor of Henry's arrival, I joined him and my parents in the dining room.

Howard and Henry began talking about motorcycles and even my mom — who hates motorcycles — joined the conversation. I had nothing to say about the subject, so I just ate my food and occasionally slipped Spike a piece of gooey cheese under the table.

"Lissa, have you ever ridden a motorcycle?" Henry asked.

"No. Just horses."

"A friend of hers drove Liss to Wellington recently so she could spend some time with her horse," Mom informed Henry.

"Oh, really," Henry replied. "Did you ride?"

"No,' I shook my head slowly. "I can't. Not like this."

"Well," Henry continued, "can't you ride behind someone or have somebody lead you around?"

Recoiling from Henry as if he'd slapped me, I sneered, "No, absolutely not. How would you feel if the only way you could ride your motorcycle was to sit in the back, clinging to the driver?"

"Wouldn't it be better than not riding at all?" Henry pressed.

"I would never get on a horse behind someone," I replied haughtily. "And being led around is also out of the question."

"Why?" Henry asked.

"Because it's not who I am. None of this is who I am. I'm so sick and tired of pretending I don't notice everybody holding their breath when I walk into a room, terrified that I'm going to trip over something or walk into a wall."

Several seconds of shocked silence followed my outburst. Then my mom said hesitantly, "I was looking at some of your options on the web. I discovered a place in Baltimore that trains people who are blind or have low vision to read Braille and walk with a white cane."

"That was a gigantic waste of your time," I snarled. "Do you honestly think that it's a good idea to put something that can double as a weapon in my hand? As for reading a book with my fingers, I don't foresee that in my future either."

I could hear Howard and Henry shifting in their chairs as the tension at the table grew.

"Fine," my mom said. "Then please tell me what you do see when you think of the future."

"I don't know, but it definitely isn't filled with books in Braille and white canes," I proclaimed. "Why is everyone but me so ready to accept that this is who I am now?"

"Because we have to," she explained patiently. "Until you are more independent, I'm the one looking out for you. I'm the person clearing a path for you so you don't trip over anything. I'm the one taking care of Spike and making sure you eat. I'm your mother and I love you. It's my job to get you through this the best that I can. However, at some point, you're going to have to learn to take care of yourself."

The more my mom pushed me to accept my blindness, the more I pushed back, until finally the fighter inside me erupted.

"I get it that you're exhausted but I'm sorry, I'm not ready to wave the white flag. I cannot accept a life without light. I will not go to school and learn how to exist in a world I can't see. There must be something out there that will help me, but I don't know what it is or how to look for it without sight. You need to find it, because I refuse to live like this anymore. If you can't discover whatever it is that will bring my vision back," my voice hitched and I hated myself for what I said next, "you'll have no choice but to let me go."

Hot tears burned a path down my cheeks, but I ignored them. Turning in Henry's direction, I reminded him that he had a role in this, too. "You've been trying to save my vision for most of my life, Henry. I need you to save it, and me, one more time. Please, you and Mom go online and find something somewhere. Because this," I placed my hands over my eyes, "is not my fate, and I will not sit back and pretend it is."

My mom got up and began clearing the table. She said a few words to Howard and Henry but not one word to me.

If I had a tail, it would have been between my legs as I shuffled back to my bedroom. I was disgusted with myself. What had I just done and said to my mother? I'd asked her for a miracle and threatened to end it all if she couldn't deliver. I was more ashamed of myself than I'd ever been. Although I'd meant what I said, I regretted making such terrible threats and wondered why I couldn't have kept that part to myself.

When I finally fell asleep, I slept badly.

"Are you awake yet?" my mom asked the next morning as she opened my door. I sat up to make room for her at the foot of the bed. She didn't sound angry, which surprised me.

I immediately launched into an apology. "Mom, I am so sorry—"

That was as far as I got before she stopped me. "You were right," she said.

"No, I wasn't. I should never have threatened you. That was completely unfair of me."

"Do you remember what you said last night about knowing there was something out there that could help you, we just had to find it?"

"Yes," I replied, baffled.

Leaning forward, my mom wrapped her hands around my thin arms and pulled me closer to her.

"You were right," she said in a low yet triumphant voice. "There is something."

My heart stopped for a second and when it started up again, it pounded like a hammer in my chest. I was feeling light-headed and if not for my mom's grip on my arms, I probably would have collapsed against her.

When the full force of what my mother said hit me, everything seemed to go still. Then I began to chuckle, picking up speed until my body shook with laughter. Moments later, I was crying. My mom's words had set off an emotional bomb in my head, and I was having trouble landing on a single reaction.

"How?" I managed to ask between hiccups. "What is it?"

Giddy with excitement, my mom described last night's events after I'd gone to bed.

Once I left the kitchen, Mom and Henry began scouring the internet for anything that could raise my eye pressure. Around 2:00 a.m., Henry turned to my mom and, pointing to the computer screen, said, "I think I've found something."

He had come across a medication called Trazyl, which was available only in Italy. Used to dilate pupils before an eye exam, some patients experienced a significant increase in eye pressure after repeated doses.

Henry left sometime after his pre-dawn discovery but said he'd return as soon as possible to talk to me about Trazyl.

"Henry had to spend the morning with his father but promised to be back here by one o'clock this afternoon," my mom assured me.

"What time is it now?"

"Almost noon, which doesn't give you much time to shower and get dressed."

I was already swinging my legs over the side of the bed when I realized I had forgotten to do something important.

"Thank you, Mom. This is incredible. Thank you for trusting me and helping me when I couldn't help myself."

"You're very welcome. But Henry was the one who found Trazyl online."

I was in a daze as I made myself ready for the day. I almost pinched myself to make sure I was really awake and not dreaming about a miracle medicine called Trazyl. My mom's words came back to me. All this time, there was a cure for my blindness just waiting to be unearthed.

"I knew it," I said out loud as I brushed my hair. "I knew it."

I felt so lighthearted that had I been able to see, I would've skipped from my bedroom to the den where my parents were waiting for Henry and me. Instead, I walked slowly, deliberately, as I went through my mental checklist — *six paces to the right, turn left, five paces straight ahead, carefully feel for the single step down* — until I reached the couch and sat on it.

Anticipating my favorite question, Howard said, "It's five 'til one."

I tapped my toe and chewed my nails until the sound of a car, slowing down as it neared our driveway, made me freeze.

"He's here," I announced.

My parents had grown used to my heightened sense of hearing and didn't question me. Seconds later, the doorbell rang and, finally, Henry arrived.

He and my mom were discussing a local restaurant as they walked into the den. I allowed them about thirty seconds more before I interrupted them.

"Do you think you guys can chat about food another time? I have a lot of questions for Henry." I was being a little bratty, but it wasn't time for small talk; it was time to discuss the drug that might restore my sight.

"Of course," Henry said, pushing a chair closer to my end of the couch and sitting down. "Unfortunately, I don't have much to tell you. I'd never heard of Trazyl before today. But the article I read stated that several patients, who had been given Trazyl to dilate their eyes, wound up with glaucoma."

This surprised me. I needed clarification. "So, they started with normal eye pressure and ended up with glaucoma. I'm starting with zero pressure. Does that mean the medication could increase my pressure enough for me to see?"

"Correct," Henry confirmed. "But it's a rare side effect, and I can't guarantee how your eye will react."

"Oh, it's going to work," Mom declared.

"And Italy is the only place in the world that has it?" I asked incredulously.

"Also correct," Henry said quickly.

"Are we going to Italy then?" I asked.

"No," my mom answered for Henry. "It just so happens that Jane has a friend, Franco, who, at this very moment, is staying in a small town outside Florence."

"Aunt Jane?" I asked, referring to one of my mother's best friends.

"Yes. Jane called me this morning as I was booking my flight to Italy, and when I told her what was going on, she said she'd ask Franco if he could get the medicine before he returns to West Palm tomorrow."

"Today is Friday," Howard piped in, knowing that I struggled to keep track of the days as well as the time.

"How is Franco going to buy it without a prescription?" I wondered.

"He won't need one," my mom said. "Trazyl is sold in pharmacies over-the-counter. The problem is that Italy is six hours ahead of us, and by the time Jane spoke with Franco, pharmacies had closed for the weekend. However — and this is truly amazing — Franco is visiting a good friend who happens to be a pharmacist, and he was delighted to open his store and retrieve his last bottle of Trazyl for you."

She paused to catch her breath. "If everything goes according to plan, Franco will be back in Florida tomorrow afternoon, Trazyl in hand."

I jumped to my feet, spreading my arms wide like a bird in flight. "I can't believe this is really happening!" I fell back down on the couch. Franco and his friend had gone out of their way to help me, even though I was a complete stranger. Their act of genuine kindness almost brought me to tears, but I kept them at bay, for I still had one more question to ask, even though I dreaded the answer.

"Henry?" He had been quiet for so long I wasn't sure if he was still in the room.

"Right here."

"You know my eye better than anyone. Do you think there's enough life left in it for it to respond to this drug?"

Henry cleared his throat. "I don't know. I'm not making any promises. We need to keep in mind that the prolonged lack of pressure has surely damaged your eye. If Trazyl gives you some pressure back, and that's a big 'if,' you still have to consider your retina and what kind of shape it's in. There's a possibility it's already detached."

The nighttime choir of tree frogs was still singing when I woke up the next morning. My inner clock estimated the time to be between five and six. I pressed the large button on my talking clock for confirmation. A gift from Howard, its hollow, tinny voice announced, "It is 5:22 a.m."

"Drat," I grumbled, disturbing Spike's slumber. I still had hours before Jane would meet Franco at the airport and deliver the Trazyl to me.

Spike stretched and moved from the foot of the bed to the pillow beside me where he was asleep again within seconds. *Lucky dog*, I thought.

Time dragged on and it felt like an eternity had passed before the aroma of freshly brewed coffee lured me out of bed and into the kitchen.

"Good morning," Howard greeted me brightly as he filled a mug from the coffee pot. "Where would you like this?"

"Counter, please."

"Here you go," Howard said, setting the cup down in front of me. "Your mom's been on the phone with Jane. I think I heard her say the flight from Italy was landing early."

"Wow. How early?"

"Pending traffic, Jane should be here around two this afternoon," my mom answered as she entered the kitchen. "She promised she'd speed all the way from the airport."

Smiling, I slid off the bar stool to go back to my room to retrieve my new audio book.

"Where are you off to?" Howard asked.

"I thought the day would go by faster if I had company, but talking about the medicine's arrival is making me even more anxious. I think the only way I'm going to survive the day is if I lose myself in a good book."

Eventually, I settled down on the living room sofa, headphones on, portable CD player in my lap, and Spike rolled up in a little ball next to me. I was starting chapter four of the latest Harry Potter adventure when I felt a light tap on my arm.

"Wishing you could press fast forward and speed up time?" Henry asked once I'd removed my headphones.

"Yes," I grimaced. "Exactly that."

Henry had stopped by on his way to the airport to say goodbye and tell me how to use the Trazyl.

"You're to take it only three times a day, one drop each time," he instructed. "No more than that until we have a better idea of how your eye is going to react. If there is a change in your vision, call me immediately. I don't care what time it is, call me. Oh, and if you have any allergic reaction or pain, let me know as soon as possible."

"And if nothing happens?"

"Keep taking it and we'll update our plans when I see you in about a month," Henry said, reminding me that the end of March and my return to Maryland were not far off.

"One month," he repeated. "I'll see you when you get home."

Three hours later, I was so engrossed in my book I didn't hear my mom enter the room. In fact, I was completely unaware of her presence until she plucked the headphones from my ears and crowed, "It's here!"

"Jane's here? Does she have the medication?"

"Yes, she's here and of course she brought it with her," my mom laughed as she herded me toward the kitchen.

Howard and Jane were laughing about something but fell silent the moment they saw me. My mom positioned me directly in front of Jane. I could smell her perfume.

"I have something for you," Jane said, and I put my hand out. "It's going to work," she whispered confidently as she placed a glass vial into my opened palm.

Before she could pull her hand away, I squeezed it and said in a voice brimming with love and gratitude, "Thank you, Aunt Jane."

I closed my fingers securely around the bottle. *Is this my salvation?* There was only one way to find out. *Please work*, I thought as I unscrewed the cap and gingerly held the dropper to the corner of my eye and squeezed.

A single drop of liquid flooded my eye and my lid snapped shut, trapping the medicine behind it.

I counted to ten before I opened my eyes.

"It isn't a magic potion," my mom said, reading the disappointed look on my face. "You have to give the medication some time to work."

"I know, I know," I replied. "But the part of me that believes in fairy tales was hoping the curse would be lifted instantly."

"I was hoping for the same thing," she said, "but it took longer than an instant for you to lose your vision and I suppose we'll have to be patient until your eye shows signs of improvement."

Every day, I placed three drops of Trazyl into my eye: one drop first thing in the morning, another drop no later than one o'clock in the afternoon, and the last drop at night before I got into bed. After each dose, without fail, I returned the bottle to its designated spot on my bedside table.

This went on for two weeks and my vision hadn't shown even the smallest sign of improvement. Sometimes I would swear that my eye felt firmer or more defined, but the feeling didn't last.

With five days left before our departure, the house was buzzing with activity. The electrician and plumber were fixing some last-minute issues, the housekeeper was giving everything a final cleaning, and my mom was ridding the refrigerator and cabinets of all perishable food.

"What time is it?" I asked her.

She stopped filling a garbage bag with opened boxes of chips and crackers long enough to consult her watch.

"Ten past one. Why?"

"I need to put my afternoon drop of Trazyl in my eye but I'm not comfortable going into my room while it's being cleaned. Too many things for me to step on and trip over."

A succession of vicious barks and growls could be heard coming from my room and I shook my head, remembering how irritating Spike's never-ending desire to kill the vacuum cleaner could be.

"Crazy dog," I grumbled.

"I'm sure Joan can handle Spike," my mom said indifferently. "If you need your medicine right this second, I'll get it for you."

Before I could accept her offer, the whirr of the vacuum ceased, and I heard Joan wheeling it down the hallway.

The air in my bedroom was thick with the noxious odors of bleach and ammonia. I wondered if I should wait for the air to clear before putting a drop of Trazyl into my now-irritated eye. But it was already past one o'clock and I didn't dare deviate any further from my schedule.

My fingers tapped lightly against the nightstand's glass top as I felt for the bottle of Trazyl. Since going blind, I'd come to understand the importance of putting things back where they belonged, and I always made sure to return the Trazyl to the front left corner of the bedside table after each use.

The bottle wasn't in its usual spot. Joan must have moved it before cleaning the table. My open palm glided across the glass from corner to corner until I'd covered every square inch of the table top. With each pass, I grew more agitated. Hadn't Joan been told not to touch the bottle of medicine? I was sure I'd overheard my mom making that request.

The table had three drawers and I searched each one thoroughly but came up empty handed. *It has to be here.* My hands were moving faster now as I double-checked the areas I'd just inspected.

I was getting very close to not being okay. *Stay calm. It must be here somewhere.*

"Joan!" I called out loudly. I waited for five seconds and then called for her again.

I heard heavy rubber-soled footsteps coming toward me, and then from my doorway Joan asked, "Did you need me for something?"

"I'm missing my bottle of eye drops." My voice was sharp and accusatory. "I always leave it on the table next to my bed. Did you move it when you were cleaning in here?"

Joan didn't answer right away, and I supposed her silence meant she was trying to remember where she'd put the bottle.

"I didn't touch anything that looked like medicine," she said defensively. "Where was it?"

"It was right here, on the table. Where it always is."

My mind was spinning, making it impossible to think clearly. My chest tightened, making it difficult to breathe. *This can't be real.*

Sick with dread, I barely heard Joan ask, "Are you all right?"

I tried to answer but my mouth had gone dry.

No, I wasn't all right. I licked my lips twice and, instead of answering her question, I asked in a raspy voice, "Can you get my mom, please?"

Scarcely aware of Joan's swift retreat from my room, I bent my knees and sank stiffly to the floor.

I was still there, sweeping my hands wildly over the cool tiles when my mom found me.

"What happened?" she asked, her alarm evident as she rushed into the room and crouched beside me.

"I can't find the Trazyl!" I wailed. "I had it this morning and now it's gone."

CHAPTER TWELVE

After my mother picked me up off the floor and calmed me down, she launched a methodical search for the Trazyl.

"It has to be here somewhere," she maintained. "The bottle didn't sprout legs and walk away. Joan probably bumped into the table while she was vacuuming."

"I felt all around the nightstand and under the bed."

"I know you did, but it could have rolled anywhere. Don't worry, it'll turn up."

Starting with the table where the bottle usually sat, she opened and closed each drawer, then pushed the nightstand to the side and pushed it back. I heard the sequence repeated with the nightstand on the other side of the bed and with each piece of furniture in the room. The only thing I could do to help was stay out of the way. I sat in a corner, my knees drawn up to my chin and my back against the wall.

As time wore on and the Trazyl remained at large, my mom's search became more desperate. Opened drawers stayed that way. Sheets snatched from the bed and vigorously shaken were left in a heap. Hangars emptied of their clothing rattled in the closet. Shoes tossed from shelves landed on the floor with a thud. I imagined that by now, my room must resemble a crime scene.

"What are we going to do?" I asked despairingly. "Is it time to give up?"

"Why would you ask that?" my mother demanded crossly. "This is little more than a setback. Definitely an inconvenient one but certainly not a reason to give up."

Mom's plan to devote her day to packing was put on hold while, instead, she scoured the entire house for my missing medication and interrogated every person who'd been inside in the past twenty-four hours.

By dinnertime, she stopped looking for the Trazyl. She made a plate for me but took her dinner into the office so she could look up flights to Italy and book a hotel.

My stomach was in knots and my face ached from wearing a permanent frown. I managed only a few bites of salad before I pushed my chair back from the table and just sat there, holding my forehead.

The last-minute trip overseas was going to be expensive, exhausting, and time-consuming. I was so full of guilt and shame for being such a burden, it's no wonder I lost my appetite.

Mom's phone rang but the office door must have been closed because her voice was muffled, and I couldn't decipher what she was saying. Not that I enjoyed eavesdropping on her conversations. I was just hoping for something to listen to other than my self-recriminations.

"Change of plan," she announced as she entered the kitchen moments later. "Your Aunt Karen has volunteered to fly to Italy tomorrow so I can stay here and finish packing up the house."

My mom's sister, Karen, had always been one of my favorite people. Fun, fashionable, bright, and beautiful, Karen was the epitome of a cool aunt. The trip would be easier for her than for my mother; Karen had studied piano in Siena, Italy, and spoke Italian.

"Wow, it's really nice of Karen to do that for me." Not quite guilt-free but greatly relieved, I felt my brow unfurrow as the muscles in my face relaxed.

Karen flew from Baltimore to Italy the next day. On the way to her hotel in Rome, she stopped at two pharmacies where she purchased a total of four bottles of Trazyl.

Less than twenty-four hours later, she was on a flight back to Baltimore.

With some creative planning, my mom had arranged for Howard and Karen to cross paths in the BWI airport. Howard, who was there to catch a plane to Florida, met Karen outside the international terminal. My travel-weary aunt handed him a zippered, canvas pouch containing four carefully wrapped bottles of Trazyl.

My mom left the house to retrieve Howard from the Ft. Lauderdale airport and when they returned, I was waiting for them by the door.

The bottle my mom placed in my hand felt exactly like its predecessor. I crossed my arms over my chest, hugging the bottle to my heart, and silently sent thanks to my Aunt Karen.

"I'll hold on to the rest of the bottles for safe keeping," my mom said, leaving no room for argument.

"Thank you," I said sincerely. "You, too, Howard. Thank you for going to all of that trouble to get this to me so quickly."

I was already tearing into the bottle's protective packaging with my teeth when my mom and Howard replied in unison, "You're welcome."

During dinner that night, my mom took advantage of my good humor to discuss my future.

"Howard and I are going to be spending more time in Baltimore this spring," she said pointedly between bites.

I considered what that meant for me, given that I was essentially homeless. Everything I owned was in storage or in my suitcase. Surely Mom wasn't suggesting I live with them in their Baltimore condo.

"Don't you think that will be close quarters for the three of us? Sorry, Spike, I meant three-and-a-half."

"For a little while, it will be," my mom said, her tone serious. "But we'll have to make do until we figure something out. Howard knows of a few condos for sale in our building. I think it would be easier for you and me if we lived in the same complex."

"You want me to live in Baltimore?" I asked sullenly. I hoped my question didn't offend Mom and Howard, who loved the city, but it had never held much appeal for me. I found it noisy and dirty.

"We want you to live wherever you'll be happy," Howard said diplomatically, "but we thought it would be more convenient if we were an elevator ride away."

I chewed on my lower lip and nodded in agreement. I knew the transition to being on my own would be smoother if my mother lived a few floors above me. Even so, I hated that this decision was being made for me. But I had no choice.

Without a job, controlling my own life was a luxury I could, literally, no longer afford. My mom managed the money from the sale of my house and car, which would soon be spent on my new place. She was also in charge of Milo's lease money. I hoped she'd let me use it to cover Milo's costs when his lease was up, but that would leave nothing for my expenses.

I relied on my mom for everything, which made me wonder if I deserved a say in where and how I lived.

Will I ever have control over my future again? When I got into bed that night, all I could think about was the Trazyl. If it didn't work, any hope of regaining my independence would vanish.

We were leaving Florida in two days and although I wasn't embracing the idea of living in Baltimore, I was ready for a change of scenery…so to speak.

Urban living did not suit me. Although I learned to appreciate the ease with which I could move around in my parents' condo, the nonstop noise from the streets below kept me up at night. We were fourteen floors up, but when a motorcycle roared by, it may as well have been in the room with me. Cars honked, trucks rumbled, sirens screamed, and I heard it all.

We'd been back in Maryland for three days and the city that refused to sleep wasn't letting me get any, either. I yawned, momentarily interrupting the examination Henry was trying to conduct in his office. "Sorry," I mumbled.

He ignored my apology and continued to study my eye. This was my first appointment with Henry since I started using Trazyl three-and-a-half weeks ago. Henry noticed the improvement in my eye's shape and size even before I sat in the exam chair. My eye pressure had crawled back up to two, which would have elated me had I been able to see. But it would seem that, despite the elevated pressure, we were too late to save my vision.

The heat of a high-powered light warmed my cheek, and I knew from experience that Henry was looking at my retina.

"Is it still there?" I asked, getting right to the point.

"It's showing some signs of damage, but your retina is miraculously still intact. It's in better shape than I thought it would be." Henry continued to describe his findings. "Your optic nerve, on the other hand, is looking very pale, which is worrisome. A healthy nerve is pinkish, but the lack of pressure restricted the flow of blood to yours, turning it white."

"Is that why I still can't see? Because my optic nerve is dead?"

Henry's answer painted a disturbing picture. "I don't know exactly why you can't see. Your eye is so badly damaged that one thing or many things could be causing your blindness. All I know is that the back of your eye looks like a train wreck."

"Should I continue to use the Trazyl?" I asked bleakly.

"That's up to you. I don't want to tell you to stop, but it doesn't appear to be making a difference in your vision. On the other hand, what have you got to lose?"

"Nothing. I have absolutely nothing left to lose."

Mom and I left Henry's office and battled beltway traffic for the next two hours. It was late afternoon when we arrived back in Baltimore. I greeted Spike, who followed me into my room where I picked up the bottle of Trazyl and threw it into the metal garbage can. It landed with a resounding thwack.

The bottle sat in the trash for three hours before I retrieved it, squeezed a few drops into my eye, and placed it back on my dresser. I wasn't ready to admit defeat. I doubted I'd ever be able to do so. It wasn't who I am.

My time in Baltimore was spent much the same as it was in Florida. Audiobooks and television kept me occupied most days. At least once a week, I called Bob so he could amuse me with stories of Milo. I was thrilled when at the end of April, he called me for a change.

"Well, the horses and I got back from Florida a week ago and If you want, I'll bring you out to see Milo and the new barn," Bob offered.

"New barn? I don't remember hearing anything about a new barn."

Bob spent the next ten minutes describing the larger facility he was renting. It sounded palatial and I was glad that his business was growing.

"It's about thirty-five minutes east of Baltimore. A little bit of a hike but absolutely worth it. Wait until you see it, you'll love it."

There was an uncomfortable lull in the conversation. In his excitement over his new barn, Bob forgot that I'd probably never be able to see it.

"Is the new medicine working?" he asked soberly.

"Not yet. I was hoping I'd be able to see again by the time Milo got home, but it looks like it'll take a while longer." I didn't want to give Bob any reason to bring up the subject of selling Milo, so I kept the results of my last eye exam to myself. Instead, I said, "As soon as I can see, I'll call you for that ride."

I was thinking about my chat with Bob as I put my pajamas on. I missed my friend, and I really missed my horse, but I wasn't ready to visit him. Unfamiliar places still scared me, and a new barn was no exception. I would give myself more time to get used to the idea, but soon, with or without sight, I knew I would need to be with Milo.

Stupid medicine, I thought, picking up the Trazyl and giving it a vigorous shake as if I were wringing its neck.

That night, the Trazyl stung a bit more than usual and as my eye twitched painfully, I regretted taking my frustrations out on the bottle.

The din of morning rush hour was making it impossible for me to sleep. Annoyed, but not enough to leave my cozy bed, I snuggled closer to Spike, who happily shared his warmth with me. I was considering spending the day in bed, or at least in my pajamas, but my mom had other plans for me.

"Are you awake?" she called while simultaneously knocking on the door and opening it.

"Mmmph." My reply was swallowed by the pillow covering my face.

"Put some clothes on so you can walk Spike with me," she said, and I knew this was not a request but an order. "After our walk, we're going to look at some condos. I think you'd agree that it's time for you to start living on your own."

I was glad I was still lying face down in the pillow. My mom's comment, though innocent, made me feel like an intruder and I didn't want her to see my pained expression.

I stretched lazily, turning my head toward the window, and my eyes popped open. "Oh!" I cried out. My eyes snapped shut and I ducked my head.

"What's wrong?"

"The light," I protested and covered my eyes with my hands. "It's really bright."

"The what?" my mom asked, her voice low and tense. "Why are you covering your eyes?"

"Because the sun must be shining directly into—" I stopped talking when I realized what I'd said.

"The light," I repeated, slowly moving my hands away from my face. The back of my neck began to tingle and my arms and legs broke out in goose bumps. I opened my eyes and was again assaulted by a sickeningly intense light, but this time I forced my lids to stay open.

When I moved my head, waves of bright light swirled around me. Suddenly overcome with nausea, I took a deep breath and held it until the feeling passed.

I must have turned pale because my mom worriedly repeated, "What's wrong?"

"Nothing." I smiled. A second wave of nausea threatened and fighting back the urge to be sick, I reluctantly closed my eyes, shutting out the light. "Nothing at all is wrong," I said, smiling crazily and beginning to cry tears of joy. "Mom, I can see."

I'd lost nearly all hope that I'd ever say those words again. But the beams of light, which glowed so intensely that they were, ironically, blinding, proved that Trazyl had brought my eye back to life.

Tilting my head back, I laughed until I was howling. "Holy shit, it worked! The Trazyl worked. I can see!" I shouted over and over until I collapsed against the pillows, out of breath and unable to hold myself upright.

Happiness, unlike any I'd ever known, ran wildly through me like bolts of electricity.

There was a noise on my left, something between a sigh and a sob. Slowly turning my head toward it, waves of light danced in front of me, dipping and swaying until they came together to form an unrecognizable shape. Mesmerized by the glob of light that seemed to be floating in my direction, I reached out to it and shyly asked, "Mom?"

I heard a sharp intake of breath followed by, "Oh my God, you can see," as she threw her arms around my shoulders. The sudden movement caused the light around her to scatter and spin.

"I can't believe it," she cried, squeezing me tighter against her. "What is your vision like?"

I hoped my answer wouldn't disappoint her. I didn't truly have vision. At least not yet.

"All I can see are lines and waves of light. When you walked toward me just now, the lines came together and were much brighter but not really recognizable. But it's okay because it'll keep improving, and it's a lot better than being stuck in the dark."

"This is the best thing that could ever happen. I'm so happy for you." There was a hitch to her voice, and I knew she was close to tears.

I pulled out of her embrace but loosely held onto her arms.

"This is all because of you. I'm going to see, for real. You found the Trazyl and made all of the arrangements so I could have it as quickly as possible. I'd still be blind if not for you. Thank you, Mom. Thank you for getting my sight back."

"Don't forget Henry, he's really the one who discovered Trazyl. Speaking of Henry," she said jumping to her feet, "we need to call him." Mom left my room saying she'd be back as soon as she called Henry and Howard.

Henry was flabbergasted and insisted on seeing me that day. "He didn't sound entirely convinced," my mom said when she was off the phone. There was laughter in her voice, and I was glad to hear it.

A few hours later, my mother and I were in Henry's office, and he was still having trouble believing the miracle that was sitting in his exam chair.

"Amazing," Henry kept saying as he studied my eye.

"Will my vision continue to improve?"

"I hope so, but keep in mind, your retina is damaged. I doubt you'll have a full recovery. Although at this point, it seems anything is possible."

"You know what?" Mom asked me as we left Henry's office. "This is the first time in almost a year that we've walked out of here and neither of us is crying."

"It's a nice change," I replied, watching beams of light whirl about as the elevator doors opened.

Though I had no right to be, I was disappointed when I woke up the next morning and my vision hadn't improved. My mom suggested we look at some of the condos for sale in the building but I declined.

"Maybe next week," I said grouchily.

My foul mood didn't last long because over the next five days, there was marked improvement in my sight. The bands of light stopped their drunken dance, allowing my queasy stomach to settle. Objects took shape and, best of all, I was beginning to see colors.

At first, I glimpsed a flash of red that took my breath away. Soon reds, blues, and greens returned to dazzle me with their brilliance. I embraced the bright hues as one would a lost love, timidly at first, then rapidly becoming greedy for more.

For the last five months, I'd lived like a ghost. A transparent likeness of myself, living in the dark and haunting a house full of life. I existed, but I wasn't present.

But now, surrounded by shapes and colors, I felt real again. I participated in conversations, I laughed, and I made others laugh. I wanted to know what was happening in the world and occasionally glanced at the TV screen as I listened to the news instead of sitcoms.

Once a week, my mom took me to Henry's office so he could track my eye's progress. My sight improved continuously for a month, and there were days that I felt so light, I could have been filled with helium. Then a week went by without any change in my vision, and I slowly began my descent back to Earth.

Don't quit on me now. I could see color, and, with my contact lens, I could barely make out certain objects such as tables and chairs. It was better than being blind, but my vision was, by no means, sufficient to enable me to function outside my condo.

"My sight seems to have plateaued," I reported apprehensively to Henry during my latest appointment.

Reminding me of the considerable damage my eye had sustained, Henry, to my dismay, agreed with me.

"Then, I'm truly never going to have my life back, am I?"

I allowed a single tear to fall and, realizing how I must appear to my mother and Henry, I immediately wiped it away.

"I'm sorry, I didn't mean to sound ungrateful, and I'm not. I am frustrated, though. Henry, I know you warned me about getting my hopes up. I guess I thought once some vision came back, it all would. Pretty stupid of me to assume I could ever have a life again."

"Your life is going to resume," my mom said confidently. "No, it won't be the same as before, but you'll get used to it and you'll make it work. You just need to take it one step at a time."

On the way home, my mom said nonchalantly, "I'd like to look at some condos for you." Now that we understood how little vision I'd have, there was no denying my new residence should be in her building.

"That's fine," I said dully.

I should have been excited or at least interested, but I only felt stuck. I was stagnant, and it didn't matter where I lived. I'd be stuck there, too.

After two days of looking, we found a nice place on the fourth floor. The open layout worked well for me and, as an added bonus, the bedroom didn't overlook the busy street.

"Won't it be nice to have a place of your own again?" my mom asked expectantly after the closing date was scheduled.

I pictured my furniture. *Will it make me feel better to be surrounded by my old things? Do I care anymore?* I was no longer the same person who'd chosen my couch and bedroom set years earlier.

While my mom was tied up at the closing, I was left to supervise the movers as they unloaded boxes and furniture into my new home. A long time had passed since I was in charge of anything, including myself. Constantly being asked, "Where do you want this?" was unnerving. Thank goodness my mom had diligently labeled each box with its precise contents and the room it belonged in. She arrived in time to ask the movers to take several unmarked, mystery boxes down the hall to the private storage locker assigned to my condo.

"What's in those boxes and why aren't they labeled?" I asked.

"Actually, they were my boxes that somehow got mixed into your things." Before I could ask her any more questions, she said, "Let's get your bedroom set up and unpacked so you have somewhere to sleep tonight."

After several hours of unpacking, organizing, and cleaning my belongings, my mother was more than ready to return to her apartment.

"Will you be okay?" she asked uncertainly.

"Of course," I said, taking a seat on the couch. Spike jumped up next to me and I scooped him into my lap. "I'm fine," I insisted

"Call me if you need anything," Mom said, opening the front door. "I'll be back down in a few hours to help you take Spike for a walk."

The door clicked shut and the brave face I'd been wearing crumbled. At that moment, sitting on my couch, clutching Spike to my chest, my life had never felt so empty.

I had a home full of my things, but there was nothing for me to do. I had no plans, no job, no friends nearby, no purpose in this world.

I'd lived in my condo for about a week and had yet to receive a visitor who was not my mom or Howard. So, when I heard the digital chimes of my doorbell at 7:30 on a Thursday morning, I was stumped. *Who in the world is at my door?*

Warily, I approached it and in my most assertive voice asked, "Who is it?"

"Oh, for heaven's sake," the man on the other side of my door grumbled. "Do you ever listen to the messages I leave you? Why do you even have a phone?"

"Bob!" I exclaimed happily, opening the door. "What are you doing here?" I ignored his comment regarding my poor phone etiquette. "You called? When?"

"Last night," he replied, giving me a quick hug. "You may have been asleep."

"Probably. Well, now you can tell me in person, what brings you here so early in the morning?"

"I was hoping you'd come with me to the barn today," Bob said somberly, causing my nerves to prickle.

"What's wrong with Milo?" I felt the blood drain not just from my face, but from my entire body.

"He's stopped eating," Bob said, fatigue and concern evident in his voice.

"Who won't eat? Milo? My Milo is refusing food?" I couldn't control the spasms of fear that were making it difficult to think.

"He hasn't touched his food or hay in three days. I've tried everything. Carrots, apples, he refuses it all. The vet believes that he has at least one bleeding ulcer. He put Milo on two medications that should have worked by now, but Milo still won't eat."

"An ulcer?"

"Many ulcers, actually. Unfortunately, it's fairly common for a horse to develop problems with its gut. I've had the vet out twice to give Milo several bags of fluids, but if he doesn't start eating…" Bob's voice trailed off, but I knew he was talking about Milo's low chance of survival.

"Give me three minutes." Moving faster than I had in a very long time, I raced to my room to get dressed.

CHAPTER THIRTEEN

B ob's car wove in and out of traffic as we sped along the highway. As he drove, Bob did his best to engage me in conversation, but thoughts of Milo in pain and starving to death made it impossible for me to manage anything other than one-word responses.

After a while, Bob gave up and we rode in silence until finally he announced, "We're almost there."

"Good," I said.

"I'm sorry I've upset you. I didn't know what else to do. I hate for you to see Milo like this, but I also know if anyone can convince him to eat, it's you. He's already lost so much weight. I'm not sure what you can see, but you should prepare yourself. Milo won't look like the horse you remember."

As though on cue, my brain summoned an image of Milo from my visit nine months ago, the last time I had enough vision to see him. Well-rounded and heavily muscled, he was the epitome of a horse in perfect health.

I swallowed hard, and although I knew the answer would devastate me, I still asked, "How much weight has he lost?"

Bob pushed on the accelerator harder than necessary as he exited the highway. My back pressed against the passenger seat and I righted myself in time to turn around and watch Spike's lumpy, black shape slide across the leather back seat.

"My guess is he's lost close to three hundred pounds. His hair is starting to thin and fall out in some places, and he'll most likely be lying down when we get there. As far as I know, Milo didn't get up at all yesterday. Tom has been watching over him. He checks on Milo every other minute and I wouldn't be surprised to learn that Tom has been spending the night in the barn."

My appreciation for Tom's devotion to Milo was immediately replaced by feelings of guilt. "I should have been the one in Milo's stall," I said wringing my hands. "He's my horse and he needed me."

Bob cleared his throat and I turned my head toward him. I'd gotten out of the habit of looking at people while we conversed and lately I'd been trying to rectify that.

"How could you have known that Milo was sick? I didn't tell you right away because we thought this would be an easy fix. Maybe I should've gotten you sooner, but you're here now and you need to forget about everything else and focus on your horse."

The car bounced along an unevenly paved country road and we slowed noticeably as we pulled up to something very large and very yellow. When Bob stopped the car, we were probably less than twenty feet from the building, close enough for me to see the white trim outlining every door and window.

"We're here," Bob said at the moment I located the giant white X that marked the barn's front entrance. Milo was somewhere behind that X, and I had every intention of leaping from the car and finding him. But Bob's strong hand on my shoulder stopped me.

"Wait for me and I'll take you to Milo. I know you're anxious to get to him, but it will be faster and safer if you let me help you."

I exhaled through pursed lips, making a soft popping sound, and opened the passenger door. Spike bounded into the front seat and, yapping excitedly, dove out of the car ahead of me.

Bob gathered what he needed from his car before taking my elbow and leading me into the cool, dark barn. I blinked several times but my eye couldn't adjust to the dim light. I stayed close to Bob as he guided me down a cement floor padded with thick, rubber matting. We walked by open doorways but the unrecognizable objects inside the rooms remained a mystery to me.

When the aisle widened, allowing in more light, brown doors appeared on either side of us, and I knew we'd reached the stalls.

I stared into each one, desperate for my first glimpse of a horse in almost a year, but they were empty.

I assumed the occupants must be turned out in their paddocks for the morning. All except Milo. He was in here somewhere and I had to fight the urge to whistle for him.

"Hold on a second." Bob dropped my arm, walked away, and called out to his barn manager.

"In here," Tom replied just loud enough to be heard, which made me suspect he was in Milo's stall.

"How is he today?" Bob asked.

"The same," Tom exhaled wearily. "He didn't touch his dinner last night or his breakfast this morning."

Unable to wait one more second to be with Milo, I coughed loudly. "Where is he?"

"Come on, I'll take you." Tom moved to my side and put his hand on my shoulder. "I'm glad you're here," he said, placing a carrot into my hand. We hardly walked ten feet before Tom stopped in front of a stall. The door had been left open and I stared at the unresponsive, brown figure inside.

Milo was lying on his stomach on a bed of shavings that looked like snow, his head drooping so low his chin touched the floor. I shivered involuntarily.

"Milo?" I walked toward him, but he remained motionless and mute. The closer I got, the more of him I could see. The finer details still escaped me, but I could tell by his shape that he'd lost weight.

I sat cross-legged on the ground facing him and leaned in until I could rest my forehead against his.

"I'm here, Milo. I'm right here and I won't leave you again. I'm going to take care of you and everything will be all right." There was no reaction to my whispered declarations, and had it not been for his slow, shallow breaths, I would have thought Milo had already left me.

"Milo," I repeated his name several times in an attempt to call him back from wherever he was. "Please come back to me," I implored while running my hands up and down his neck.

Milo's body felt rigid and cooler than usual. His once soft coat was now rough and sparse in some areas. He had the look and feel of a malnourished animal, and it wouldn't be long before his ribs were showing under his skin.

"Please, Milo," I sobbed. "Please don't leave me now. I know it hurts but you have to eat." I held the carrot under Milo's mouth, but he ignored it.

I tried showing it to him, but his eyes were half-closed. I even pretended to eat it myself. The only attention I captured was Spike's. He had entered the stall unnoticed by Milo and now was attempting to take the carrot for himself.

"Come on, Milo. You have to eat or you're going to die. Please, M, I lived for you, now you do the same for me."

I brought the carrot back down to his mouth and tried using the pointed end to pry his lips apart. He refused to take it, but something was different, His breathing was less labored and, if I wasn't mistaken, Milo's body temperature was rising.

These were the first signs of hope since I entered the stall about an hour ago, but I needed more. Milo had to start eating.

My thoughts were interrupted by a wet nose on the back of my hand. Annoyed, I broke off a piece of carrot and gave it to Spike.

"Obviously, you have no problem eating."

I broke off another chunk of carrot for Spike and even I could see Milo's ears rotate toward the sound.

A memory tickled the back of my brain, and in a flash of insight, I began to bite the carrot into little pieces and spit them into my palm. I'd prided myself on knowing Milo better than anyone else, yet I'd forgotten that in times of stress, he would refuse all treats unless I chopped them up.

I nibbled my way through half of the carrot until my hand was full of orange morsels. "Try it now," I said encouragingly, as I presented the pile of carrot mush to Milo who pushed at it with his lips but still wouldn't eat it.

Undeterred, I kept my hand where it was. "That's a start but not good enough. I know you're hungry, and my legs have gone numb from sitting here for so long. Do us both a favor and eat."

Milo's prickly chin whiskers brushed against my wrist as he again played with the mixture of saliva and carrot.

"Stop playing with your food and eat it," I demanded in my sternest, motherly voice. And, suddenly, Milo did as he was told.

"Thank you," I breathed, never enjoying the sound of a horse chewing as much as I did at that moment. Each bite Milo took and every mouthful he swallowed were cause for celebration. The fear that had been twisting my insides all morning relaxed its hold on me. Milo nudged my hand holding the bitter end piece of the carrot and making a face, I bit into it.

Milo was still munching on his last bite when Bob returned to check on us.

"I was wondering…" His voice trailed off as he took in the sight of Milo greedily licking my open palm in search of more food.

"Is he eating? Oh my God, he's eating," Bob repeated excitedly. "You got him to eat!"

I smiled but remained focused on Milo. "It was only one carrot, but I think he's hungry for more."

Before Bob could reply, a second set of footsteps approached, and I heard Tom tell Bob that the vet had arrived.

"Perfect timing. Let him know that she got Milo to eat and see if we can give him some grain."

I wished I could see the expression on Tom's face. "I knew he would eat for her!" he rejoiced before running off.

Minutes later, Tom was back with another person I supposed was the vet. Bob introduced us as Tom set a bucket of feed next to me.

"Just a little at a time," the doctor cautioned as I scooped up a small handful and presented it to Milo. Although he didn't find the tiny pellets as enticing as the carrot, Milo ate the grain out of my hand.

"I'll be darned," the vet said, walking into Milo's stall for a closer look. "I can't believe this is the same horse that, just yesterday, looked half dead. How did you do that?"

"I don't know," I said looking up at the stunned man. "Maybe the medicine started kicking in."

"Or maybe he's eating because you told him to," Tom said, chuckling.

I blushed, knowing the vet would never accept that as a reason for the return of Milo's appetite. I didn't completely believe it either, but whatever the cause, the doctor assured me that as long as Milo continued to eat, he would fully recover.

On the way home, Bob offered to take me to and from the barn every day until Milo was eating on his own. I responded with a grateful, "Yes, please."

Bob also reminded me that Milo's lease to Wendy ended in a week and he would be back in my care. He would also be my financial responsibility and I would have to ask my mother for help. I worried about how I could convince her to keep Milo without leasing him out again, especially when I wouldn't be riding him. I'd have to discuss this with her as soon as possible.

I didn't have to wait long. I'd been home for no more than ten minutes when my mom burst through my front door. "How's Milo?" she asked worriedly, charging into the kitchen to find me sitting at the table.

I'd called her that morning on the way to the barn to let her know where I was going and why.

"He's better now, but it took forever for me to get him to eat something." My voice held a mixture of pride and relief as I described my day. Leaning against the counter, my mom listened quietly until I reminded her that Milo's lease would be up at the end of the month.

"I know," she said. "Does Bob think he has anyone else in the barn who would lease him?"

Oh, crap. She's already thinking of leasing Milo again. "I don't know. We were too upset about Milo not eating to talk about anything else. Even if Bob does have someone in mind, Milo can't be leased right now because he isn't in any shape to be ridden."

Without being able to read her face clearly, I had no way of knowing if Mom was angry, disappointed, or okay with this turn of events. But if she insisted on leasing out Milo again, I was prepared to beg, if that's what it took for me to keep him.

I heard her take a deep breath. "I think it would be better for both you and Milo if we forget about a new lease for now. Better for the two of you to spend time together. Heal each other's wounds."

"Really? You don't mind?" I asked, astounded by her generosity. My hand clutched my throat, which had tightened with emotion. "Thank you for understanding how much I need him, especially now."

It was getting late, but before she left, I thanked my mom again and hugged her.

She was almost out the door when she turned around. "Don't worry about Milo's bills," she said. "I'll take care of them."

I closed the door behind her and, alone in my condo, I did a little dance. Milo would soon be mine again.

Having a purpose and a place to be took some getting used to. It had been ages since I'd set an alarm, but now I needed to wake up at 6:30 a.m., six days a week, to get out the door by 7:15.

Forcing myself out of bed was nowhere near as daunting as taking the elevator to the lobby and stepping out into the world. Spike marched along next to me, his leash wrapped tightly around my fingers. Bob's car was dark green, which could be a tricky color for me to see. I banked on him seeing me first and honking or yelling to draw my attention and, to my consternation, the attention of everyone else on the street.

Either Bob or Tom had to guide me to Milo's stall, where a bucket of grain would be waiting by the door. Once I was safely inside, I stayed there all day. Spike would join me when he finished zooming around the property, but for the most part, I was left alone with my horse.

Ordinarily, Milo could wolf down a bucket of grain in twenty minutes but feeding him his breakfast by hand took an hour. I sat next to him, the bucket between us, and fed him one handful of grain after another. Sometimes he eagerly lapped up an entire handful at once; other times he suspiciously sniffed at my cupped hand before taking the grain in two or three bites. Either way, he chewed in extreme slow motion before swallowing each mouthful. Dinner was a replay of this incredibly repetitive and time-consuming routine. Nonetheless, I relished every second of feeding time.

I didn't know if it was pain or lack of strength that kept Milo from standing up more than a few times a day. Most of the time he wanted to lie down in a deep pile of shavings and rest his head on my lap. Usually I'd let him sleep, but sometimes I'd tell him stories about how it felt to be blind and how I got my sight back. He, too, had suffered at the hands of others, and while I spoke of the torturous surgery that eventually blinded me, I rubbed the areas around his belly where whip and spur marks had once been.

Preferring not to socialize, I hid in Milo's stall until Bob finished teaching and it was time to go home. Since the days were often long, I packed a cooler with drinks and snacks for myself, Milo, and Spike. Besides the apples I brought for him, Milo liked to share a bag of Fritos and a bottle of Sunny Delight with me.

As each day passed, Milo grew stronger. His appetite was increasing, he was more alert and wasn't sleeping as much, and he was standing up for longer periods of time.

I'd been hand feeding Milo his grain for a week when I decided to see if he would eat on his own. He watched while I poured his breakfast into the feed tub hanging in his stall, staring at me and then at the empty bucket in my hand. When Milo realized that I wasn't going to feed him, he snorted, stuck his head into the tub, and started chomping.

Now that it was no longer necessary for me to feed him, I feared Bob and Tom would find something else for me to do that would take me away from Milo. I let them believe I was still feeding him by hand until Tom walked by the stall one morning and witnessed Milo, head buried in his feed tub, munching away.

"When did you stop hand feeding him?" Tom asked.

I was standing in Milo's stall watching him eat and hadn't realized Tom was looking in on us.

"Four days ago."

Tom walked off but returned a few minutes later carrying something I couldn't really see.

"What is that?" I asked, pointing at the blurry, black object.

Tom dropped it at my feet with a clunk. I guessed by the sound it made that it was a bucket.

"Brushes. Now that Milo is eating and standing, here are all the grooming tools you'll need to put the shine back on him."

"Thanks, Tom," I said merrily, and rummaged through the bucket until I felt a rubber curry comb.

Milo loved to be groomed. I indulged him for at least an hour twice a day, his puckered lips quivering the entire time. I was mindful of the areas where the hair was growing back and used a soft towel on those spots.

He recovered quickly. A month later, he looked, felt, and sounded like his old self, greeting me with a whinny every morning when I entered the barn and called his name. I loved the time I spent nursing him, but nothing compared to how good it felt to see Milo healthy, shiny, and as handsome as I remembered.

Three weeks since his last visit, the vet returned to the barn to check on Milo's progress. Bob, Tom, and I hovered outside Milo's stall while the vet went over every inch of him.

"I can't believe this is the same horse," he said when he was finished with his exam. "He was on death's door the last time I saw him, and now he looks ready to walk into the show ring."

I smiled, enjoying the praise. "It helps when you have such a good-looking patient." I walked into the stall and patted Milo's neck, appreciating how soft and smooth his hair felt.

"Speaking of the show ring," Bob said, "when can I start riding him?"

"Any time you want," the doctor replied. "Take it easy until he builds up his stamina and keep him on his medication. Other than that, I'd say Milo's good to go."

Bob began riding Milo lightly at first, until he felt that Milo was ready for more. I pretended to watch, moving my head as though tracking them with my eyes when it was actually the rhythmical sound of Milo's hoof beats that told me where they were. It was like old times, except now I knew it would never be my turn to ride.

We were already midway through July when I decided to be adventurous.

"I'm taking Milo for a walk and a little bit of grass," I said nonchalantly to Tom as we walked past him. The slack lead rope dangling from my hand allowed Milo to be a few steps ahead of me, leading the way.

"It looks like Milo is walking you," Tom quipped. "Are you sure this is all right with Bob?"

"I don't see why not. What could go wrong?"

Milo led me out the barn door and down a grassy pathway, walking slowly but with purpose, as Spike scampered alongside me. We made it safely to a spot where the grass was so high, it brushed against my knees, and Milo barely had to lower his head in order to graze. While he ate, I leaned against Milo's shoulder, so I knew the moment his body tensed. Spike took a break from chasing insects and came to stand by me.

The sound of trotting hooves made me tighten the hold I had on Milo's lead. A horse was coming toward us, and I hoped it hadn't escaped from the barn. This happened occasionally and it was always an ordeal until the horse was safely back in its stall.

A large, dark shape emerged from the distorted haze, and I was relieved to see that the horse had a rider.

"What on earth are you doing out here?" Bob huffed belligerently. "I don't know if I like you hanging out in the field by yourself."

I appreciated his concern, but I was enjoying this taste of independence.

"Thanks, but I'm perfectly safe," I grinned. "Tom knew I was out here, and Milo took good care of me."

"Are you sure?" Bob didn't sound convinced.

"I promise, I'm fine. Nothing at all to worry about. I have my two bodyguards with me."

"Well, don't spend too much time out here. I'm supposed to ride Milo next, and I imagine Tom would like to start getting him ready."

"Okay, I'll bring him in."

I followed Bob back to the barn. One of the grooms took charge of his horse while Bob walked into the tack room. Tom collected Milo from me, and I apologized for holding everyone up.

"We actually weren't waiting for you," Tom replied, laughing. "Bob's just giving you a hard time. He was really worried and would have told you anything to get you to come back here where he could keep an eye on you."

"I should have known Bob was trying to hide that he cares," I groaned as I clipped a crosstie onto Milo's halter.

I rubbed Milo's face with a towel while Tom brushed bits of dirt and grass from his legs. Bob resurfaced from the tack room, his arms loaded with items of various sizes and colors.

"What have you got there?" I asked.

He ignored my question and walked over to Tom. Handing him the largest of the items, he said, "Use this one."

"Are you sure?" Tom asked as he wiped off the top of what I guessed was a saddle.

"Yup," Bob replied tersely. Then turning to me, he draped a pair of stiff, leather chaps over my shoulders.

"This, too," he said, and placed a riding helmet in my hands.

"Why am I holding your hat and chaps?" I asked, perplexed.

"You're not," Bob said. "You're holding your hat and chaps."

"Mine?" I frowned.

Bob leaned against a wooden rail in the middle of the grooming area.

"Yes," he said, reaching across the railing and giving my chaps a light tug. "These are your things."

Shaking my head, I stepped out of Bob's reach and asked, "Why?"

Bob straightened and took a deep breath. "It's time for you to start riding again," he stated, taking the hat from my hands and setting it on my head.

I yanked the hat off. "Bob, I can't," I said, thinking he must be joking and not finding it funny. "You know I can't."

But Bob wasn't kidding. "If you can traipse about the countryside with Milo in tow, I see no reason why you can't ride him. More importantly, I know you want to ride. You and I both know Milo would never allow anything to happen to you. So, what's stopping you?"

I looked at my boots while I considered my answer. When I looked back up, Bob was staring at me. "In order to ride, I need to be able to see."

Bob marched around the railing, stopped inches away from me, put his hands on his hips, and glared down at my face. "Where in the world did you hear that bit of nonsense?"

"You don't think I need to be able to see where I'm going? Of course, I do. All riders do."

"It's time for you to stop making up these rules so you can hide behind them," Bob said sternly. "You're deciding what you can't do before you've given it a chance. You're braver than that. Now, put on your hat and chaps and get on your horse."

Had Bob lost his mind? Or maybe I'd lost mine, because without giving any thought to my answer, I said, "Okay," and buckled my chaps around my waist.

CHAPTER FOURTEEN

I couldn't remember the first time my mom lifted me onto the back of a horse, though she has a photo of it in one of her albums. The three-year-old version of me looks completely at ease on the large, chestnut gelding, a rein in each little hand and a big smile on my face. According to my mother, I was a cranky child, and my temper tantrums were legendary. At the time, she didn't know that my eye disease gave me severe headaches. But as soon as I got on a horse, the pain faded away.

With my hiatus from riding about to end, I thought of that photo and had faith that getting back on Milo would diminish the pain of the past fifteen months.

Milo sniffed my hair, apparently appreciating the apple-scented shampoo I'd used that morning. "I can't believe I'm doing this," I said softly as I tucked my hair under my riding helmet.

"Did you say something?" Tom asked, adjusting my saddle so it sat in a better spot on Milo's back.

"I haven't been on a horse in over a year."

"That's a long time," Tom said with a touch of concern in his voice.

"Considering I thought I'd never ride again, it really isn't." Not that I expected to do much riding. I assumed Bob would have me walk Milo in a big circle once or twice before giving him back to Tom.

Having been locked in my tack trunk for such a long time, my chaps were dry and tight on my legs. I was trying to stretch the leather by doing a deep knee bend when Tom took my hand and placed Milo's reins in it.

"All set?" he asked, still holding onto Milo's bridle.

He didn't let go until I bobbed my head up and down and said, "Yup."

Under normal circumstances, Tom would've left me alone to take Milo to the ring myself. But today he walked ahead of us, leading the way to the indoor ring where Bob was already riding.

When we got to the mounting block, Tom made sure Milo stayed still while I stepped to the top of the block and, in a well-practiced, fluid motion, got on his back.

Gathering the reins in both hands and sinking slowly into the saddle, I savored the feel of the leather cradling me. For the first time in so many months, I was where I belonged. I was home.

I looked down at Tom, who remained rooted to the ground by the mounting block, still loosely holding onto Milo.

"It's okay, Tom." I smiled at him. "I'm fine. Really fine."

"Are you sure?"

"Absolutely."

Tom stepped to the side and Milo walked into the ring, where the only other occupants were Bob and his horse.

"Take care of me, M." I spoke softly so only he could hear me.

My upper body automatically moved in time with each footfall as Milo's powerful shoulders lifted, stretched, and dropped, then repeated the cycle. The motion served as a wake-up call to muscles in my legs and stomach that had long been asleep.

I couldn't remember a time when I'd been so mesmerized by a horse's walk. I relaxed my fingers on the reins and, while we walked around the ring, I began to adjust to the view from Milo's back.

My sight was still a distorted mess, but at least while I was on a horse, I didn't have to worry about tripping over curbs, falling down stairs, or walking into walls.

Bob trotted past us then slowed his horse enough to look back at me and ask, "How does it feel to be riding?"

"Liberating, like I can breathe again. Although I don't know if I would call this 'riding.' I feel more like Milo's passenger."

"That's not a bad thing. Especially when you have a horse who knows his job as well as he does."

The next time Bob caught up with Milo and me, he started circling around us. "You don't think you're going to get away with just walking, do you?"

"That's exactly what I think." It never occurred to me that Bob would have me do anything but a slow walk. I pursed my lips while considering the risks. "I don't know. What if I steer Milo toward a fence and he bumps into it, he could get hurt. Or worse, what if I don't stop him in time and he jumps it, we could both get hurt. I think I'm happy to stay at a nice, safe, slow walk."

Bob slowed his horse until he matched my pace.

"You know what I think?" he asked rhetorically. "I think that not long ago, you told me you couldn't come out to the barn. Yet here you are. You also told me more times than I can count that you'd never ride again. But look at you now. If you really want to ride, you'll figure out how to do it. Even if you can hardly see anything."

I was a little hurt that Bob wasn't more sympathetic to my situation. I was about to tell him as much when my subconscious whispered something truly disturbing.

He has a point, said the little voice inside my head. *You can do this.*

"What if I look like a fool?" I asked meekly.

"I'm the only one here and I don't care how you look. Besides, you'll probably ride just like anyone who hasn't been on a horse in a while, and there's no shame in that."

Bob was growing aggravated with me. I could hear it in his voice.

"What do you think, Milo? Do you feel like trotting?" I pushed my heels down and pulled my shoulders back into the correct posture for a posting trot. "Okay, Bob, but if I wind up impaled on one of the jumps, it's on you."

"In that case, I suggest you steer as little as possible. Remember, the key word is 'passenger,'" Bob said before leaving my side at a canter.

Pressing my tongue against my teeth, I made a clucking sound and Milo began to trot. I was too weak to hold myself in the proper position. Instead of keeping tight against the saddle, my legs swung back and forth, making it impossible to control the rise and fall of my seat in time to Milo's pace.

Off balance and unable to see where I was going, I resisted the urge to pull back on the reins and make Milo walk. I refused to give up so easily. I needed to prove I could still ride.

Shadows loomed ahead and as we neared them, I realized we'd reached the ingate. Some horses would have taken advantage of my lack of control and slowed to a walk or left the ring. Milo did neither. Instead, he followed the rail, passed the ingate, and continued his steady trot down the long side of the ring.

Putting my trust in him, I took a deep breath and loosened my grip on the reins until I was barely holding onto them, literally giving Milo free rein to go where he pleased. I braced myself, knowing this was dangerous. Milo could have bolted, stopped short, or turned too sharply, and I would have fallen off.

But my good boy just kept trotting.

I never realized how much strength it took to post up and down. Twice around the ring, I was gasping for air and had to bring Milo back down to a walk.

Bob had stopped in the center of the ring where he could keep track of me.

The last time we rode together, in Florida, I boasted I was in better shape than he was. He laughed then almost as hard as he was laughing now.

"I'm glad you find me so entertaining," I wheezed.

Still chuckling, Bob allowed his horse to lazily walk toward me.

"It looks like your eyes aren't the problem," he said when he met up with me on the rail. "You, my friend, are weak and out of shape. We need to make you strong and fit again. But for now, go ahead and canter. At least you can sit in the saddle and not worry about posting. It's less work so it'll be easier for you, although it'll be less fun for me to watch."

I shifted my body weight to my leg next to the rail, signaling Milo to pick up a canter. As Bob predicted, the canter, a much smoother gait than the trot, was easier. I managed five laps around the ring before I gently pulled back on the reins, letting Milo know it was time to walk. My face was burning with both exertion and pleasure. As much as I hated to admit it, I couldn't go on anymore.

"It won't take long for you to feel like your old self again," Bob assured me as he dismounted and began leading his horse back to the grooming stalls. I tried to mirror his actions, but when I slid off Milo and my feet hit the ground, my worn out legs buckled like cooked spaghetti.

I grabbed the saddle's flap to keep myself upright. Milo turned his head, saw me clutching the saddle, and let out a loud snort, sounding very much like he was laughing at me.

"You, too, Milo?" I wagged my finger at him before lifting the reins over his head and leading him back to Tom. "I expect a little teasing from Bob, but not from you."

"It felt so good to be on a horse again," I sighed, as I fed Milo a handful of mints while Tom removed his tack. "I'll probably be too sore to move tomorrow, but it will be the good kind of pain."

"There's a good kind?" Tom asked as he released Milo from the crossties. He snapped one end of a lead rope to Milo's halter and handed the other end to me.

"Sure," I said as we walked Milo to his stall. "My aching muscles will be a constant reminder that I rode today."

When we got to Milo's door, Tom stopped at the threshold. "Will you be okay if I leave you alone? I have to get dinner ready for the horses."

"Of course, go do what you have to do. See you tomorrow."

Milo lowered his head so I could remove his halter. As I pulled the strap over his ears, I leaned in to kiss his nose.

"Thank you for taking such good care of me, M." I dug a bag of Fritos out of my backpack. "I'd feed these to you myself, but I have to go. I'll pour them into your feed tub instead, which I don't think you'll mind one bit." As soon as I did, Milo forgot that I existed, and his head disappeared into the bucket. The sound of his crunching made me smile. I wished I could spend the rest of the day in his stall, perfectly happy just to be near him. But I knew Bob was waiting for me by the barn door, and I could hear the toe of his boot tapping impatiently against the gravel.

I spared another minute with Milo, patting his neck and listening to him eat.

The sharp beep of a horn told me my time was up. Shutting the stall door behind me, I made my way to Bob's car as quickly as I could.

He spent most of the trip back to Baltimore on the phone, giving me forty minutes to come up with the right words to express my gratitude. If Bob hadn't all but forced me into the saddle, I'd never have gotten on Milo today. If ever. I massaged my leg muscles while I thought of a hundred different ways to say, "Thank you."

I waited to speak until we were in front of my building and Bob was staring at me. With my hand on the door handle, I stared back and took a deep breath.

"I never thought I'd ride again," I began, but saying it out loud triggered painful memories and I turned away, pretending something outside had caught my attention. When I was sure I wasn't going to cry, I turned back to Bob who was uncharacteristically silent.

"All that time I spent in the dark, I couldn't stop thinking about everything I'd lost." My eyes burned but I refused to look away from him. "Driving, friends, my job...all of it, gone."

Bob shifted in his seat. "I know it was hard for you."

"Hard," I repeated in a low tone. "Yes, it was hard. Except I knew I could go on with my life without those things. But without riding, my life wasn't worth living."

I paused for a second to catch my breath. "I rode my horse today." I smiled through my tears. "Because of you. I can't imagine you'll ever understand what you've done for me. Thanking you isn't enough, but it's all I have. So, thank you, Bob."

I opened the car door, letting in the sounds of the city during rush hour. Horns blared and brakes squealed, but I was still able to hear Bob's brusque, "You're welcome. Now get out of the car."

I smiled at him, nodded my head, collected Spike and my backpack, and walked into the building. Sentimentality didn't come easily to either of us.

Had it been any other day, I wouldn't have seen my mom until she ventured downstairs to make sure I was still surviving on my own. But today was different. So, instead of getting off the elevator at my apartment, Spike and I rode to the top floor where I was hoping I'd find my mom at home.

On the ride up, I thought of several clever ways to break the good news to her, but all was forgotten when she opened the door. Bouncing on my toes, I blurted, "I rode today! I rode Milo! I walked, I trotted, and I even cantered."

My announcement was met with silence. Her fixed stare made me self-conscious and keenly aware that I was filthy and smelled like a horse. I started nervously wiping my hands on my jeans when my mom stepped aside to let me in the door.

"I'm sorry," she said, following me into the kitchen. "I don't mean to be unsupportive, but are you sure it's safe for you to ride? You can't cross a street without my help. How did you ride a horse?"

"Bob was there the whole time, and I was never in any danger. It's amazing, Mom. Milo took care of me. He seems to understand that I'm different." I smiled, recalling how Milo had taken charge of our route, sidestepped the poles in our way, and kept his gait smooth and consistent as I fought to maintain my balance. She drummed her fingers on the counter, and I imagined she was weighing what I'd said versus what her protective instincts were telling her.

"I'm proud of you and I'm happy that you're happy. But please promise me that you'll be careful. I know you, and the next thing you're going to want to do is jump over fences."

I laughed and dismissed the idea with a shake of my head. "Believe me, I won't be doing that, at least not any time soon."

My mother made me promise to be careful three more times. Before I left, I tried to assure her that my riding was a cause not for fear, but for celebration.

"You should come watch us after I get in shape. I think you'll feel better when you see how Milo protects me."

Each day that I rode — six days a week, 35 minutes a day — was a gift. I practiced steering in big circles, little circles, and figure eights until Milo could second-guess me and do them automatically. I practiced transitions from a walk to a canter and back down to a trot until Milo changed gaits with my slightest pull on the reins or lightest nudge of my heel. And I worked on shifting my weight to keep Milo's hind end lined up with his front.

Bob watched it all, constantly reminding me to look up to keep my balance, using the axiom usually reserved for beginners, "If you look down, you'll end up on the ground."

Most days I rode early in the morning so I would have the ring to myself. Every now and then, other clients would ride with me, but Bob made sure to let them know to stay out of my way.

Sometimes my friends from the barn came to the ring to watch. I could feel them staring at me and I could hear them talking.

"It's great that she's riding again."

"Yeah, but how does she know where to go?"

They weren't comfortable asking me directly, so Bob fielded most of their questions. It always made me smile when he would tell me he answered, "I don't know. She just does."

By mid-July, temperatures were hitting triple digits and, if we weren't careful, the afternoon sun could cause horses and riders to become ill. To avoid heatstroke, I rode Milo in the morning while there was still a nice breeze and before the sun was out in full force.

Bob usually rode with me but that morning he chose to stand in the middle of the ring so he could focus all his attention on Milo and me.

I had the entire ring to myself, and I was able to relax and concentrate on my riding without fear of getting in the way of another horse. Bob was pleased and even a tad impressed with my progress.

"You look really good," he said more than once. His praise gave me the confidence and strength I needed to push my heels down further and raise my chin up higher.

Milo and I were cantering in a large circle when I felt the slightest hitch of his hind end followed by a noticeable surge in his stride.

"Did I just canter over a pole?" I asked, slowing Milo to a walk and looking on the ground for whatever we'd cantered over.

"You sure did," Bob replied, nudging the end of a white pole with his boot so I could see it.

I patted Milo's sweaty neck and proudly announced, "We jumped!"

Cantering over a pole on the ground was certainly not the equivalent of going over a fence, but it was the closest I'd come to jumping in a long time. I couldn't stop smiling and praising Milo for his valiant effort. Even Bob's sarcastically uttered "hardly" in response to my announcement didn't bother me.

"Don't even try to steal my thunder," I teased. "There was an obstacle on the ground and Milo and I went over it. That's jumping in my book."

"Hmm," Bob said distractedly. "Whatever you say."

Believing my lesson was over, I loosened my hold on Milo and allowed him to walk around the ring until his breathing became less labored. The hollow thunk of wooden objects knocking together caught my attention, and I turned my head toward the sound.

"What are you doing?" I asked Bob, who was pulling things out of a pile of poles and jump standards.

He ignored my question. The only sounds he made were a few low grunts as he dragged the things closer to me.

I was about to repeat my question when he nonchalantly replied, "I'm building you a jump. A real one."

Had I misheard Bob, or did he really believe I was ready to jump a fence? Suddenly, I was feeling neither strong nor confident.

Clumsily, I shortened my reins and steered Milo to the spot where Bob was bent over a wooden box filled with bright red, plastic flowers. Now that I was closer, I realized I had heard Bob correctly. The jump he'd assembled consisted of a long white pole, held horizontally between two white standards. I estimated the pole to be about two feet off the ground with the box of red flowers centered under it.

The jump wasn't high. Young children on their ponies tackled bigger fences than this. Of course, they could see where they were going.

Bob's phone rang and while he was otherwise occupied, I thought, *Now is my time to escape.* Milo and I could have walked out of the ring and back to the barn. I knew Bob wouldn't have come after us. He may have called out to me, but I could have ignored him.

Instead, I remained in the ring, running my hands through Milo's mane, until Bob ended his phone call.

Making a few last adjustments to the fence, Bob turned his attention back to me. "What do you think?"

Think? I had the jitters too badly to think. I couldn't even tell if my adrenaline overload was due to excitement, fear, or both.

I was still trying to decide what to do or say when Bob made my mind up for me.

"Just give it a try."

"All right, but how?"

I stared at the red flowers sticking up from the white, rectangular box. Milo and I had jumped much bigger than this. The jump itself wasn't the problem. Locating it while Milo cantered around the ring, was.

"I don't know," Bob said. "I think this is a matter of trial and error since I can't tell what you can or can't see."

My vision had stopped improving since my last appointment with Henry two months ago, when he had taken me off the Trazyl. I couldn't read and I couldn't recognize anything unless I knew what I was looking at.

"I can see shapes, colors, and movement, which is a lot better than nothing."

Realizing this was all I needed, I gritted my teeth. Milo, sensing my tension, shifted nervously until I loosened my hold on him and allowed him to walk in a small circle around the jump. I never took my eye off of it. I stared at it until I'd committed every inch of it to memory, especially the red flowers.

An idea started to take shape, and I turned Milo away from the jump and walked in a straight line back to the rail. Just as I had memorized the jump, I studied the brown wooden fence outlining the ring.

"Got it," I said as I noticed one of the boards had been replaced and was much lighter in color.

"Got what?" Bob asked and I realized he was standing beside Milo.

I explained my strategy to him as well as I could. "This new board on the rail happens to line up perfectly with the jump. So, when we're cantering around the ring, if I turn here to start my approach to the jump, I'll be heading right to the middle of it. All I need to do is find the board and not ride past it."

It sounded simple enough, and I was anxious to put my plan into action.

Bob stepped away as I turned Milo around and squeezed him into a canter. I followed the rail, with my head cocked to the right so I wouldn't miss the lighter piece of wood. I held my breath until, finally, I spied it. The air pushed past my tightly closed lips in a whoosh as I squeezed my fingers against the rein in my left hand. Obediently, Milo turned to the left and we cantered in a straight line toward the jump. At least, I hoped we were aiming for the jump.

I resisted the urge to call out to Bob and ask if I was going the right way. I wanted to do this on my own and I needed to keep my mind on finding the red flowers. It felt like hours had gone by when, at last, I caught a glimpse of red, but it wasn't in front of me, it was to my left.

I had miscalculated my approach. I cursed under my breath as I cantered past the jump.

"Try again," Bob called out.

Without slowing down, I circled Milo back to the rail and repeated the exercise. Again, I passed by the fence instead of jumping over it.

Milo was huffing and puffing from the heat, and I was breathing just as hard from frustration.

"Whoa, M." Milo immediately came back to a walk and we went over to Bob who was watching from the middle of the ring.

"What am I doing wrong?" I could feel sweat dripping down my back, and I could see Milo's neck was drenched. We had one more try in us before I'd have to call it quits.

Bob rubbed his palm against his brow while he considered how to solve my problem. "Try turning earlier. I think after you find your marker, you're waiting a second too long to turn toward the jump."

Irritated but determined to make my last attempt count, I scouted the rail for a new landmark. My eye didn't pick up on anything on the railing that would work, but there was a chair leaning against it and I decided it would do.

"This time for sure, M," I said as Milo pushed off into a canter.

I found the gray, metal chair and had barely touched my left rein when Milo turned away from the rail and headed for the jump. His ears were pricked forward. I looked between them and was gifted with a spectacular sight. They were blurry, but there was no mistaking the fiery red flowers in front of us. Beneath me, I felt Milo's muscles flex and with little effort on his part, we sailed over the tiny jump.

We landed on the other side, and I felt electricity shoot through me. The kid in me wanted to whoop and shout, but the experienced rider won out, and I kept my composure. For the most part. Still cantering, I bent over Milo's neck, grinning and patting him with both hands as I repeated several times, "We did it."

"It worked!" Bob yelled, his voice a mixture of pride and excitement.

Even Milo, now walking, seemed to have a little swagger to his gait.

"That was fantastic," shouted a voice I recognized as Linda's, and after a second, I managed to locate her. She was on her horse by the gate, staying out of the ring and out of my way.

Linda was one of Bob's students and also his office manager. I hadn't spent much time with her, but I'd always enjoyed our conversations.

"Thank you," I called back to her feeling a little shy. I wasn't aware that I had an audience.

Milo heaved a sigh, and I loosened his girth so he was more comfortable. Bob walked up to us and patted Milo's neck.

"We'll practice more tomorrow," he said, smiling.

"Sounds good," I replied, matching his grin.

I slid off Milo and walked him to the barn. He rested his chin on my shoulder as he trailed closely behind me. When I stopped in front of the grooming stall, he lifted his head and blew a stream of hot air over my cheek.

"I know, Milo," I said, leaning against him. "You can make miracles happen."

As promised, Bob gave me another lesson the next day. He said very little. Mostly he left it to me to figure out how and when I would approach the jump. By the end of the lesson, I was finding it about half the time.

Whenever I made it over the fence, I was ecstatic. Had it not been so hot, I would have begged Bob for "just one more jump," but the sun was relentless, and I couldn't push Milo too hard.

The following week, during my third lesson, Bob built two jumps on opposite sides of the ring that were a little higher than the one we used the week before. I didn't know their exact height, but I could feel it in the extra effort Milo made when he pushed off the ground in front of them. I practiced the approach to one fence until I was finding it every time. I did the same with the second fence. Then Bob had me put the two together. After clearing the first one, I cantered back to the rail and kept going until it was time to turn toward the second fence, which we jumped as well.

By the end of my fourth lesson, I could jump a course of four fences placed strategically around the ring. Bob outfitted each jump with a box of brightly colored flowers and set all four near the rail, making it easier for me to find them.

The simple course was a wonderful confidence booster, but I knew it wouldn't be long before our lessons became more demanding. I was up for the challenge. In fact, I was hungry for it.

After the lesson, Bob and I were in the car, preparing to go home, when Linda ran up to the driver's side window and handed Bob a piece of paper. "Here's the list of horses going to the Middleburg Classic."

"Oh, I love that show," I said. "They always have the prettiest jumps, and the outdoor course is incredible."

Bob had won his division at Middleburg the year before on Milo. The outdoor course was an immense grass field full of birch and pine jumps, built to mimic a hunt field in the countryside. It was glorious to watch the horses gallop on the grass, as opposed to the dirt and sand usually found in riding rings.

Bob was looking at the piece of paper while Linda waited for him to approve the list.

"I've always wanted to show there," I said wistfully.

"Then, why don't you?" Bob asked.

"Very funny," I replied dryly. "I managed to jump four fences in a row today. That doesn't mean I'm ready to compete at one of the country's most prestigious horse shows, where I'd have to jump eight fences in an unfamiliar ring."

Bob handed the paper back to Linda. "Add Milo to the list."

"No, no," I protested. "Don't add Milo to the list."

Linda cleared her throat impatiently. Her pen hovered over the paper while she waited for Bob and me to have a meeting of the minds.

"Relax," Bob said turning toward me. "We have a little while before we have to commit to anything. For now, it's easier for us to enter you and, if you decide you don't want to show, we can scratch your entry."

"Do you think I'm ready to show?" I couldn't hide the hope bubbling up inside me.

"Not right now," Bob replied, "but I think you're close. Look how far you've come in only two weeks, and the show isn't for another two months. That's plenty of time to practice jumping. If Middleburg is something you've always wanted to do, then I think we should give it our best shot."

As long as I could back out of it, I saw no harm in entering the show. After all, Bob wouldn't put me in danger, and if he believed I could compete, then so did I.

"All right," I said to Linda, who'd already put pen to paper.

With that, Milo and I were on the list for the Middleburg Classic. The decision, made in just a few minutes, would change my life forever.

CHAPTER FIFTEEN

Either Bob had powers of persuasion that bordered on magical, or I had a death wish. Regardless, I was beginning to seriously question my decision to compete in a horse show. The progress I'd made in a ring I knew so well didn't surprise me. But it would be insane to try to navigate a strange ring full of obstacles I'd never seen before.

Have I lost my mind? On the other hand, if I could figure out how to find my way around a course of fences at home, what's stopping me from doing the same at a show? It was a simple matter of geography. Besides, I've already signed up for it.

Entries for the Middleburg Classic had been sent in two weeks ago. I was so busy vacillating between wanting to go and fearing for my life, I'd yet to discuss the plan with my mom.

She'd been less than thrilled the day I proudly announced that I'd started jumping Milo. It wasn't until she watched me successfully complete a course of fences that she shared in my excitement. She'd even agreed that if Bob and I didn't take any unnecessary risks, then I was free to do whatever I wanted on Milo.

I had a strong feeling that my mother would consider competing in a horse show an unnecessary risk. I had to admit, there was a small part of me that hoped she would forbid me to show.

I was running out of time to talk to her. On the drive back to my condo, Bob reminded me that entries for the Middleburg Classic would close soon.

"If you wait until entries close and she won't let you go, you'll have to pay a fee for scratching," he warned me.

Groaning, I reached for the phone and dialed after I got out of the car.

"Well?" Bob greeted me the following morning.

"Well, what?" I replied adjusting my seat belt.

"Did you have the talk?"

Bob quickly pulled away from the curb and began maneuvering through the rush hour traffic like Mario Andretti.

"If you mean the talk with my mother then, yes, I did."

The conversation had not gone at all as I had expected. Not only had my mom been thrilled that I wanted to compete, she also readily agreed to cover all the costs of showing.

"Aren't you going to lecture me on safety?" I'd asked before we'd ended our call. "I mean, when I told you I was jumping, you were sure I was going to break every bone in my body."

She knew I was teasing but she'd answered my question as though I had asked it in earnest.

"That was before I saw you ride. You need to keep in mind, I've seen you fall down flights of stairs, walk into glass doors, and trip over cracks in the sidewalk. Can you blame me for being terrified when I found out that you're riding and jumping your horse?

"Now that I've watched you ride, I think you're safer on Milo than you are on your own two feet. What you can do on that horse defies reason. I don't understand how someone who can get lost in an elevator can jump course after course without making a single mistake. All I know is that when it comes to you and Milo, there are no limits to what you two can accomplish together. I'm looking forward to finding out."

Dead air had hung between us while I struggled to hold back the tears gathering in the corners of my eyes.

"Thank you for believing in me," I said huskily. "Even when I don't."

"This is great news!" Bob said bringing me back to the present. "I was sure I was going to have to step in and do some convincing. I'd already planned what I was going to say to your mom."

I pictured Bob practicing his speech in front of a mirror and laughed.

Bob's phone rang and I assumed Linda was on the other end of the call, because he spent the remainder of the drive discussing his latest invoices.

His call ended as we arrived at the barn. I was already gripping the door handle when Bob stopped me.

"Hold on, I need to talk to you about something."

My hand fell away from the door as I settled back in my seat.

"Umm," Bob stalled, clearly uncomfortable. "Would you mind if I asked Linda to help you once we get to the show? I'll be too busy to keep an eye on you. You'll also need to share a hotel room with someone. If it's all right with you, I'll ask Linda if she'd be willing to room with you and Spike."

Embarrassed and annoyed that Bob thought of me as an invalid, I turned my back to him.

"You don't think she has better things to do than babysit me?" I asked bitterly.

"I didn't mean it like that, but you can't deny that you need help."

"I know," I said, feeling deflated. "I'm sorry. If you would ask Linda, I'd appreciate it."

Needing some distance from Bob, I opened the door and slid from my seat. Except for a few mishaps, I could find my way around the barn better than my own apartment. Here, among the horses, I could easily forget that I was impaired, and I'd foolishly hoped others would, too. Bob's insistence that I have help at the show was an unwanted reality check. I wasn't fooling anybody, least of all Bob. No matter how great my accomplishments, I would never escape being labeled handicapped.

Our uncomfortable exchange left me with a knot in my stomach that didn't go away until I walked into the barn and called to Milo. The sound of my voice was met with a shrill neigh followed by a few guttural noises that reminded me of an engine turning over.

I didn't see Bob again until an hour later in the tack room. I was already dressed in my hat and chaps when he walked in and sat on one of the trunks.

"Linda said she'd be happy to help out as long as you split the room charges with her."

"Thank you," I smiled. "I hate having to depend on my friends for so much so often. But if I'm going to show, I'll have to learn to ask for help."

"Okay. Now get over yourself." Bob got up and walked to the hanging saddle racks, chose a saddle, and, carrying it over an arm, presented it to me.

"This is yours, right?"

I ran my hand over the saddle's seat feeling for familiar indentations. I found one by the pommel and nodded.

"Good," Bob said and began removing my stirrups from the saddle. "When you aren't having a lesson, I want you to ride without stirrups. You may be fit but you still need to be stronger."

Riding without stirrups would force my legs to work harder to keep my balance. I knew that would be good for me, so I simply nodded in agreement.

When he was finished detaching the stirrups, Bob placed the saddle on top of the trunk. As he turned to leave, he grabbed his chaps off the hook by the door where they always hung.

"That's what friends are for, you know," he said, swinging his brown leather chaps over his shoulder.

"What?" I asked, confused.

"Helping each other. It's what friends do," Bob said and left the tack room.

That was a lesson I'd need to get used to.

With the show about six weeks away, I worked on strengthening my body with new intensity. After two weeks of riding without stirrups, Bob told me I could have them back. I refused, continuing to ride without their support unless I was jumping Milo in a lesson.

Bob reconfigured the jumps in the ring each week so I could get used to jumping different courses. With each new course, I had to pick out new places along the rail that would line me up with each jump. I had lessons that ended in tears and just as many that ended in triumph. When it came to the technical aspects of coaching, Bob was brilliant. But he had no idea how to ride with limited sight, so when it was time for me to find my way around a course, I was on my own.

The more I rode, the better I got. By early September, I was stronger and tighter in the saddle. Milo's take-off over a jump no longer threw me forward, and when he landed, my recovery time was faster. Instead of taking several seconds to reconnect with the saddle and his canter rhythm, now I regained my balance immediately.

Even so, I obsessed over all the things that could go wrong at Middleburg. As the show got closer, fear of failure began to keep me up at night.

Scenes of disaster ran through my head on a continuous reel. In one scenario, I'm lost in the show ring and can't find my way to the first fence. Over the loudspeaker, the announcer excuses me from the ring, and I exit in disgrace. In another, I manage to find the right fence but jump it in the wrong direction, and again, I'm told to leave the ring. In the most disturbing vision, I never make it to the show ring, because in the practice ring I walk Milo in front of a fence as someone's jumping it, and we all die.

I don't think I would have gone through with the show if not for the nights when I pictured Milo adorned with blue ribbons and me beaming with pride.

"Quit yawning," Bob chided me one afternoon as we drove home from the barn.

"Sorry," I muttered, my hand still cupped over my mouth.

I told Bob how my visions of all that could go wrong in the ring were keeping me up at night. He merely shook his head and suggested I "get over it."

"What time do you want to leave in the morning?" I asked, clipping a leash onto Spike's collar. I could hardly believe it was already mid-September and tomorrow we were bound for Middleburg, Virginia.

Bob wanted to leave early, which I'd been expecting.

"Try and get some sleep," he said as I stifled another yawn. "And don't forget to pack the coat you bought for the first time you showed Milo. It's been two years but you're finally going to have a chance to wear it."

I pictured the finely tailored wool coat, along with all my other show clothes, neatly folded in a cardboard box with DONATE written across the top in black marker.

"Oh, no," I gasped, "I don't have my show clothes anymore."

Bob stared at me. I held his gaze for a few seconds before looking away.

"You've got to be kidding me," he said.

"I'm not. I gave them all away."

"Why?" he thundered. "Why would you do something so stupid?"

"As you may recall," I said stiffly, "I gave my riding clothes away because I'd just been told I'd be blind for the rest of my life. So, you see, at the time, it didn't seem at all stupid. Just practical."

If only I had thought of this earlier. Then I would've had time to borrow clothes from a friend or buy used ones at a consignment shop. But I'd been so focused on re-learning how to ride that I forgot I had nothing to wear in the ring.

We sat in the car for another thirty minutes trying to solve my clothing crisis but couldn't come up with a single remedy. No one at the barn had clothes that would fit me, and my size six feet and skinny legs required custom-made boots.

"There will be vendors at the show," Bob said.

I was already shaking my head before he could finish his sentence.

"You don't have any other choice. I know you don't want to, but you have to ask your mom if you can buy some clothes."

"Okay," I said, dejectedly gathering Spike in my arms and climbing out of the car. "I'll call you later."

My mom wasn't due home for an hour or so, which would give me a little time to think of some way to beg, borrow, or steal show attire by morning. Anything would be better than asking my mom for the nearly two thousand dollars it would take to buy a brand-new outfit at the horse show.

Almost two hours later, there was a knock on my door, and I knew it was my mom coming to take Spike and me for a walk. My stomach twisted and turned. There was no way to avoid asking for her help.

We were in the elevator when she said, "You're awfully quiet. What's going on?"

Exiting the elevator, I explained the situation while we walked through the lobby and out the door. It was past five, but I could still feel the heat of the day radiating from the bricks beneath us as we walked along the Inner Harbor canal.

"I hate to ask," I was saying as my mom reversed our direction. "Bob and I tried to think of another solution, but the only way I can show is if I buy new clothes."

Passing a hotel, I heard the clatter of dishes coming from its restaurant and caught the fragrance of garlic in the air. It was a poignant reminder of how life rolls along while mine keeps running into roadblocks and stalling.

"The boots alone are around nine hundred dollars," I explained painfully, "and that's not even for a custom pair. They'll be too big in the ankles and legs, but I'll have to make do."

"That's a lot of money to spend on something that doesn't fit," my mom said, holding the door to our building open for Spike and me.

"I know, I'm so sorry," I said, looking away from her. "I shouldn't have asked you for the money."

The elevator doors slid shut behind us and my mom punched the button for the fourth floor.

"I'd happily buy you whatever you need to show if I thought that was your best option," she said.

"I think it's the only one." I sighed heavily as I bent down and freed Spike from his leash.

Spike ran ahead of us and stopped in front of my condo door. Reaching in my pocket for the keys, I felt a tug on my arm as my mom dragged me past my door and down the long hallway.

"Where are we going?" I asked, bewildered.

We walked by five tan doors that were identical to mine before we stopped in front of one that was gray. Using one of her many keys, my mom unlocked it and held it open for me. The room was dark and smelled musty, like a thrift store.

"What's in here?" I asked hoping the sound of tiny paws scuttling around the concrete floor came from Spike and not a rat.

"Options," she said, clicking on the lights.

We were in a large storage room filled with junk. My mother's grip on my arm tightened as she led me through a maze of stacked suitcases, piles of books, and mounds of furniture. Along the wall, metal cages stretched from floor to ceiling, each one jam-packed. In a few of them, my neighbors' belongings were neatly arranged, but most of them were a disorderly mess, as if a bomb had gone off inside.

My mom steered me around a heap of stereo equipment and then stopped in front of one of the cages. For the first time since we'd entered the storage room, she let go of my arm so she could unlock the door.

I followed her into the locker and was pleased, though not surprised, that the several boxes inside were neatly stacked.

"I don't understand what we're doing in here," I said, taking a seat on the only box not piled on another.

Mom, who was busy scanning the labels on each cardboard container, replied, "You will, as soon as I find what I'm looking for."

The strong smell of mothballs was beginning to make me nauseous, and I was about to suggest we take a break when something prickly brushed against my leg. Imagining a gigantic hairy spider or worse, I jumped up in a panic.

"It's just Spike," my mom said pointing at my feet. I followed her finger and sure enough, my little black dog was standing next to me happily wagging his stumpy tail.

"Wait a second," she said as she grabbed the box I'd been sitting on and turned it over.

"What is it?" I asked moving in for a closer look.

It appeared that something dark had spilled on the box, but when I squatted next to it, I realized it wasn't a stain; it was a word printed in black marker. The scrawl was familiar, but it took me a few seconds to realize it was mine. Now, more confused than ever, I stared at the word until I could make out the first letter.

"'D?" I asked, looking at my mom for confirmation.

"Yes," she said smiling, "as in 'donate.'"

CHAPTER SIXTEEN

Over a year ago, I had watched my mom load the box I was now staring at into her car and drive away. We'd argued about my decision to donate my show clothes but in the end, I managed to convince her to take the box of riding attire to Goodwill. Or so I thought.

In a daze, I looked up at my mom whose smile had grown broader. "You're amazing," I said. "I can't believe you kept all of this."

Expertly, she used a key to slice through the layers of tape that sealed the box. "I couldn't bring myself to get rid of it. I had no problem tossing all of your other boxes into the donation bin but when I came to this one, it felt wrong. It wasn't just riding clothes I was giving away. There was a part of you in this box."

She tore the tape off the box but left the honor of opening it to me.

"It's like Christmas," I said, sliding the cardboard panels apart. I reached into the box and began pulling out its contents.

"My boots!" I squealed, hugging them to my chest.

Before I could empty anything else onto the floor, my mom suggested we drag the box back to my condo. Once we got it into my bedroom, she helped lay its contents on top of the bed. It had been more than a year since my riding clothes had seen the light of day and they reeked of neglect.

"They're clean," Mom said, shaking out one of my white show shirts. "Let them air out overnight and they'll be as good as new."

After the box was empty, she helped me pack for the horse show. When she offered me a light gray show coat, I shook my head and selected the black jacket that had been slung over one of my pillows.

"It has to be this one," I said, giving the fine wool coat a vigorous shake.

Mom hung it inside a garment bag, along with my riding shirt and pants. She stared at the blue bag for a minute before turning her attention back to me.

"I have to admit, when I made up my mind to keep your riding clothes, I never imagined you'd be wearing them again," she said, taking a seat next to me on the bed and wrapping her arm around me.

I inhaled deeply and rested my head on her shoulder.

"I didn't think I'd ever see these clothes again, much less wear them."

With her free hand, my mom smoothed the wrinkles from one of the shirts on the bed. She was quiet, which usually meant she had something on her mind. Given the suitcase we'd just packed and the riding clothes that surrounded us, I could guess what was bothering her.

"I'll be okay," I said attempting an air of confidence.

"I know," she said resting her cheek against the top of my head, "but you can't blame me for being worried. Especially when I think about what you're attempting to do with such little vision."

I heard the breath catch in her throat, and I took her hand and held it tightly against my heart. I could think of nothing to say that would put her mind at ease. Even with Milo taking care of me every step of the way, I was still placing myself in danger.

"I have to try," I said. "Even knowing that I'll probably suck, I still want to try."

She sat up straight and pushed off the bed. Standing in front of me, she said, "I'm sure you're not going to suck. But if you expect to walk into the ring and be perfect, then you're setting yourself up for failure."

"I'm not expecting to be perfect. I'll settle for respectable."

She stared at me, one eyebrow raised. "No, you won't. I know you, and you've never settled for anything. At least not when it involves horses."

I looked away from her. She was right. In the past, I wouldn't have been happy with anything but a blue ribbon. But now, so much had changed, I didn't know whether I could compete at any level, let alone win a ribbon.

My mom had to start dinner. I hugged and thanked her before she left, then called Bob to tell him we needn't worry about outfitting me.

"Your mother is certainly full of surprises," he said, chuckling, before reminding me we were leaving at seven sharp the next morning. "I'll leave without you if you're not waiting outside when I get there."

He was kidding, but I knew he'd be furious if I was late, and he'd never let me forget it. I swore to be ready to go the moment he arrived.

While my dinner cooked in the microwave, I hung the remainder of my show clothes in the closet. Staring at the dark wool coats and bright white shirts, I wondered if I'd have the chance to wear them again, or if my show career would end in Middleburg.

Three sharp beeps rang out from the kitchen. I wasn't a fan of the microwave meal plan, but I'd have to make do until I was confident that I wouldn't burn down the building if I attempted to cook.

"I suffer to keep others safe," I said to Spike, who'd positioned himself under my chair, patiently waiting for me to finish eating so he could lick the plastic dish clean.

Before going to bed, I double- and triple-checked the contents of my suitcase and then made sure my alarm clock was set for the correct time.

Next morning, I rolled my suitcase out to the curb in front of my building a full five minutes before Bob arrived. He was already on the phone and simply waved his hand toward the back of the car signaling me to load my things in the trunk.

For the next hour and forty-five minutes, I was forced to listen to Bob's one-sided conversations, barely able to get a single word in between calls. It wasn't until we reached our destination that he was off the phone long enough to talk to me in a full sentence.

"Take what you need and leave the rest in the car, for now." He'd parked his car in a grassy field next to several blue and white striped tents, and I assumed our stalls were inside one of them.

"Where…," I began to ask Bob which tent would be our home base for the next few days, but the insistent trill of his cell phone cut me off. "Never mind," I mumbled to Bob's back as he exited the car, already engrossed in conversation.

Quickly, I collected the few things I needed. I threw my purse over my shoulder, but, remembering my cell phone and the cash inside it, I decided my bag would be better off in Bob's locked car. "All set," I said as I pressed the lock button and closed the door.

Spike stood still while I bent over and clipped a leash to his collar. Straightening, I looked around for Bob, but it was soon apparent that he'd been distracted by the phone call and had forgotten about my need of his assistance.

"Super," I mumbled while staring at the three massive tents.

Without a clue as to which one Bob had disappeared into, I elected to start with the one on the far left. Moving slowly, I managed to reach the back of the tent. Squaring my shoulders, I took a deep breath. *You can do this.*

Luckily, it was a warm day, and the back flap was rolled up, giving me room to walk from one aisle with its row of stalls to the next. The first aisle was empty, except for a tall, white pyramid resembling an iceberg in front of each stall. Had I not known from experience what I was looking at, I would never have guessed that these were plastic bags full of shavings, piled one on top of the other.

"This can't be our aisle," I said to Spike. "Our stalls were bedded early." I knew Tom and the other grooms had already spread bags of wood chips inside each stall so the horses would have soft beds waiting for them.

I walked slowly to the next aisle, straining to hear a familiar voice. Music blared from several radios, making it difficult for me to zero in on anyone in particular. I passed a young man sitting on a bale of hay and hesitated, thinking that if he worked for Bob, he would acknowledge me. When he didn't, I smiled and moved on.

The rest of the grassy aisles were full of people leading horses into and out of stalls. I nodded my head in greeting as I passed by each stranger, hoping I looked like I knew where I was going. The only thing worse than being lost was being pitied because of my blindness.

I could hear men and women talking and laughing with one another. They seemed to be friends or at least barn mates. But, unfortunately, not mine.

My head was pounding as I continued my search for someone or something I belonged to. When Spike and I reached the eighth and final aisle and I still hadn't seen or heard anyone I knew, I had to admit that tent number one was a bust.

Halfway through the second tent, Spike began whining piteously and pulling on his leash. Believing his superior canine senses had picked up on a recognizable voice or scent, I gratefully allowed him to take the lead.

"Good boy, Spike! Go find Bob!"

Spike sniffed the air and began pulling me until we were out of the tent. He took a sharp right and I continued to praise him until he stopped in front of a paper bag on the ground containing a rotting, half-eaten burger.

"You're useless," I griped.

We were standing in back of the third and final tent and I could hear voices coming from inside. Frustrated, I cupped my hands around my mouth and yelled Bob's name. I waited expectantly, sure Bob or Tom would hear me and come to my rescue. But neither man appeared, nor answered my call. I was considering my options when I heard a sound that made me breathe a sigh of relief.

A familiar whinny reached out to me like a siren's song. Obviously, I had shouted the wrong name.

"Milo!" I sang out gleefully. Instantly, I was answered by more nickers and neighs. Smiling broadly, I began walking toward the sound of Milo's greeting. Every few steps, I stopped, called to him, took a few more steps after he answered, then called to him again. Our bizarre version of Marco Polo brought me to the place I'd been so desperate to find, right in front of Milo's stall.

Bob was in the stall across from Milo's, sorting through the bridles.

"Where did you go?" he asked as if I had purposely evaded him. "I've been looking all over for you." Bob was already wearing his helmet and chaps and I found it hard to believe that his search for me had been overly extensive.

"I'm sure you did," I said in a low, tired voice.

Ready to get on his first horse, Bob brushed past me. "Linda should be here soon. She'll do what she can to help you between riding her own horse and organizing the office work. I have to talk to some people and ride some horses, so stay close to the stalls until Linda retrieves you, all right?"

As he marched off, I was left to ponder whether all adults with disabilities are treated like children. I knew Bob didn't do it on purpose. No one did. But that didn't negate the fact that, more often than not, I was given orders as if I were a troublesome ten-year-old.

"It's no wonder I prefer your company to any human's," I told Milo and Spike. They were the only two creatures in the world that still relied on me.

My babysitter came to collect me an hour later. Linda was carrying something in her right hand and, although it took me a moment, I finally recognized what it was.

"Numbers," I said out loud without meaning to.

"What?" Linda asked. "Oh, right." She fanned the air with the small stack of laminated, cardboard rectangles. "I just picked them up from the show office."

"Is mine in that pile?"

"It should be." Linda shuffled through the stack and as she neared the end, plucked one of the numbers from the group. "Here you are," she said, holding up proof of my official entry in the show.

With the greatest of care, I took the number from Linda and cradled it in my hands as if it were made of glass instead of paper. Staring at the black symbols, I tried, unsuccessfully, to make sense out of them.

"What is it?" I asked and handed the number back to Linda.

"Two, two, one. I'm going to hand these over to Tom for safe keeping. Then, I'm going to take a walk around the grounds. Would you like to come with me?"

My narrow zone of comfort didn't extend much farther than the interior of Milo's stall. Plus, still rattled by my abandonment, I found myself resisting her invitation. *I don't want to get lost again. I don't want to run into anybody I know because I won't recognize them. And I sure don't want to make a mistake and feel like an idiot.* The more possible mishaps my brain conjured the more my stomach churned.

"We can take a look at the ring you'll be showing in," Linda offered.

Now that was tempting, so much so that I found myself setting my angst aside and agreeing to join Linda on her walk. I was scheduled to show in two days. That wasn't much time to memorize an entire ring. The sooner I began the process, the better.

"That would be great," I smiled. "Thank you." I collected Spike and waited while Linda shared a private word with Tom.

"Let's go," she said.

Expecting her to rush ahead of me as Bob had, I prepared myself for a brisk game of follow the leader. But Linda surprised me. She stayed close by my side, keeping an eye out for holes and other hazards that threatened my stability. "There's a small ditch to your right," she cautioned as we passed several show rings, which were already full of horses and riders making use of the one day of practice before the competition's official start.

"Over here," Linda pointed to our left. "This is the ring you're showing in. Ring 3."

It was a fairly small, unremarkable, rectangular ring with a wood railing, much like the ring at home, with one exception. This railing had been recently stained dark brown, and when I leaned against it to get a closer look at the ring, I could feel that the wood was still tacky.

Ring 3 was primarily used for divisions of horses and riders that shouldn't jump fences higher than 3'. The fences in my division, the Low Adults, were only 2'9". Milo was overqualified for this division and, frankly, so was I. With its low jumps and uncomplicated courses, this ring should have been easy for me to show in. But now it would be the greatest challenge of my riding career.

Pushing back from the rail, I glared at Ring 3, resenting it for reminding me that like everything else in my life, I had to start over with this. My twenty-six years of riding experience didn't amount to anything.

While Linda rushed off to tend to unexpected business, I decided to put my bitterness on hold and spend the rest of the day studying the ring. I may be starting over, but I knew I was lucky to be here at all. Spike and I set up camp on a grassy bank, where I could see the entire ring and bits and pieces beyond the rail.

Four riders entered the ring and I watched them for a while. Their horses were obviously young, and I couldn't help smiling at their antics as they snorted and backed away from the unfamiliar jumps. I thought of Milo and how exceptional he'd been as a young horse. My boy had never bucked or spun around like these horses. He wasn't one to act out or ever put his rider in danger.

Horses and riders seemed to come and go in waves. When the ring became crowded, it was impossible for me to tell one horse from another. Indistinct bay, chestnut, and gray figures whirled around. The sound of hooves striking the sand and dirt was hypnotic. I might have fallen asleep had it not been for the sharp cries of the riders.

"Heads up!" they yelled, warning each other to stay out of the way.

After an hour or so of watching and listening to what was happening inside the ring, it was time to focus on what was surrounding it. After every day of competition, the fences in each ring would be arranged into a brand-new course. I wouldn't know the layout of my courses until the day I showed. But if I could find some objects outside the rail to use as turning points, I'd be a few steps ahead of the game.

It wouldn't be easy. This landscape was new to me, and it would take time to make sense of it.

Eventually, I found my markers.

From where I sat, I could see that the shiny metal bleachers to my right would line up perfectly with any jumps placed close to that part of the rail.

"I'll definitely be using those as a guide," I said to Spike who was lying on his back with his legs sticking straight up.

On the opposite end of the ring, a row of recently planted trees against the rail would come in handy, as well.

I scanned the rest of the rail for more landmarks and found a large white trashcan with a bold blue stripe around it.

That will work, as long as no one moves it.

The last item to join my catalogue of markers was a nearby telephone pole. Although it wasn't right next to the rail, it was large enough for me to see it from inside the ring.

I spent the following day in a similar manner, splitting my time between studying the ring and being with Milo. While Linda was busy coordinating with Bob and the show office, she managed to make time to check on me. After two nights of sharing a hotel room with Linda, I concluded that behind her cool exterior was a warm and trustworthy friend.

Wednesday night, the eve of my debut on Milo in the show ring, Linda and I ordered Chinese take-out and brought it back to the room. As we slurped our soup sitting cross-legged on our beds, we were walled within our own thoughts.

Suddenly, Linda asked, "On a scale from one to ten, how nervous are you about tomorrow?"

"Right this second, I'm standing firm at seven," I answered honestly, "although that number can change at any minute."

We knew that by 6:00 a.m. a diagram of the courses would be posted. Linda wisely suggested we leave the hotel by 5:30 so we'd have plenty of time to follow the diagrams as we walked around the ring.

I hit the sheets early, but sleep played cat and mouse with me all night long. By 4:00 a.m., I gave up and slipped quietly out of bed and began preparing for the day ahead.

An hour later, Linda woke up and, seeing that I was dressed in my white show shirt, tan pants, and tall black boots, asked, "Did you sleep at all?"

"Not much," I shrugged and fed Spike a little breakfast. Linda was a quick dresser, and we were out the door dragging our suitcases behind us well before the appointed time. As we reached the show grounds, we were treated to a spectacular view of the sunrise. Pink and blue streaks cut through the dark sky.

"Ready?" Linda asked as she opened the car door.

I was competing in two classes, and I had to memorize a course for each one. Linda looked over the two diagrams depicting the order in which I was required to jump each fence, while I stood next to her seriously questioning my sanity.

Once Linda knew the courses, we stepped inside the ring so I could begin my version of a course walk.

"Red flowers on my left," I said out loud as, fence by fence, I committed each one to memory.

"So, that's how you know the order of the jumps?" Linda asked.

"Yes, but the hardest part is finding each fence in the first place."

"How do you do that?"

I pointed to the telephone pole outside the rail. "Since I can't see the jumps until we're right on top of them, I have markers like this all around the ring that tell me where to turn to head toward each fence. I think of them as my breadcrumbs."

"That's a lot to remember," Linda observed.

You have no idea.

Together, Linda, Spike, and I walked around the ring several times as I reviewed the jumps and the markers I'd use to find them. After our fifth time around, Linda looked at her phone and said, "I have to take care of a few things. Do you want to go back to the stalls or stay here?"

I took one more look around the ring. "I think I'll go back with you. I need a little Milo time."

I could hear the smile in her voice as Linda said, "Of course, you do." Then her tone turned serious. "Are you sure you're okay with the ring?"

We had walked around the course until my boots had rubbed a blister on every toe. There wasn't a grain of sand in Ring 3 that I hadn't memorized.

"I know where I'm going," I replied optimistically. "By now, I think Spike does, too," I joked as I bent over and brushed sand off his snout.

On our way back to the stalls, we passed the hospitality tent where a line of people waited for free coffee and bagels. Many of them were dressed in show attire like mine, but despite our similar outfits, I could guarantee our mornings had started very differently.

While I'd been cramming my brain with descriptions of jumps and markers, these folks had been thinking about breakfast.

Noting where my attention had gone, Linda asked, "Are you hungry?"

Ordinarily, I would've loved a good bagel, but today I had no room for one. I was filled to capacity with fear, nerves, exhaustion, and images of flowers, bleachers, and telephone poles.

"No thank you," I replied wearily.

We were almost to Ring 1 when the announcer's voice boomed over the loudspeaker, letting us know it was 7:30 a.m. and the show would start in thirty minutes. He rattled off the day's agenda. My classes were scheduled to begin around one o'clock and I wondered if I'd be able to hold onto everything I'd memorized for that long. Riders rushed past us, and I caught myself wishing I wasn't the only one with low vision. Maybe that way, I wouldn't feel like such a misfit.

Linda deposited me at the front of our tent while she went to find Bob and Tom. I could feel my nerves gnawing away at my delicate sense of confidence. Rattled, tired, and feeling a little sorry for myself, I took sanctuary in Milo's stall.

Milo was waiting for me at his door. We were both oddly quiet when I entered his stall. Instead of greeting me with his usual nicker, he gently rubbed his head against my shoulder. Wordlessly, I stroked his neck, until I realized something felt strange.

"What's different about you?" Stepping to his right side, I ran my hand up Milo's neck and counted thirty-six perfectly formed braided knots.

"Well, Mr. Handsome, at least one of us is ready to show."

I rested my cheek against his neck, recalling the first time Milo was braided and I was the one soothing his nerves.

"It's funny how quickly life can change, isn't it, M?"

He curled his neck around me until his nose touched my hip.

"Milo, I'm really scared," I whispered, finally giving in to the feelings I'd worked so hard to hide. Hugging his neck, I began crying. Hot tears streamed down my face. "I need you more than ever," I sobbed, tasting the salt on my lips.

I cried until I was so drained, I could barely hold myself up. Had it not been for Milo's support, I may have collapsed in a heap.

Except for my ragged breathing, the stall was quiet. Even Spike, who'd burrowed into a pile of hay, hadn't made a peep. Still a little unsteady on my feet, I let go of Milo and joined Spike on the bed of hay. My breathing grew less haggard and as my eyes closed. *I'll just rest for a couple of minutes.*

I awoke with a start. The mountain of hay I'd fallen asleep on had been nibbled to nothing. *I must have been asleep for more than two minutes. Even Milo doesn't eat that fast.*

Milo was standing over me, chewing on a few strands of hay. Spike's snoring grew louder as I stood up on numb legs.

Voices were coming from the front of the tent. I tickled Milo under his chin, picked up Spike, and left the stall to investigate. I discovered Bob, Tom, and Linda, all talking at once.

"What's going on?" I asked innocently. The three of them froze at the sound of my voice.

Crap. Whatever they'd been talking about involved me and I suspected I wasn't going to like it.

"What?" I asked in a toneless voice, bracing myself for the worst.

Bob turned to me, and I took a step backward, instinctively wanting to put some distance between myself and whatever he was about to say. Then, in a caring voice, he said the four words I'd heard enough to last me a lifetime: "I have bad news."

Bob paused and took a deep breath.

"Ring 3 was running behind schedule," he continued, "so they switched your classes to another ring."

CHAPTER SEVENTEEN

I waited for someone, anyone, to laugh and say, "Just kidding."

When no one did, I blurted, "This is a joke, right?"

Linda and Tom shook their heads. Bob kicked the ground. "I wish," he said.

"The only one available was Ring 2," Linda grumbled.

"That's not fair," I wailed, even though I knew perfectly well that the show manager had every right to switch the rings and the schedule. "I'll never be able to find my way around that course. Even if I had all day to memorize it, I'd still get lost."

Ring 2 was the enormous outdoor course. The grass field lacked an actual rail. In its place was a thick yellow rope defining the perimeter of the ring. I could hardly see the rope when I was standing just inches away from it. Once I was on Milo, it would be useless as a guide to help me find my way around the course.

I looked down at my tan breeches and the black boots I'd painstakingly polished until they would have passed a military inspection. *All dressed up and nowhere to go.* The adage popped into my head, making me wince.

"No one would blame you if you scratched," Linda said, looking through her notebook most likely for the form she would have to fill out if I decided not to participate. "There will be plenty of other shows for you to go to."

"No," I said, defiantly folding my arms in front of my chest, "it's now or never. I'm mentally and physically prepared to do this today. Do you think the manager would let me walk around the new ring?"

Looking up from her book, Linda was thoughtful for a second before saying "maybe." After giving it more thought, she added,

"We can ask but even if she allows it, you won't have much time to memorize anything."

I was sick with fear, but my mind was made up. I had to try. "Let's go."

We hustled to the show office but the manager, Nancy, wasn't there. After Linda explained my situation, one of the staff members called Nancy and requested she meet us at Ring 2.

"As soon as possible," I heard the show secretary whisper into the phone.

While Linda and I waited for Nancy by the ring, I had my first glimpse of the outdoor course. It had been a couple of years, and the field was larger than I remembered. I could tell that the jumps closest to me were white and brown, but from where I was standing at least twenty feet away, they were a monochromatic blur, and I couldn't distinguish one from the other.

Linda had been standing next to me, but when I turned to ask her to describe the jumps, she was gone. I found her examining two pieces of paper posted on a board next to the ingate. I couldn't see what was written on them, but I knew they were the course charts. The diagrams on each chart depicted the order and direction in which all eight fences were supposed to be jumped for each class.

I looked at the blurry images in the ring and wondered how on earth I would be able to find one jump much less eight of them. I was about to tell Linda I'd changed my mind, when I heard an authoritative voice from behind us ask, "What can I do for you girls?"

I spun around to face a woman of medium build wearing a yellow shirt and dark slacks.

"Hi, Nancy," Linda said, giving the manager a friendly embrace.

I wasn't aware of their friendship, but I hoped it would work to my advantage. After she introduced me, Linda explained the circumstances that had brought the three of us together.

"So," Linda concluded, "if it's all right with you, we'd really appreciate it if we could have as much time as possible to walk around the ring before her classes begin."

I could feel Nancy's eyes on me as she digested Linda's request. "Let me get this straight," she said. "You're legally blind?"

"Yes," I replied, disliking the shame in my voice.

"And you're going to compete in this ring?"

"Not if you don't let me walk around in it first."

Linda added, "She's been camped out at Ring 3 for the past two days and this morning we spent about an hour in there learning her course. But, with the ring change…" She let her voice trail off.

"I am sorry about that," Nancy said. "We'd be here until dark if I hadn't switched the rings."

"I understand," I said glumly. I chewed at my bottom lip, certain she was going to deny my request. Instead, she placed her hand on my shoulder and gave it a little squeeze.

"Follow me," she said and led us to the ring's entrance.

"I wish I could give you more time, but we'll need to kick you out in about thirty minutes," Nancy said, stepping aside so we could enter the ring ahead of her. "That's all the time we have before the next class begins."

As I walked past her, I could hear Nancy's walky-talky crackle and a man's voice on the other end frantically ask, "Can you hear me? We need you back at home base."

"I'd love to stick around," Nancy said, "but duty calls. You're a very brave young woman and I wish you the best of luck." She hugged me and rushed off.

Unused to such kindness from a stranger, I stood in a daze until Linda took my hand and dragged me to the jump closest to us. Now a few inches from it, I realized the jumbled disarray I'd been trying to make sense of was actually three separate fences. Each one had white standards and white and green poles. Instead of flower boxes at their base, there were piles of pine branches.

The green and brown stalks blended with the ground. Luckily, the next group of fences we came to were painted blue and white and decorated with boxes of multicolored flowers.

With only a yellow rope instead of an actual fence rail to guide me, it would be nearly impossible to locate the ideal spot where I should begin my approach to each jump. However, I did find a few markers alongside the rope line, such as a blue and yellow porta-potty and three tall metal stakes that secured the rope.

We made it around the course once before the main announcer began calling the next class over the P.A. system.

"We have to go," Linda said, her voice tinged with regret.

"I know," I said, taking one last look around the ring.

Bob met up with us and sent me back to the stalls with Tom. As I walked away, I heard him ask Linda, "Is she going to be able to do this?"

Instead of stopping to hear her answer, I walked faster. Whether or not I made it around the ring was not up to Bob or Linda. Milo and I were the only ones who could answer that question.

Despite my faster pace, Tom stayed by my side as we trudged down the slight incline to the front of our tent. For three days I'd walked the same route and, like everything else, I'd committed this path to memory. We were only a few feet from the tent when I heard a woman's voice, much like my own, talking to Spike, who had been left behind, tied to a tack trunk.

"Mom!" I yelped happily.

She'd promised me she would be here before I showed, but I was so distressed by the ring change, I'd forgotten to look out for her. Now she was waiting for me in the open area of the tent, in front of our stalls.

"I'm so glad you're here," I cried, leaping into her arms.

"As if anything could stop me from being with you and Milo today."

Hugging her close, I inhaled deeply and was comforted by the familiar scent of her perfume.

"Are you okay?" she asked suspiciously. She gently extracted herself from my hold and took a step backward. "What's wrong?"

Everything. "Nothing," I said. I'd made up my mind to show, but if my mom knew about the ring calamity, she might not let me.

I could hear a stall door close, and a few seconds later Bob was walking toward us. Stepping over Spike, he asked, "Did you tell your mom they changed your ring?"

"No, I hadn't gotten to that yet," I growled.

"What ring change?" my mom asked as Bob gave her a hug.

If I were to tell her, I doubted I could keep the fear out of my voice, so I decided to let Bob explain, knowing he'd tell her I'd be okay.

"I'm going to finish getting dressed," I announced, though neither Mom nor Bob was listening to me.

The first stall on the left had been made into a junk room and housed trunks, horse tack, and miscellaneous items including my garment bag. Milo was directly across from it, and he grunted disapprovingly when I turned left instead of into his stall.

"I'll be right there," I called back to him.

I grabbed two carrots from a bag that was on top of a trunk, took my show coat off its hanger, slung it over my shoulder, and walked into Milo's stall for a quick visit.

"I'm trying to stay clean," I said, tossing the treats into his feed bucket. "If I get too close to you, I'll be covered in orange drool."

I hung out with Milo for a few minutes before returning to the front of the tent. Mom and Bob were deep in conversation about where to go for the best cheeseburger in Baltimore. I smiled as I slid my arms through the satin-lined sleeves of my show coat.

Clang! The sound of a stall door slamming shut made me jump, and I turned around to see Tom leading Milo into the grooming area. "Sorry," Tom said as I joined them, "the latch sticks on that door. I didn't mean to scare you."

Milo gave me a low nicker, his way of asking for treats and my undivided attention. But I could see the bits of orange that covered his mouth and I refused to get any closer to him. I had some mints in my pocket and I handed them to Tom.

"No more," he admonished, "he's had enough sugar for now." Looking me up and down, he smiled. "Look at you all dressed to show. I bet you never thought you'd do this again."

"No, definitely not."

Tom had a towel draped across his arm and I grabbed it before he left to retrieve my saddle. I needed to have a last-minute pep talk with Milo, but first I had to wipe off his mouth.

Milo rubbed his now clean muzzle against my shoulder. I leaned my cheek against his and caught myself wishing I'd never agreed to compete. I desperately wanted to be back home, safe inside Milo's stall and feeding him treats, unmindful of the mess they created.

As if he'd been reading my thoughts, Milo lowered his head and blew a warm, carrot-scented breath across my face. His body was soft and relaxed, but his large brown eyes, locked on my green one, were full of fire.

Milo will keep me safe. This is the one thing about today that I know for sure.

"I'll see you up there," I told Milo, giving him a final peck on the nose and sneaking him a forbidden candy.

"I saw that," Tom said. I pretended not to hear him and kept walking.

I went back to the front of the tent, where Mom and Bob were still chatting, and found my hat, gloves, and number on a chair where I'd left them. In need of some normalcy, I put myself on autopilot and mechanically went through the final motions of getting ready to show: I gathered my hair into a ponytail, covered it with a hairnet to contain any loose strands, and tucked it under my helmet; pulled a well-worn, black leather glove over each hand; and placed my number against my back, then drew the strings attached to it across my midsection and tied them in a bow.

I tugged on my shirtsleeves so the white cuffs peeked out from my jacket and looked down at my boots to check their shine. I didn't need a mirror to know that I looked great. I could feel it.

Turning to face my mom and Bob, I waited for a pause in their conversation.

Mom noticed me first and stopped talking. I looked from her to Bob and smiled at them both.

"I'm ready to go," I announced with as much confidence as I could muster.

We walked to the ring together in silence, Bob and my mother on either side of me with Spike, whom I'd decided to bring along for luck, on his leash leading the way.

My class had already started but there were at least ten horses in front of me, so I didn't have to get on right away.

"Can you see well enough to watch the other riders jump the whole course?" Bob asked, pointing to a horse as it entered the ring.

I knew that I couldn't. Nevertheless, I leaned over the rope barrier and watched until the horse and rider became nothing more than a smear of color. I could hear them as they cantered to the first fence, but bit by bit they disappeared from my sight, their color evaporating until all that was left was a quiver of movement cutting through the green background.

"No," I replied. "I do know that the first fence is green and white and has pine brush decorating it." I could see the fence perfectly, in my head. At least I knew what to look for.

"That's good," my mom said encouragingly. "Do you know what the other jumps look like?"

I did and spent the next ten minutes describing all eight fences in the order I was supposed to jump them. When I was finished, Bob walked over to the schooling ring where Milo was waiting for me to get on.

Lissa Bachner

Mom kissed my cheek and wished me "good luck." I could tell she wanted to say more but held back.

Tom gave me a leg up, grunting as he always did as though I weighed two tons instead of a little over a hundred pounds. On any other occasion, I would have laughed or at least replied with a sarcastic "ha, ha." But today, I was far too worried about the other horses and riders to joke with Tom. All I could manage was a perfunctory "thank you."

Bob walked Milo and me into the warm-up ring which, to my dismay, was full of horses. The ring was large enough to accommodate two jumps. Each rider selected a jump to practice over until they were ready to go into the show ring.

It was a mob scene. I did my best to stay out of the way, which meant I was concentrating more on the horses around me than on the one under me. I had to pull up twice in order to avoid crashing into another horse. I could tell by Milo's choppy canter and pinned back ears that he was upset.

When one of the jumps became available, Bob lowered its height. "Ready?" he called out.

I waited until there was a clear path to the jump. When it looked safe, I squeezed Milo into a canter and jumped back and forth over the fence two times before Bob raised it. Twice more and he raised it a final time to 2'9", the height of the fences in the show ring and the same height I used to practice at home.

Pleased that I'd managed to survive the warm-up without any incident, I forgot to look to my left as I exited the ring, and I couldn't see the gray horse that was barreling toward me. I heard several loud gasps and a shriek, but having no idea they were directed at me, I didn't react. Luckily Milo did, halting in his tracks and saving us from a potentially devastating collision.

"I am so sorry," I told the other rider who had pulled her horse to a stop.

"You need to watch where you're going," she snapped viciously before riding away.

Trust me, I would if I could.

Having observed the near-crash, Bob ran over to make sure Milo and I were all right. Milo hadn't moved, but I was trembling. Bob led us from the ring, instructing me to "keep breathing" and reminding me that I was okay. When we got to the show ring, there was only one horse in front of me waiting for its turn.

Bob and I went over the course one last time, but I barely heard a word he said.

Yellow flowers, blue flowers, red flowers, the colors swirled through my memory until I was dizzy and couldn't breathe. I felt like everything I had memorized was stuck in my throat, and it was making me choke. My system for finding each jump had broken down. I was lost even before I entered the ring.

My heart was racing and my shirt was damp with sweat. Somewhere in the back of my head, a man's voice was telling me to walk in, but I was frozen in place.

I could feel Milo growing restless. His back twitched, his tail swished, and he chewed on his bit. Tired of my indecision, he began walking onto the outdoor course.

I took a very deep breath and let it out slowly, then squeezed the reins lightly to slow Milo's walk and give myself as much time as possible to gain my bearings. I looked all around and tried to make sense of the shadowy objects surrounding me. *How in God's name am I going to do this?* I asked myself before I picked up a canter and followed the yellow rope to the first fence, which was alongside it.

We were better than I expected. My pace was slow, but Milo jumped it in good form and after a smooth landing, I allowed him to canter forward.

When I had walked the course with Linda, the fences had seemed far apart. Now, as the scenery flashed by, I realized I hadn't taken Milo's speed into consideration. By the time I recognized my marker, I had passed the spot where I planned to turn toward the second jump.

I started to unravel. I slowed down and, guessing where the jump was, turned Milo and began our approach. I couldn't see the fence until we were almost on top of it. That's when I realized we were so far to the right, we were going to run into the standard instead of over the poles attached to it. Milo shifted sharply to the left. Because we were going so slowly, there was no power to his take-off, and he had to hurl himself over the fence. Despite his effort, my right foot hit the standard, shaking the top pole loose. We landed and I heard a thud as the pole hit the ground.

I wondered if my trip around the outdoor course could get any worse. Thankfully, the third jump was six strides directly in front of us, and all I had to do to get to it was canter in a straight line and count to six.

We flew over the fence and as we cantered away from it, I waited for the yellow rope to appear. I followed it to our left and there, shining like a beacon, was the blue and yellow porta-potty.

"Found it," I said to Milo and turned to begin our advance to fence number four. Everything fell into place. We met the fence in perfect unison and landed, I counted to eight, and like a couple of pros we jumped over fence number five.

I cantered back to the yellow rope until I reached the metal stake in the corner of the ring, signaling it was time to turn left and keep riding until jump six came into view. We were dead center and Milo effortlessly cleared it. My fingers relaxed against the reins. Milo glided eight strides to the seventh fence and we soared over it.

"Almost finished," I said more to myself than to my horse as we cantered back to the rope.

The last jump was the easiest to find, because as soon as I came to the metal marker and turned, I could see the fence only four strides away. But before we got to the marker, Milo caught his toe on a divot and almost went down to the ground. Luckily, he caught himself, but the disruption was enough for me to lose my focus and my stirrup. I had no choice, I had to pull up.

As much as I wanted to leave the ring, I forced myself to finish what I had started. Returning my foot to the stirrup, I walked Milo in a circle back to where he tripped, making sure to avoid the hole in the ground before picking up a canter. I came upon the metal stake, turned, and saw the shape of the final fence. Milo's ears pricked forward, and I knew he'd sighted in on it, too. Holding the reins loosely, I rested my hands on the crest of his neck and did something I should have done seven fences ago.

I let Milo take over.

"You do it," I said. We surged forward and arrived at the fence in five strides. I dug my hands into his braids, giving Milo free rein. Rocking back on his hind end, he fired off the ground and I felt every muscle in his body push, flex, and arc over the fence. He landed lightly on his toes, like a dancer.

"Thank you," I whispered, in awe of my extraordinary horse and relieved that the first class was behind us.

We exited the ring to the sound of polite applause. For a rider, there are few things worse than retreating from the ring after a mediocre performance. Granted, I had extenuating circumstances, but still I was frowning when Bob and my mom reached me outside the gate.

Before Bob could say anything, my mom grabbed him in a hug. "Wasn't she wonderful!" she crowed. Bob placed his hand on my leg, and I prepared myself for his critique.

"That was incredible," he said, staring up at me with moist eyes. In a few seconds, he collected himself, gave my leg a squeeze, and offered some advice for my next course.

"You need to commit to your rhythm and let Milo take care of the rest for you. Keep in mind, he sees the fences before you do, so pay attention to when he pricks his ears."

"What do I do if his ears don't go forward?" I asked anxiously.

"In that case, don't guess where the fence is. That's when you get into trouble. Trust that you've found the marker and you're heading toward the jump. Then let Milo do his job. If you're a little crooked, he can straighten you out. Are you ready to go back in?"

God, no. "Sure," I nodded.

We reviewed the second course and, once again, I was sent into the ring.

The first time, I was scared to death, and I just wanted to finish the course in one piece. This time, mindful of Bob's advice, I felt confident that Milo would take care of us. I made a few mistakes in my second course but nothing major. All the fences were jumped in the correct order, and I didn't have to pull up. No "fly-bys" as I like to say.

Physically and mentally exhausted, I loosened my hold on the reins. Milo, also worn out, dropped his head until his chin almost touched the ground as we slowly walked out of the ring. My rounds hadn't been good enough to win a ribbon, but that had never been my goal. Making it through two courses with only a few mistakes was good enough for me, and I was leaving the ring triumphant.

I could hear boisterous clapping and the piercing sound of Tom's whistle.

"I love you, M," I said leaning forward and stroking his neck. Filled with gratitude for Mom's support, Bob's expert training, and Milo's devotion, I smiled. Despite my relief that I'd survived the outdoor course, a small part of me was disappointed that I was finished. I'd worked so hard for so long, and in a little more than four minutes, my time in the show ring was over. Most likely, forever.

Tom took Milo from me and led him back to the stalls. Bob and Linda had work to do, leaving my mom and me at the ring.

"Do you mind if we stay a little while?" I asked her. For me, the show grounds were a safe haven where I wasn't identified by my handicap. Only my friends knew I was almost blind. To everyone else, I was just another rider, and I was in no rush to get back to reality. Mom agreed, and we walked to a shaded corner with a view of the ring.

We watched the last riders complete their courses and when my class was finished, the ribbon winners were announced. As I'd suspected, my name was not among them, but I didn't care. My sense of accomplishment was reward enough.

"I'm so incredibly proud of you," my mom said, putting her arm around my shoulders. "I'm sure it won't be long before you and Milo are winning tons of ribbons."

My stomach heaved as I imagined myself at another show, and I shook my head vehemently. "No. I don't have it in me to do this again, and I wouldn't put Milo through it. It was much too difficult and way too terrifying. I'm glad I did it, but I'll never be able to compete at this level."

Mom gave me a quick hug. "I understand, but you may change your mind one day. So do me a favor and don't get rid of your riding clothes this time."

We took a detour to the concession stand on our way back to the stalls. Neither of us had eaten all day, but I was too wound up to think about food. While Mom waited for her sandwich, I sat at one of the picnic tables with Spike.

Three women were sitting at a table several feet away. My table's umbrella blocked me from their view, but I could easily hear what they were saying. Their conversation centered on some poor rider who'd made a fool of herself in the ring. Playing with Spike, I did my best to ignore them until I realized I was the poor fool they were talking about.

"I feel badly for Milo," I overheard one of them say. "He's such a nice horse and she's just awful."

I bent my head so no one would see the look on my face as humiliation and pain ripped through me. I thought about getting up and walking away, but I didn't want to attract attention. Wrapping my arms around my middle, I stayed where I was, hugging myself tightly.

"Honestly," another chimed in, "half the time, she didn't look like she knew what she was doing or where she was going."

All three of them hooted with laughter and I hugged myself harder. I thought I had ridden pretty well, sighted or not, but according to these three, I was nothing more than a laughingstock.

"Maybe she was drunk," one of them snickered.

That doesn't even make sense. But, absurd or not, their words ruined what had been such a proud day. My hurt feelings turned to rage. How dare they say these things when they knew nothing about me. I silently vowed to reclaim my self-worth and prove that Milo and I were not a joke. Unfortunately, the only way I could do that was to win in the show ring, and that seemed impossible.

My mom placed her tray of food on the table and sat down next to me. The trio got up and left without another word. I was grateful my mom hadn't heard their heartless comments.

"Are you all right?" she asked popping, a fry into her mouth. The smell of sweet potato fries teased my nose, and my stomach growled. I took one from the top of the pile and chewed thoughtfully.

"Fine, why?"

She handed me a bottle of water. "For a second, it looked like you wanted to murder someone."

"Murder?" I chuckled. "No, I don't have murder on my mind. I was thinking about what you said, and I think you're right. I do need to keep showing. It's the only way we'll get better."

I wasn't sure how I was going to do it, but Milo and I would be unstoppable. And I was going to make damn sure that no one, ever, would laugh at us again.

CHAPTER EIGHTEEN

Bob and the horses returned from Middleburg late Sunday night. They had Monday off and on Tuesday morning, Spike and I were back in Bob's car on the way to the barn. I hadn't seen Milo in three days, and I missed him terribly. While Bob caught up on his business calls, I stared out the window, letting my mind wander.

There were so many things I could have thought about but, hard as I tried, I couldn't get those three women and what they'd said about me out of my head. Bullies had been the bane of my childhood. I thought I'd outgrown them, but even at age 29, I still let them get to me.

We were zipping along the highway when I noticed a tall, gray office building on my right. *Our exit is coming up on the left.* Once we made it off the exit ramp, there would be a yellow and green house on our right. We would take a right there, which would put us on the road to the barn.

Bob and I had traveled this route so often, I was positive I could get to the barn and back to Baltimore on my own by following the trail of landmarks I'd identified. It was similar to my method of jumping a course of fences, except instead of one marker pointing the way to a fence, I had dozens of them to guide me to the barn. Essentially, one landmark along the drive led me to the next one, and so on.

All at once, an idea took shape and I understood what I'd been doing wrong in the show ring. More importantly, I knew how to fix it.

We'd just driven by a farm stand, and I knew our destination would be coming up on the left.

Bob was wrapping up his phone call and the second he hung up, I pounced. "I need to jump today," I said, without preamble.

"It's Tuesday," Bob said, as though I needed reminding that we didn't usually jump the horses this soon after a show.

"Please," I said, willing him to give the okay. "I want to try something. I'll make the fences so low, all Milo has to do is step over them."

My arms and legs were rigid while I waited for Bob to make up his mind. He knew I'd never ask for something like this without a good reason.

A minute ticked by and Bob still hadn't answered me. My request didn't deserve this much thought, and I realized he was making me suffer in silence on purpose.

"Well?" I huffed. I wasn't in the mood for one of Bob's pranks.

"Fine," he drawled, as if he were doing me a big favor.

We got out of the car at the same time, but Bob headed toward the barn and I started off for the ring.

"Where are you going?" he called after me. "I thought you were in a big hurry to get on."

Without stopping or looking back I said, "I need to do a few things first."

Someone had recently driven a tractor with a drag attached to it around the ring. I could see the lines in the white sand where the metal drag had scraped the ground. Climbing over the fence, I could smell the salt coming from the freshly turned sand.

The ring was empty. All the jumps had been disassembled and taken out of it. Now poles, standards, and flower boxes sat in piles shoved against the railing.

I expected to have to rearrange some of the fences, but I hadn't banked on starting from scratch. I took another look at the jump standards. Some were standing up while others were on their side in the tall grass outside the ring.

I was definitely going to encounter a creepy-crawly or two if I went ahead with my plan to set up a course of fences for myself. Briefly, I contemplated waiting until Tom and Bob designed a new course and then, with the help of a few other guys, put the jumps back in the ring.

But who knew when that would happen? It could take days, and I wanted to put my idea to the test immediately.

In a little over an hour, I lugged twelve standards, eighteen poles, and four flower boxes into the ring. I already knew where I wanted to place each jump, so once all the pieces were inside the ring, it didn't take long to build a course of six two-foot jumps.

Now for the hard part. I wiped sweat from my face with the back of my hand. If the daily drive here had taught me anything, it was that I needed more than one marker to guide me to a jump.

Bob rode into the ring on a gray horse named Wendall just as I began to walk and talk my way around the course.

"Enter the ring and turn left. Track right at the walk until we reach this corner." I stopped and stared at the rail's corner post. "Then walk across the ring toward the opposite corner. Aim for the white and green standard. Keep it off my right shoulder when we pass it. When we hit the corner, start cantering to the left." Trying to mimic Milo's stride, I took three big steps along the rail as I searched for my next marker.

"What are you doing?" Bob asked as he passed me, walking Wendell on a loose rein. "I thought you only needed one marker for each fence."

Unhappy with the interruption, I quickly explained why I was talking myself through the entire course.

"My vision is too limited for me to rely on just a trash can or a tree to tell me when I need to turn toward a jump. It's too easy for me to miss a marker and get lost. I need to know where I'm going at all times." I leaned against the railing and pointed to the footprints I'd left in the sand. "I need to have a complete inventory of markers that begins with our first step into the ring and continues until the last one."

Bob looked around the ring and then back to me. "It sounds good, but isn't that too much to remember?"

I started walking again. "I'm pretty sure the more I do it, the easier it will be. Plus, memorizing the entire ring is way easier if I talk myself through it."

"Okay, I'll leave you to it then."

Bob rode for another half-hour while I continued talking my way from one fence to another, identifying and memorizing each marker as I came upon it. With every step I grew more confident. After walking the course a second time, I could picture it perfectly in my head, the string of markers guiding me through it. I was no longer worried about missing a turn or a jump, and I couldn't wait to get on Milo to put my new way of navigating a course into practice.

Bob was leaving the ring. I climbed over the railing, ran up the hill to the barn, and scooted by him to go into the tack room.

"I'm going to get on," I called out.

Bob had gotten off Wendall and was handing the reins to one of the grooms. "Don't start jumping without me."

"I know, I know. It isn't safe for me to jump unsupervised."

I was already halfway to Milo's stall when Tom brushed past me carrying Milo's bridle. "I'll get him out for you," Tom said throwing his shoulder against Milo's door until it slid open.

By the time I returned to the grooming area, Bob was getting on his next horse. "Actually," he said as he checked to make sure the girth was tight, "I know you're safe on Milo. I just want to see if this works."

Behind me, Milo was being hooked up to one of the crossties and grunting like a goat.

"I think somebody wants you," Bob laughed. He walked his horse out the barn door, calling back, "I'll meet you down there."

The minute Milo and I walked into the ring, I began to recite my landmarks from start to finish. Milo's ears twitched back and forth at the sound of my voice.

I was eager to begin jumping, but first Milo needed to walk, trot, and canter until his muscles were warm and loose. I was cantering to the left when Bob barked, "Hurry up, I don't have all day. I'm very important, you know."

His self-mocking made me chuckle and I let Milo walk for a few seconds so he could catch his breath. I was glad Bob was sticking around. I had a good feeling about my plan, but I still wanted Bob to watch so we could celebrate together if all went well, or he could tell me how to fix it if something went wrong.

"We're trying something new today, M," I said pressing my left leg against Milo's side, signaling him to pick up his right lead canter.

We rode past a standard and I checked it off my list of markers. "White standard on my left," I said out loud. Then to myself, *three more strides and we'll canter by a yellow jump, go straight to the railing, and turn left.*

I was in heaven. For the first time since I lost my vision a year-and-a-half ago, I knew where to go every step of the way. The rail appeared in front of me exactly when I thought it would, and I couldn't help smiling at it.

Concentrate, I reminded myself. *In five strides, turn left at the break in the rail, pass two jumps on the right, and the one we want will be directly in front of us.*

We turned to the left and I peeked over my right shoulder to make sure I was lined up with the jumps on my right side. It was the first time I was using other fences to guide me and, as expected, our first jump was straight ahead. We hopped over it and the tension left my body. *This is going to work*, I thought as I let out a breath.

By the fifth fence, I hadn't made a single mistake, and my enthusiasm was picking up speed. Each turn was accurate, and every jump was met at the ideal spot. I was so excited that for a moment, I forgot where I was going and missed the next marker. Luckily, there were two more on the way to the sixth and final fence. With perfect timing, we met it exactly at the center, proving beyond a doubt that as long as I had Milo, I didn't need even one good eye to ride better than ever before.

I pulled Milo up in front of a stunned Bob who, like me, was speechless. Neither of us spoke for a solid minute. All we could do was sit on our horses and grin at each other.

I broke the silence. "I think it works," I said, brimming with pride and happiness.

Still smiling, Bob said, "That was awesome."

"I know," I said softly as though Bob and I were sharing a secret.

He asked if I wanted to jump the course again, but I declined. I didn't need a repeat performance to tell me that Milo and I were capable of putting in a winning round.

On the way home from the barn, Bob and I kept smiling at each other and reminiscing about my course.

"Remember the third fence? That was the best one." Bob took his hand off the wheel long enough to give me the thumbs-up sign. "I don't know how you did it, but your turn was perfectly square."

"It was a good one," I blushed, unused to such exuberance and high praise from my trainer.

"You kept your canter pace, too. I don't think you slowed down once."

Chuckling I replied, "It's hard to slow down when every brain cell is busy trying to remember what to look for and where to go. What about the last fence? Could you tell that I almost missed it?"

"No, not even a little bit."

The reminder of my near mistake was sobering.

"It's okay," I said after an uncomfortable silence. "Nothing comes easily for me anymore, and there isn't much left in my life that I'm good at. Today was a game-changer. If I keep riding like this, all the extra effort will be worth it."

Bob made an unexpected appearance at the ring the next morning. It was a crisp, fall day, perfect weather for riding. I had Milo in a nice, relaxed canter, and let him carry his head low to stretch his neck and back muscles. Something blue caught my eye, and I pulled Milo up to get a better look. It was Bob, perched on the rail and wearing a bright, royal blue shirt. He had more horses to ride and we hadn't scheduled a lesson, so his presence was a mystery.

Seizing the opportunity for attention, Milo took a few steps to the rail and rested his chin on Bob's leg. Helpless against my horse's charms, Bob brushed Milo's forelock aside and kissed the swirl of white hair in the middle of his head. Not to be outdone, I scratched Milo behind each ear.

"What brings you down to the ring?"

"Nothing." Bob cocked his head to the side. "I thought I'd watch you jump the course again."

"Why?" I sat up straighter in my saddle and smiled coyly at him. "Do you think yesterday was beginner's luck?"

In fact, I knew I could jump the course again and probably better this time. In the fifteen minutes since I'd entered the ring, I found several new markers to help perfect my riding.

"Actually, I'm sure you can do it again. That's why I want to watch."

Gently, Bob pushed Milo away so he could jump down from the fence. He strode to the first jump and raised the top pole.

"Let's try something a bit bigger this time."

When Bob had adjusted all the jumps, I asked how high they were.

"About three feet," he replied nonchalantly.

I'd jumped much bigger fences, but never with so little vision. I could get away with making a mistake when jumping two-foot fences, which were small enough that Milo could jump them from a standstill. However, a bigger jump called for a more accurate ride. Any error in judgment on my part would make Milo's job of getting to the other side more difficult. But I knew as long as he was carrying a good pace, he'd have enough power in his hind end to clear the fence even if the take-off wasn't perfect.

Confident that we would be fine, I shifted my weight to the left and Milo began to canter.

Powerhouse that he was, Milo shot off the ground as I guided him to the perfect take-off point in front of each jump. His canter rhythm from fence to fence never changed. Each stride was even and balanced, and it felt like we were gliding.

It was easy for Milo, but not for me. I had forgotten how much strength it took to hold my position over a higher fence. I had also forgotten the thrill of hovering in the air. The higher the fence, the higher you fly, and each jump gave me an adrenaline rush.

Bob told me to jump the course again. Then he had me start the course with a different jump. I was still going in the same direction and using the same markers, so the new order didn't faze me.

I was panting by the time I finished the third course. I pulled Milo up and we walked over to Bob, who was standing in the middle of the ring.

"Are you going to make it?" he teased.

"That was so much fun," I wheezed. "I feel like I just got off of a roller coaster."

"It was fun to watch." Bob pressed his hand flat against Milo's chest. "He's still a bit warm. You should walk him."

"I'm a little warm, too," I said, fanning my face with my gloved hand.

"Your cheeks are bright red. Why aren't you in better shape than this?"

I stared down at Bob. "Well, excuse me, but you try talking yourself around a course of fences. It makes it really difficult to breathe."

"Right," he said apologetically. "I guess it would. I forget that you can't see, especially after watching you ride better than most people with two good eyes."

"Thanks, that's the idea. I don't want to be known as 'a good rider for a blind person,' I just want to be a good rider, period."

Milo pawed at the dirt, which was his way of telling me he was bored with our conversation. "All right, M, I'll take you back."

We were almost to the gate when Bob called after us, "You know I'm going to start dragging you to shows again."

A little thrill shot through me, and I turned in my saddle so Bob could clearly hear me. "Good. I'm planning on that."

Two weeks passed without another word from Bob about showing. I rode every day. Whether or not I was jumping, I practiced using my markers to lead me around the course and honed this skill until it became second nature.

One morning in early October, we got to the barn right after sunrise so Bob could take down the basic course I'd built and replace it with a more challenging one. I asked if he wanted my help and was relieved when my offer was refused, even more so when the sky turned dark gray and it began to drizzle.

While Bob, Tom, and the rest of the grooms worked on the course, Spike and I hung out with Milo in his dry stall. During the night, the temperature had dropped into the thirties and Milo was still wearing his navy blanket. I leaned on his shoulder where the blanket stopped and could feel his soft fur against my cheek. Heat radiated from his body and as I snuggled closer to him, his warmth enveloped me.

Gradually, the pinging of the rain against the barn's tin roof slowed, and I left the comfort of the stall to bring Bob and the guys a stack of towels.

When I was halfway down the muddy path to the ring, I could see that the fences had been set. By now, I'd become quite adept at recognizing people by their body shape, and I spotted Bob and Tom standing at the far end of the ring. They were deep in conversation and, wordlessly, I handed them a couple of towels. I gave the rest to the grooms as they walked by me, carrying armloads of fresh pine brush to decorate the fences.

When I'd first returned to the barn after regaining some vision, I hid in Milo's stall, afraid the rest of the world would see me as I saw myself: pitiful. But since Middleburg, I was spending less time with my horse and more time with my human friends. My new ability in the ring boosted my confidence and self-esteem, and I started seeing myself as a competent rider. As the men smiled and thanked me for the towels, I felt a connection to them. We all belonged to the same team, and I was overjoyed to be an active member.

The strong scent of pine followed me as I toured the ring, studying the new course and memorizing the markers that would point the way to each jump. I counted nine fences, all covered with brush and fake flowers. Bob wanted this course to resemble one we'd jump at a show, but I thought the grooms overdid it. Piles of green brush were everywhere, and, to me, the ring looked and smelled like a forest.

"When you're done here, why don't you go get on Milo," Bob said, catching up with me.

Confused, I looked up from the fence post I'd been considering using for a marker.

"I'm not supposed to have a lesson today, am I?"

"No," Bob replied walking over to the rail and using the lowest board to scrape the mud from his boots. "I think it would be a good idea though. We're here early enough for you to have the ring to yourself."

During a lesson a few days ago, I realized my way of riding wouldn't work if there were other people in the ring because the slightest noise or movement could distract me. Two other riders had been by the rail, waiting for me to finish the course. Though they weren't near me, I had to pull up twice when my concentration was broken, first by the sound of their laughter and again by one of their horses kicking at a fly.

Rushing through my final walk around the ring, I bolted up the hill, eager to get on Milo and try out this new, more difficult course. With Tom's help, I was on in record time. I passed Bob on his way into the barn as Milo and I were walking out.

"I'll be right back," he said stopping for a second to plant a kiss on Milo's cheek. "If I'm not there in five minutes, start hacking."

Experience had taught me that Bob wouldn't make it back to the ring for at least ten minutes. There was always someone or something that required his immediate attention.

Putting the extra time to good use, I circled Milo around each jump, letting him smell the brush and stopping him when he tried to eat it. When it felt like five minutes had gone by, I did as Bob had asked and began working Milo on the flat, walking, trotting, and cantering but not jumping. I hacked Milo to the left and then to the right. Every so often, I would sneak a peek at the barn, hoping to see Bob emerge from its wide doors.

Cars were beginning to bounce down the uneven driveway and it wouldn't be long before I was sharing the ring with other riders. I was running out of patience when I heard Bob yelling," I'm here, I'm here!" as he charged down the hill.

"Ready to talk about the course?" he asked as he strode to his customary spot in the center of the ring, where I joined him.

"The first jump is off of your left," he said pointing in the jump's direction. "I noticed when you're on your left lead, you lean to the inside of the ring as Milo canters around the corner."

That would explain why I could feel off balance when we were going to the left. "How long have I been doing that?" I whined. "Why is this the first time I'm hearing about it?"

"Because," Bob said looking up at me, "before, my main concern was getting you around the course in one piece. But now that I know what you and Milo can do, my job is to make you the best rider you can be. I have to say, I don't think we've even scratched the surface yet."

No one had ever told me I was a good rider, and I could have leapt off Milo's back and hugged Bob with all my might. However, the ring was no place for a display of emotion.

"I'll do my best," I promised Bob solemnly.

"I know you will." He patted my leg and pointed to the first jump. "By the way, I'd hold on tight if I were you. All the extra brush makes the fences wider, and I have a feeling Milo's going to jump them like they're on fire. Now get going or we'll run out of time."

Clearing my head of everything except my mental map of the course, I rode to the far end of the ring and picked up a canter. I reminded myself to stay in the center of the saddle and fought the urge to lean in as I came around the corner to the first fence. Beneath me, I could feel Milo's hind end propelling us forward and I relaxed my hold on the reins to let him set our pace.

Ears forward, Milo aimed for the middle of the jump and pushed off the ground with so much force that I felt like I'd been shot out of a canon. With my upper body thrust forward, I braced against Milo's neck and struggled to hold myself still as we cleared the fence by a foot.

The impact of our landing jostled me out of position. The second fence was coming up quickly and I pushed my heels down to regain my balance. Milo's canter was more energetic than usual, and I had less time between jumps to locate my markers. Luckily, the vivid emerald brush stood out against the white fences and the contrast made it easier for me to see them.

Our final jump was a short ride from the corner and at some point, Bob had moved closer to it for a better view.

"Show him what you got, M," I cheered him on as we rounded the turn.

Milo's ears perked forward, and I buried my hands in his mane and concentrated on staying on as he blasted off the ground. We hung in the air, suspended over the jump. Milo's back folded as he arched his muscles and then we were landing, like a ton of bricks, on the opposite side.

Bob's low whistle of approval trailed us as we cantered away from the jump.

I slowed Milo until we were walking. He lowered his head and I let the reins slip through my fingers until I was barely holding onto them.

"Unbelievable!" Bob crowed. "He looks like he's wearing springs on his feet."

"He feels like it, too," I laughed and hugged Milo around his neck. "That's my boy," I whispered, as he looked back at me, snorting proudly. My eye locked on Milo's, and I could see the fire in his, burning brightly.

We weren't finished yet. Bob wanted me to work on my position in the air so we'd have a softer landing. "I know Milo has a big jump and it's hard to stay with him, but you're leaning too hard on his neck. Your landings will be much smoother if you drop your weight into your heels and hold yourself closer to the saddle. Let him catch his breath before you start again!" he called out to us.

Milo and I were walking alongside the rail, not too far from Bob, but the wind had picked up, making it difficult to hear.

"Weight in my heels and don't lean on his neck. Got it!" I yelled into the wind.

Clouds of dust whipped around us as the wind grew stronger. We approached the first fence, and I detected the slightest hesitation in Milo. Bits of pine bark and needles pelted us as we cantered through the wind. My eye burned, but with the jump looming ahead, I dared not blink.

Milo was even higher over the first fence. I shoved my heels down as far as they would go and clenched my stomach muscles to hold myself off of his neck as we flew over the jump.

Compared to the first time around, our landing was much lighter and, having started in the correct position, I was able to hold it and maintain my balance.

"Much better!" Bob hollered.

Milo and I were on a roll and even Bob's outburst didn't distract me. But as I was tracking my markers to the fourth fence, I began to fall apart.

We were on the right lead and cantering into the wind when, without any warning, my contact lens shifted, and the world became a swirling mass of muted colors. The markers I so heavily depended on were unidentifiable and the jumps may as well have been invisible.

I snatched at the reins, stopping Milo more abruptly than I should have. He threw his head up in protest but did as he was told. "I'm so sorry," my voice cracked, making my apology barely audible.

"What happened?" Bob demanded, running to Milo's side. Then seeing the frown on my face, he asked, "Are you okay?"

I tried blinking my contact back into place but the tiny piece of plastic slipped past the front of my eye and settled, uselessly, in the corner.

"My contact again," I said, closing my eyes against another gust of wind.

Earlier that week, Bob had been in the ring with me when the same thing happened. I was trotting and since my contact had never moved around before, I didn't give it much thought.

Now that it had happened again, and this time while I was jumping, I realized it was a serious problem that could ruin everything.

Frustrated and angry, I didn't bother stopping the tears that filled my eyes. Rehydrated, my contact slid back into place and the world around me took shape.

"Don't worry about it," Bob soothed. "You were fantastic until you pulled up."

Bob was running late and several riders stood outside the gate waiting for me to clear the ring. "We're out of time," he said. "Try not to worry. We'll fix this and then you'll be unbeatable."

I smiled at Bob's attempt to make me feel better. He was right. Milo and I had been exceptional, but that wouldn't matter at a show, where I'd be automatically disqualified if I had to pull up in the middle of a course. My shoulders slumped forward as we left the ring.

Bob spent the rest of the day teaching and riding. We didn't leave the barn until after three and little Spike was so exhausted from running around all day, I had to carry him to the car. Worried about my eye, I wasn't in the mood to chat, but Bob, still excited about our lesson, was talking non-stop.

I was only half listening to what he was saying, until he mentioned the Winter Equestrian Festival in Wellington, Florida.

"Wait, what did you say about Florida?"

"I think you should consider showing in Wellington this winter. I know I wanted you to fix a few things after your first course, but I was nitpicking. That would have been the winning round at any show."

Milo had spent two winters in Wellington. Bob showed him the first time while I watched. The following year, I was losing my vision and Wendy got to ride him. Finally, after everything I'd been through, I had clawed my way back into the ring and it was my turn to show Milo in Wellington.

Bob was dangling my dream in front of me, and as much as I wanted to grab it, I couldn't. A thin piece of plastic stood in my way. Unless I figured out how to make my contact lens stay in place, Wellington was out of the question.

CHAPTER NINETEEN

That night, I waited until Mom and I sat down for dinner at her kitchen table before saying anything about showing in Wellington over the winter. I began by describing every aspect of my lesson including the part about my contact.

"Do you remember this time last year?" I asked. "I was losing my vision and we were told that I was going to be completely blind for the rest of my life."

The familiar tightness that began in my chest and spread to my stomach every time I spoke of or thought about that time in my life was already making it difficult to breathe. It was one of the reasons I rarely spoke of it. Some things were too painful to talk about.

"Of course, I remember." Mom's voice was soft and low. "I also recall you telling the doctors they were wrong and there must be something that could help you."

"Back then, all I wanted was to see again," I said, my tone somber as the frustration and grief came rushing back. "Nobody believed in me. I think that was the worst part."

"I'm sorry," she said sadly.

"Oh, Mom," I shook my head vehemently, "I wasn't talking about you. You were the only one listening to me. You saved me."

I was close enough to her to see the shadow of a smile cross her face. "I don't know about that. Anyway, what are you getting at? I haven't heard you dig up the past in a long time. You must have a reason."

Biting into a thick slice of cucumber, I chewed quickly, almost swallowing the piece whole.

"I want to show Milo in Wellington this winter."

Mom pushed her salad plate to the side, propped her elbows on the table, and rested her chin on steepled fingers. "Do you think you're ready for that?"

I wasn't sure if she was asking about my riding or whether I was ready to be on my own in the world, after living with her or just a few floors away for the past year-and-a-half. My answer to both was the same, and with as much assertiveness as I could muster with a mouth full of tomato, I said, "Yes, I do."

Without a word, she pushed her chair back from the table, collected our salad plates, and brought them to the sink. If I didn't know better, I would've thought she hadn't heard me.

It wasn't just my mother's permission that I needed. Living and showing in Wellington for three months was a luxury I wasn't sure she could afford.

After placing a plate of fish and asparagus in front of me, she sat down with her plate, speared a piece of asparagus, and let it hang on her fork while she spoke.

"I think that's a fantastic idea."

"Really?" I popped out of my seat and practically skipped over to her. I was standing behind her and when she tilted her head back, she was smiling.

"I really do. Besides, what were you planning on doing this winter after Bob left?"

"Huh, I hadn't thought of that."

She looked up at me with a raised eyebrow. "Then it's a good thing you don't have to."

"I guess so." I grinned and laid my cheek on top of her head. "You never cease to amaze me."

"I could say the same thing to you." She squeezed my hand. "Now, go sit down before your dinner gets cold."

"I don't have any of the details worked out," I said on the way back to my chair. "I may be able to share a house with Linda and we'll probably have to give her some money for driving me around. It's going to cost a lot. Between my expenses and Milo's…"

Guilt flooded me and I found myself unable to continue. I hated this part. Even more than losing my freedom and the ability to read, drive, or cross the street. Nothing compared to the loss of financial independence.

Mom noticed my sudden change in disposition and asked what was wrong.

"I hate asking you for money."

"I don't blame you," she replied. "But just know that anything I give you, including money, is done freely and happily. That's what moms do."

I was filled with so much love for my mother, I could feel it radiating from me.

"No," I said emphatically, "that's what *you* do."

That night, as I washed my face, I looked in the mirror and a stranger looked back. I couldn't recall the last time I actually saw myself. I remembered looking in the mirror when I thought I'd never see again but by then, it was too late to memorize my face.

The version of myself that stared back at me was unrecognizable. My eyes looked dark, almost black, when I knew they were light green. My hair looked short and brown, when I knew it was long and red. The skin on my face, which was smooth to the touch, looked like the surface of the moon.

I turned away from the impostor in the mirror. I didn't know who I was anymore. The only time I felt right was when I was at the barn. At least there I had a purpose. The only time I felt good about myself was when I was on Milo.

After a restless sleep, I woke up with an eye that was red and irritated.

"I'm afraid we'll be skipping the barn this morning," I told Spike while I hunted in the bed sheets for my phone. I found it under a pillow and called Bob.

"No riding for me today. I thought I'd be able to hold out for a few more days, but I need to see my doctor right away."

"That bad?" Bob asked sympathetically.

"It feels like someone was rubbing a Brillo pad across my eye all night long."

I flinched at my own description and changed the topic to a happier one.

"Great news, Mom said I can go to Wellington with you."

Bob let out an elated "woo-hoo," and I opted out of reminding him that, my mother's permission aside, I couldn't go to Florida until I had a fix for my latest eye trouble. *Why kill the mood?*

One of the perks of having the same doctor for twenty years is that you're treated like a VIP. I called Henry's office the moment it opened, and the receptionist said they'd fit me in whenever I got there. By 9:30 a.m., Mom and I were checking in at the front desk.

Henry seemed genuinely happy to see me. While he prepared his instruments, I told him how I was learning to ride with such low vision and that I hoped to show Milo in Florida in a few months.

"Of course," I added, "my eye is misbehaving again and the problem needs to be resolved before I can show."

"Oh boy, I can see how dry your eye is."

My exam didn't take long. Henry assured me that my retina and eye pressure were stable, and that my case of "severe dry eye" stemmed from my cornea.

Essentially, as Henry explained, my botched laser surgery destroyed parts of my eye that produced fluid. Corneas, which are located in the front of the eye, need moisture to maintain their shape. Mine was so dry and irritated, it was warping.

"That's why your contact lens won't stay put," Henry said. "A healthy cornea should be nice and smooth. Yours resembles a piece of sandpaper." There were several surgeries that could reverse the problem, but my eye was much too weak to withstand any kind of invasive procedure.

Before I left, Henry referred me to another doctor and gave me three bottles of eye drops. "These will help, but they aren't a cure," he warned. "I like this brand because it works well with contact lenses."

On the way home, I called Dr. Brown, the corneal specialist Henry had recommended. The receptionist placed me on hold, where I stayed for the entire thirty-five-minute drive to Baltimore.

We were standing in front of my door when a voice finally interrupted the smooth jazz loop I'd been forced to listen to. My mom took Spike for a walk while I scheduled my appointment. When she returned, I was sitting on my couch holding my head in my hands.

"What's wrong?" she asked hurrying to my side. "Wouldn't the doctor see you?"

Spike jumped onto my lap and licked my face until I picked my head up. Mom sat down next to me, and I shifted my position so I could look at her.

"Oh, she'll see me," I said sourly, "but not until the end of March."

"That long?"

I nodded my head and rubbed Spike's belly. "Apparently she's very popular and the diseases she treats are rather common. The first available appointment for a new patient isn't until March 28th."

"Oh, no. I'm so sorry. At least you'll be back from Florida by then."

I huffed cynically. "If I go."

Mom got up and I followed her to the door. "That's something you have to decide, but I'm sure you'll think of a way to make your contact sit still," she said, and then she hugged me goodbye.

I flopped back down on the couch next to Spike, where I spent at least twenty minutes asking myself, *Am I going to go to Florida, or not?*

While my mind raced with indecision, I noticed one of the bottles Henry had given me had fallen out of my pocket and onto the sofa. I held the bright green bottle up to my face for a closer look.

The drops I'd tried so far hadn't been hydrating enough to keep my contact in place the entire time it took to jump a course of eight fences. Maybe this brand would do the trick. The humidity was much higher in Florida. Perhaps that would help, too.

Who knew better than I how quickly life could change? My vision was a gift, but I had a feeling it had an expiration date. One of these days, I was going to wake up without it and when that day came, would I regret missing the opportunity to show Milo in Wellington?

"I'm going," I said with enough force to make Spike jump. He peered up at me and, patting his head, I said, "I've made my decision. Spike Dog, we'll be spending our winter in Wellington."

When Bob and I got to the barn the next day, the first thing we did was sit down with Linda to flesh out the details of my relocation to Florida. Linda was happy to share a house with me and, as long as I contributed gas money, she would make sure I had transportation. Bob and Linda were as clueless as I was about how to fix my contact, but they both said they'd try to think of something.

"We have plenty of time to work that out," Bob said. "In the meantime, you and Linda should start looking for a house to rent."

Less than a week later, Linda and I had selected a rental about four miles from the show. I couldn't see the photos online, but Linda promised me the house was clean and comfortable. By Thanksgiving, we'd sent the realtor our deposit, and I was able to check one more thing off my list.

As the weather grew colder and drier, my contact lens became more problematic, and I struggled with it every time I rode. Though I was drowning my eye in artificial tears, after thirty seconds it would become dry again and the slightest puff of wind could knock my contact out of place.

"What am I going to do?" I asked Bob one afternoon on our way home. During my lesson that day, I made four attempts to complete a course, but I had to pull up and start over each time because my contact lens kept slipping. On the last try, it fell out of my eye and landed on my nose. Somehow, I managed to catch it before it was gone forever.

I knew Bob was tired of listening to me complain about my lens, but I was so exasperated I couldn't help myself. I slid down in my seat and ran my hands through my hair until my lap was covered with the dark red strands.

"Can you wear glasses?" Bob asked.

"No," I said dully. "The lenses would be so thick and heavy, they wouldn't stay in place."

"What about trying glasses over your contact? They make pairs without a prescription. I think they call them fashion glasses. They might block the wind."

For those of us forced to wear thick, ugly glasses for years, there was no such thing as "fashion glasses." However, Bob may have been on to something.

"I hadn't thought of that. And I know exactly where I can get a pair."

When Bob dropped me off in front of my building, Spike and I got into the elevator but instead of stopping at my floor, we rode up to my mom's.

Standing in front of her door was a life-sized plastic figure. Dubbed "Sydney" by my stepfather, he was dressed as a butler in formal attire and on his wrinkled face, he wore a large pair of glasses with a thick, black frame.

I plucked them from his nose and sure enough, the lenses were plain, non-prescription plastic.

"I'll bring them back when I'm done with them," I assured Sydney in a whisper.

Mom had said she'd be out for most of the day, so I didn't bother knocking on her door. I'd let her know later that I'd borrowed Sydney's specs.

Back in the elevator, I pushed the button for my floor and thought of the many twists and turns my life had taken in the past year. "And now," I said to Spike wearily, "I've been reduced to stealing from a mannequin."

I waited until I was on Milo and in the ring to try out the oversized glasses. They nearly covered my face and I had to shove them under the brim of my riding helmet. I was trotting Milo in a circle by the ingate when Bob walked into the ring on an elegant chestnut mare named Quinn.

"Oh, my lord, what's on your face?"

Bob was hooting with laughter. I changed directions and trotted away from him. He was still chuckling when I met up with him again. "I hope you laugh so hard, you fall off."

Bob picked up the trot himself and the next time we were close enough to each other to talk, he said, "It looks like they're wearing you instead of the other way around. Where did you get them?"

"I borrowed them from a friend," I said, certain I'd never hear the end of it if Bob knew the truth.

"Do they help any?"

"I can't tell yet. So far, my contact is fine, but it doesn't usually slide around until I'm cantering. The faster I go, the more wind hits my eye."

As Bob continued trotting Quinn down the long side of the ring, I circled Milo to the left and began to canter.

At first, the glasses seemed to sufficiently block the wind from my eye. My hopes were rising and I pressed my heel against Milo's side to pick up our pace.

I cantered around the ring twice and my contact never moved.

"It's working!" I called out to Bob who was, by now, cantering at the opposite end.

We brought our horses down to a walk and met in the middle of the ring.

"You are a genius," I beamed. "The glasses were a great idea."

"Of course," Bob said walking alongside me. "All of my ideas are great."

The brim of my helmet was pressing down painfully against the frame and when I took the glasses off, I could feel the welts they'd left behind on my nose and cheeks.

"I'm really happy we found something that solved the problem," Bob said watching me rub the dents on my face. "But I think we need to find a pair that fits under your hat a little better."

"Agreed," I said smiling, "and I still need to try them while I'm jumping. That's when my contact really goes crazy."

Bob stopped at a drugstore on the way home claiming he had to pick up something. He left the car running so Spike and I would stay warm while he was in the store. Bob was gone for ten minutes and when he returned, he handed me a plastic bag.

"Here," he said gruffly. "These should fit you better."

Inside the bag were two identical pairs of wire rimmed glasses. I put one of them on. They were much smaller than my pilfered pair and the oval frame would fit more comfortably under my hat.

"How do they look?" I asked, turning toward Bob.

"Much better. They had other styles without prescriptions, but I went with the smallest ones."

"Well," I removed the glasses and carefully put them back in the bag, "that was really nice of you. Thank you."

I was still staring at Bob as we pulled back onto the highway.

He gave me a couple of sidelong glances, and when I didn't look away, he sighed deeply and asked, "What now?"

"Nothing," I replied shrugging. "I just —" my voice cracked, and I stopped talking, afraid of getting too emotional. "It means a lot, that's all," I finished, sparing us the discomfort of a heartfelt reply. Neither of us was good at those.

Over the next few weeks, all I could think about was being in Wellington. About a week before Christmas, I woke up one morning to find a foot of snow on the ground. It was Monday and, since that was my day off from the barn, I had every intention of sleeping in.

Unfortunately, Spike wasn't on board with my plan and by 7:30 a.m., he was whining to go out.

"Okay, give me a second."

Not bothering to get out of my pajamas, I pulled on my winter boots and collected my down jacket, gloves, scarf, and hat from the hall closet. Any other day, I would've taken Spike for a long walk. But today we didn't leave the building's courtyard. Despite my warm outfit, I couldn't stop shivering. Spike finished his business, and I wasted no time returning to my cozy apartment.

When I hung my coat back up, I noticed my two large suitcases on the closet floor. *What am I waiting for? Might as well start packing now.* As someone who had never liked the cold, Florida was the perfect place to spend the winter, and January couldn't come soon enough.

It took most of the day to decide what to pack for Wellington. Once both suitcases were full, I slowly zipped them shut, savoring the sound as I imagined hearing it again when I started unpacking in Florida. I set the bags side-by-side at my front door where they stayed for two weeks, a welcome reminder of all I'd accomplished to get to this point.

Bob, Linda, and the horses were leaving Maryland and heading south December 26. My mom, Spike, and I were flying down on New Year's Day. 2002 would begin with three of my favorite things: sunshine, palm trees, and Milo.

Ahh, Florida.

Spike, tired of being stuffed inside a carrier, was nestled in my arms as I stepped off the plane in Ft. Lauderdale and into a wall of humidity. While I waited for my mom to pull the rental car around, a warm breeze tousled my hair and tickled the back of my neck. By the time she arrived, I couldn't wait to get to Wellington.

Traffic heading north from Ft. Lauderdale wasn't that bad and we made it to the rental house in decent time. Linda let us in and gave Mom and me a quick tour. The house was reasonably clean;

the furniture was outdated and worn, but I tested a few chairs and found them surprisingly comfortable. My mom's phone began to chime, and she excused herself as she went outside to take the call.

Spike followed Linda and me into the master bedroom where he began sniffing wildly. I got a whiff of wet dog and assumed the last renter had a canine friend. Linda had graciously assigned the master bedroom to me since it had an attached bathroom.

"We can't have you stumbling around in the dark if you have to use the bathroom in the middle of the night," she explained.

I opened my mouth to let Linda know that I was actually very good at navigating my way through darkness, but then I saw the king-sized bed and spacious closet.

"Were you about to say something?" Linda asked.

"Umm," I stammered, poking my head out of the walk-in closet. "That was very considerate of you. Thank you."

I heard the pop of a car trunk opening and I dropped my purse onto the bed, thanked Linda for showing me around, and dashed out to collect my belongings from the car. I dragged my suitcases into my bedroom, vowing to throw away the one with the broken wheel as soon as I emptied it.

After Linda gave us a quick tour and we emptied the car of my luggage, it was time for Mom to leave.

"Did you get everything?" she asked. "It'll take me forty-five minutes to get to my house, and if I leave soon, I can avoid rush hour. So, if you want one last check, you should do it now."

On my way to the car, I stumbled on a chunk of asphalt and I frowned at the cracks and holes all over the old driveway. My mom took my hand. "You'll come to know the lay of the land here," she said in a voice full of love and sympathy. "At least there aren't any stairs for you to worry about."

"I know." I tried to smile but the sound of her jiggling the car keys brought my frown back. "I'm going to miss you," I said looking squarely into her face, recalling how beautiful she was.

"You probably can't wait to get rid of me," I joked. "I bet you don't remember what it's like not to worry about me 24/7."

She gently patted my cheek. "Do you really think a little distance is going to stop me from worrying about you? If anything, I'll be more concerned."

"Nothing's going to happen to me. I'll be just fine."

"Right. My child, with severely impaired vision, is going to jump her twelve-hundred-pound horse over three-foot fences, but I needn't give it a second thought."

"I'm not riding your average horse, though."

"Believe me, I'm aware of that." She got into the car and looked up at me through the open window. "Milo is the only reason I'm okay with all of this. I'd be a wreck if I didn't know how much that horse loves you. He takes better care of you than I do."

"I love you, Mom." My voice was raspy and I let her know that nothing, not even Milo, could take better care of me than she did. After she drove off, I stood in the driveway and listened to the whirr of the engine until I couldn't hear it anymore.

I was up and dressed by 6:30 the next morning. After racing through breakfast, I grabbed my backpack and Spike's food and bowls, and hurried out the door. There was an extra bounce in my step. I was minutes away from being with Milo.

Linda was already in her rental car at the end of the driveway. With Spike at my heels, I walked as quickly as I could through the front yard, head down and staring at the ground two steps ahead of myself to avoid anything that could trip me up.

"Come on, Spikers!" I called out boisterously as I opened the car door. "Let's go see Milo!"

CHAPTER TWENTY

When it came to driving, Linda had a lead foot, a quality I appreciated that morning as we shot onto the main road and headed to our stalls and Milo.

She switched on the radio and turned up the volume when a Rolling Stones song came on. While she sang back-up for Mick Jagger, I held Spike and stared out the window, thinking about how sight wasn't the only thing I'd lost in the past year.

My once large circle of friends had disappeared. Sarah was the only one who didn't desert me, but our longstanding friendship had changed. I wasn't the same person she had known since fourth grade. I used to be fun to be around, and I was always on the go. Nothing like the anxiety-riddled, needy person I was today.

My relationship with Milo was the only one that hadn't changed. He continued to keep me safe and give me comfort, and he was always happy to see me. When I was with him, I could almost believe that I was normal and my life was worthwhile.

I scratched Spike's belly, silently thanking him for his companionship, but what I really needed was Milo. As much as I loved my dog, it was my horse that kept me strong and made me whole.

My heart beat faster as the car jerked to the right and Linda announced, "We're here."

Three giant tents took shape in front of me, and I remembered Bob telling me we'd be based out of tent stalls this winter. The owners recently purchased the property and hadn't had time to build a barn.

Linda parked the car next to Tom's yellow SUV. I used to tease him about the color he'd chosen for his Ford. Now I wished everything was as bright and easy for me to spot.

While Linda rooted through the back seat for her belongings, Spike and I bolted from the car.

"Good, you're here!" Tom hollered and I followed the sound of his voice until I saw him walking out of the tent on my right.

"What a nice greeting," I said as Tom waved at me. Smiling, I waved back.

"Actually," Tom rushed over and put his hand on my elbow, "I was hoping you could do something for me."

Curious, I allowed him to pull me along until we came to three small paddocks.

Only one had a horse grazing in it and I knew immediately, by his coloring and shape, that it was Milo.

I yanked my arm from Tom's light hold, hurried to Milo's enclosure, climbed the fence, and perched on the top rail. A light breeze sent bits of hay, hair, and dust swirling about and I inhaled deeply, letting the strong smell of horse relax me from the inside out.

A man I hadn't noticed before was standing in the middle of the paddock, shaking a bucket full of grain at Milo and calling his name. Milo seemed more than happy to ignore him, even though his tone was low and kind. Pretty impressive considering the poor man probably wanted to kill my horse.

Tom caught up to me and leaned against the fence rail. "New guy," he explained quietly.

"He won't let me near him," the groom said apologetically when he saw Tom.

"It's not your fault." Looking at Milo, I shook my head. "He doesn't like strangers."

Tom waved the groom in and handed me a lead rope. "Will you get your horse, please?"

"Of course," I said happily and pursing my lips, let loose a shrill whistle.

Milo stopped grazing and whirled around, sending dust and large clumps of grass flying in all directions. He tossed his head until he saw me and whinnied so loudly the sound echoed in my ears.

"Hi, M," I squeaked, so elated I could hardly speak.

Milo covered the short distance between us in four strides, stopped in front of me, and dropped his head into my lap. I laid my head on his, enjoying the way his forelock tickled my cheek.

"I missed you." I ran my knuckles across his cheek before jumping down from the fence and snapping the lead rope onto his halter.

"Good lord," I heard Bob say from behind me. He was on a horse and heading toward the ring. "You both act like you haven't seen each other in years. What's it been? A week?"

Leading Milo from the paddock, I looked up at Bob and grinned. "It's been five days since I've seen either one of you, and, frankly, I'm hurt that you're not as excited to see me as Milo is."

Bob burst into laughter, and I could still hear him laughing as I entered the tent with Milo walking next to me. I realized I had no idea where to put my horse. Looking at the row of stalls on either side of us, I turned to Milo and, only half-joking, said, "I don't suppose you know which one is yours."

Milo made no response, other than to stomp his feet at the flies buzzing around his legs.

We walked toward the front of the tent, stopping at each empty stall so I could try to read the name card stapled to the door. Though I'd been getting better at recognizing words by their shape, I still couldn't decipher Tom's chicken scratch.

We got to the end of the aisle where both stalls were empty. Milo rested his chin on my shoulder while I peered into the stall to my right.

"That's definitely not your stall," I said, noticing the grain in the feed tub. Milo was a member of the clean plate club and he left food behind only when he wasn't feeling well.

I switched my attention to the stall on my left. It was a mess.

"Now this," I said kissing Milo's nose, "this could be your stall."

Hay that should have been in a neat pile was scattered everywhere and had even been dunked into the water buckets. The feed tub had been knocked over and was lying on its side, and I couldn't be sure, but one side of the tub seemed squished as if something heavy had stomped on it. The scene had Milo written all over it. I loved my horse, but there was no denying he was an absolute slob.

"Oh, good," I heard Tom say behind us. "You found his stall."

Standing on my tip toes so I could see over Milo's ample rump, I could just make out Tom's slight figure coming down the aisle. "So, this one is Milo's?" I asked, gently pushing against Milo's shoulder until he stepped back, giving me enough room to swing the stall door open.

Tom squeezed past me and held the door so I could lead Milo inside. "Bob asked me to get Milo ready for you, but why don't we let him have some water while I show you where everything is."

"That would be great," I said, scooping clumps of hay from Milo's water buckets.

Tom led me to the tack room where he grabbed Milo's bridle and my saddle. "When you've put on your hat and chaps, meet me at the grooming stall and you can get right on."

Bob was waiting for me when Milo and I walked into the ring behind the tent.

"Do you have your glasses?" Bob was on a black horse that pinned its ears back as we approached it.

"Rude," I said, wagging my finger at the horse.

I pulled my glasses out of my front pocket and put them on. Out of habit, I blinked several times expecting the glasses to change my vision, which, of course, they didn't.

Bob's horse was pawing at the ground, and I changed direction in case it decided to bite or kick Milo.

"You don't need to ride him too hard," Bob said, walking out of the ring. "Use today to let him get comfortable and to see how well your glasses work in the humidity."

The ring was at least twice the size of the one back home, and Milo and I were sweating bullets after trotting only once around. Someone had set up a few fences, but this was not a jumping day. I would worry tomorrow about finding my markers and cramming my brain with every little detail it could hold. For now, I concentrated on the glorious Florida day and the incredible horse I was lucky enough to call mine.

On my way back to the stalls, I passed Bob who was returning to the ring. "How was he?" he asked.

"Perfect," I smiled. "As always."

"And the glasses?"

"So far so good."

Bob turned in his saddle and looked back at me.

"By the way, you have more horses to ride."

It had been a long time since Bob had asked me to help out with his other horses and I was flattered that he thought I was riding well enough to exercise them.

Tom took Milo from me, and I skipped to the tack stall where the white board was hanging. Sure enough, my name had been added, in large red letters, to the group of riders. Three horses were listed under my name, but I couldn't read them. Tom would know though. Before I went back to the grooming stall, I grabbed a bag of mints from my trunk for Milo and my three mystery rides.

A little bribery never hurt when it came to horses.

Milo had already left for his bath and Tom was putting my saddle on Lucas, a sweet, brown gelding that Bob had been training for the past year.

"Hello, Lucas." I patted his muzzle and unwrapped a mint for him. "You have to be a good boy for me. I don't see very well, and you need to make me look good in front of Bob."

Tom gave Lucas a vigorous scratch behind one ear and assured me the horse would be fine.

Milo returned from his bath and was backed into the second grooming stall where he would stay until completely dry. I was petting Lucas's neck, but when I saw Milo, I quickly pulled my hand away as though I'd been caught cheating.

Chuckling at myself, I fished some mints out of the bag for Milo. He took them happily and didn't seem to care at all when I walked out of the tent with another horse.

During my first week in Wellington, I spent most of the day riding. I was in heaven and never grew tired of Tom asking, "Ready for your next one?" Every day I grew stronger and more confident in the saddle. My only complaint was I had no free time to spend with Milo. Usually, I rode him first and had every intention of grazing him afterward, but inevitably Tom or one of the other grooms would take him from me so I could get on the next horse.

On Saturday, the "weekend warriors," as people who flew in to ride on Saturday and Sunday were called, arrived to claim their horses, so I had only Milo to ride. When we were finished, I let Tom know I was taking Milo for a walk.

As we left the barn, I opened Spike's pen and he bolted out of it. I hated that he had to be cooped up all day, but I was too worried about alligators to let him run free.

My boys and I walked until we found a secluded area with plenty of grass, where I sat in the shade of a small tree. Every few minutes, Milo stopped tearing at the grass long enough to rub his nose against my arm. I suppose it was his way of checking in with me. Meanwhile, Spike found something stinky to roll in, and once he was covered with it, he stretched out next to me.

"You reek," I told him, wrinkling my nose. "I hope you know you're taking a bath as soon as we get back to the barn." Spike sighed, obviously pleased with his new scent and indifferent to my threats.

It would have been pure joy to stay in our haven the rest of the day, but we had to get back before Tom started to worry. I stood up and brushed off the bits of grass and dirt that had made their way from Milo's mouth to my lap. Somewhere in the distance, I heard the engine of a golf cart being pushed to its limit.

I tightened my hold on Milo's lead rope.

"Come on, M," I said, giving his neck a pat. I turned around to locate Spike and saw a red golf cart speeding toward us. Spike stood at attention by my side and Milo lifted his head and snorted. His nostrils flared and his body tensed.

The three of us stood our ground and waited to see what happened next. I thought the cart might pass us, but at the last second, the driver slammed on the brakes and stopped right behind Milo, causing him to jump to the side and Spike to growl protectively.

I gritted my teeth, but instead of tearing into the reckless stranger behind the wheel, I reminded myself that you catch more flies with honey than vinegar. *Be polite.*

"Hello," I said, pasting a smile on my face and ignoring the cloud of dust that was causing my eye to burn.

The large man pointed at me and snarled, "What are you doing out here?"

A powerful mixture of body odor and cheap cologne assaulted my nose and for a moment I thought I'd be sick. I waited for my stomach to stop roiling and replied, "I was just grazing my horse."

He leaned forward, causing part of his massive upper body to spill out of the cart. "This is private property! I'll give you ten seconds to get your horse, your dog, and yourself out of here!"

"Private property," I half stated, half asked. "I'm sorry, I didn't know."

I thought that my apology would mollify him. Instead, he pointed at something behind me and barked, "Well, it's printed in big letters right behind you. You couldn't possibly have missed it."

"Actually," I said turning to see what he was talking about, "I could have."

There was nothing behind me except the tree I'd been sitting under. I heard the springs of the golf cart squeal in protest as the driver pushed himself into a standing position. He stomped by me grumbling something about idiots. I assumed he meant me and if there had been a hole nearby, I would have crawled into it. He stopped in front of the tree.

"Right here." He reached up and tapped a piece of wood nailed to the tree. "See right here where it says, 'No Trespassing' in big letters?"

Now that it was being shown to me, I understood why I didn't see it before.

The board was brown, almost the same color as the tree limb it was attached to, and the writing on it was black and faded. I chewed on my bottom lip while I looked at the sign.

There was no question, I was at fault. I was about to apologize again and explain myself, but as the man stepped past me to get back in the golf cart, he did something I couldn't forgive. His massive weight made it impossible for him to squeeze between Milo and the tree, and he jabbed his beefy elbow into Milo's rump. Milo's ears went flat against his head, and he shied away in fear.

I walked him in a small circle until he calmed down, then deliberately stopped by the driver's side of the golf cart and turned to the man who had dared touch Milo.

My voice was low and steady, belying the rage that was building inside me. "Don't you ever lay a hand on my horse again," I said, stepping closer to the cart. "Do you understand me? Not ever."

Legs spread and fists clenched, I defied him to say another word, and when he did, I was ready for it.

"I barely touched him. Besides, if you saw that how did you miss the big sign hanging over your head? What are you, blind?"

Smiling, I bent forward. My face was so close to his, I could smell his sour breath. "As a matter of fact, you asshole, I am." And with that, I reached into my left socket and pulled out my prosthetic eye.

He screamed like a baby before waving me off and driving away at full tilt.

I'd never done anything like that in my life. "Worth it," I said to Milo and Spike as I wiped the prosthetic on my shirt and put it back where it belonged.

After that harrowing experience, I didn't stray far from our tent until Wednesday, when the Winter Equestrian Festival officially began. Bob had suggested I show Milo in the Adult Hunter division. This meant the fences would be three-feet high and my division would be spread out over Saturday and Sunday.

"It looks like you're in the Rost both days," Linda said, checking the show schedule Tuesday night as we were finishing dinner. "At least you only have to memorize one ring this week."

"True, but just in case things get switched on me again, I'll take a peek at the other rings where my division could end up."

As soon as I finished riding on Wednesday and Thursday, Spike and I took a shortcut to the show grounds. I spent the rest of the afternoon walking around the Rost ring, getting a rough idea of what I could use for markers. On Friday, I split my time between two other rings where I could possibly show.

Saturday morning, I dressed in my buff breeches and white show shirt. Linda was also dressed in show attire, and we looked like twins as we drove to the barn in silence, lost in our own thoughts. By 6:00 a.m., I was leading Milo down to the Rost for my last look.

The jumps for my division had been set overnight, so I could finally work out how to get from one to the other. My jacket pockets were loaded with carrots and peppermints that I fed to Milo as I studied the course, picking out the best markers.

By the time we were asked to clear the ring, my pockets were empty and long strands of drool were swinging like pink and orange vines from Milo's mouth.

"Tom is going to shoot me," I moaned. I made a feeble attempt to wipe the slobber from Milo's face with my bare hand, but I only succeeded in spreading the sticky mess to other parts of his body.

We were almost back to the barn when Milo grabbed the sleeve of my jacket between his teeth and gave it a tug. This was a game he liked to play and normally I'd laugh at his antics, but with each yank, he sprayed me with a new batch of slobber.

"What happened to you?" Linda hooted with laughter as I trudged past her with Milo in tow.

"*He* happened to me," I frowned, pointing my thumb in Milo's direction.

One of the grooms poked his head out of the feed room and gasped loudly when he saw us. He dropped what he was doing and, shaking his head disapprovingly, took Milo from me and led him toward the wash stall.

While Milo was having a bath, I retrieved Spike from his pen so he could enjoy an hour of freedom before I had to get ready to show. I parked myself in a chair in front of our tent and took advantage of my time alone to sit quietly and visualize my course. When I heard Tom take Milo to the grooming stall to tack him up, I knew it was time to get my show coat and hat out of my trunk.

I checked my pockets to make sure I had my glasses and six vials of saline. While the glasses blocked the wind much of time, they weren't perfect. Twice while jumping Milo during a lesson two days ago, the wind bombarded the side of my face, got into my eye, and pushed my contact off-center. The only thing I could do was pull up, saturate my eye with saline, and eventually blink my lens back into place. Determined to show, I'd convinced Bob and myself that with more saline and less wind, my contact would stay put.

Milo and I got to the warm-up area as the announcer called the last eleven riders in my class. Bob wasn't at the ring yet, so I walked Milo along the rail.

A familiar voice brought a smirk to my face. The high-pitched southern drawl belonged to one of the young women who'd ridiculed me in Middleburg. I could barely make out her figure leaning against the rail.

Good. I'd hoped for the chance to ride against them, and maybe today I could put at least one of them in her place.

"Perfect, you're here." Bob walked up beside Milo and adjusted a strap on his bridle. "Ready to warm up?"

"Yup." I rode Milo into the small ring and picked up a trot.

Bob lowered the rail on one of the fences and Milo and I hopped over it back and forth.

"Ready for something bigger?" Bob asked, already jacking up the height.

Automatically, my shoulders rotated back and I pushed my right leg against Milo's side, asking him for a stronger canter as we rode the same path to the fence.

Set the pace and find the jump. Don't get too comfortable. The show ring's a different breed of cat.

"Really good," I heard Bob say the fifth time we landed from the fence.

I had to admit, I was riding well. Everything Bob and I had worked on the past five months had become second nature to me. I was keeping my eye up, instead of looking down at the fence, and holding my upper body off Milo's neck, instead of collapsing on it when he jumped. I felt strong, confident, and ready to show.

Hopefully my contact will cooperate.

I loosened my hold on the reins and Milo stretched his neck out, long and low, as I walked him in a circle.

"How do you feel?" Bob came up alongside us.

Bob had asked me a similar question when I was getting ready to show in Middleburg. Back then, I'd been so worried about crashing into a fence or getting lost on the course, I was too sick with fear to answer him.

"I feel fantastic," I smiled brightly as we walked toward the ingate.

I was next to go and had to corral my enthusiasm so I could focus on my game plan. As I stared into the ring, I imagined myself riding the course. I pictured every detail along the way and recited my markers in the order I'd need them.

"Are you okay?" Bob asked. "You haven't blinked once in the last few minutes."

"Sorry." I blinked a few times and reached into my pocket for my saline. My eye was already drying out.

"Just concentrating on my course." I tilted my head back and emptied the vial into my eye. Saline dripped down my face and Bob handed me a towel to wipe it away.

"Good luck," he said, taking the towel back and stepping aside.

The rider ahead of me finished and I waited until she was out of the ring before I walked in. I took a deep breath, pushing my heels down and gathering the reins as I let it out. A calm settled over me and I cleared my mind of everything except Milo and the course.

The announcer welcomed us into the ring, but I scarcely heard him. I was too busy listening to the sound of Milo's hooves against the dirt and feeling his back stretch and compress with every step.

I leaned forward slightly and whispered, "Take care of me, M."

My first marker was a telephone pole on the opposite side of the ring. As we walked toward it, I didn't dare look away. I was so focused on it that when we came to the rail, I almost forgot to tell Milo to canter. We passed three more markers before I pulled on the left rein and began our approach to the first fence. Milo's canter was strong, but not too fast. My memory of the ring was spot on, and my efforts were rewarded with a gorgeous first fence.

One down, seven to go.

My next marker was a small tree along the rail, and I began searching for it as soon as we landed from the first jump. The wind was picking up and I could feel my eye growing dryer by the second. I blinked once and then again, trying in vain to produce a few tears.

I looked to the left just in time to see a flash of green leaves. I counted five of Milo's strides, then came to a series of markers pointing the way to the second jump.

Milo picked up his pace as he sighted in on it and I relaxed my grip on the reins, confident that my horse knew what he was doing.

Milo pushed off the ground and I closed my eyes against the wind as we sailed over the second fence. Jumps two and three were lined up against the rail with five strides between them. Milo had already taken three strides when I sensed that my contact was stuck in the corner of my eye. I squeezed my lids together again, as I felt Milo rock back on his hind end and push off over the third jump.

My eye was throbbing, my contact was useless, and I began to panic. I hadn't made a single mistake yet, but I had five fences left and about twenty markers to locate before I was finished.

By some miracle, my lens drifted back into place and stayed there while I found the next four jumps without a problem. Blinking rapidly seemed to help until I approached the last jump. The judges' booth, my final marker for the course, was on my left, and when I turned my head to find it, my contact drifted back into the corner of my eye.

Milo surged forward letting me know we were close to jump eight. I probably should have pulled up, but instead I shoved my heels down, grabbed onto Milo's braided mane, and trusted him to take care of me.

For a fraction of a second, I felt Milo sink down on his hind end and I knew it was time to get into my jumping position. I slid my hands up his neck and raised myself out of the saddle at the exact moment Milo gave a tremendous push and we left the ground.

Bob and Tom were clapping and whooping as I brought Milo down to a trot and exited the ring. My contact lens righted itself, and the first thing I saw was the smile on Bob's face as he looked up at me.

"I don't think you could have ridden any better than you just did," Bob said as he patted Milo's sweaty neck.

I was already dousing my eye with drops and almost choked on the saline running down my cheek.

"That was all Milo," I said wiping my face. "After the first jump, he had to do pretty much everything on his own."

"Well, whatever you or Milo did, you need to do it again."

I walked Milo in a small circle giving him a moment to catch his breath before Bob sent us back into the ring.

We did our best, but after four perfect jumps, my contact slipped off my pupil and I was too far away from the next fence to keep going. I had no choice but to stop mid-course and drench my eye with saline until my lens popped back into place.

Our final four jumps were excellent, but this time nobody clapped or cheered when we were finished.

"That's too bad," Bob said disappointedly. "I thought the glasses were working."

"They are," I said, my tone matching his, "but not enough."

Bob had to help a client at another ring but told me to stick around for the results. "You won't get anything in the second class, but I'd be surprised if you weren't in the top three of the first one."

Three hours later, I was back in Milo's stall feeding him carrots from a ten-pound bag.

A blue and red ribbon hung from his stall door.

"I had a feeling you were going to win that class," an exhausted but happy Bob said as he walked into the stall.

"I still can't believe it," I gushed. "My face actually hurts from smiling. When I first heard it, I couldn't believe it."

After my second course, Milo and I had staked out a shady spot next to the ring and waited for the announcer to read the class results. Resting my back against Milo's shoulder, I fidgeted with my riding gloves as I watched the last horse in the division compete.

"You're such a good boy," I murmured to Milo, whose eyes were half closed.

I envied him for being so relaxed. I was more nervous now than I'd been in the ring.

I was reaching into my pocket for a mint when the loudspeaker buzzed to life. My hand froze and I stopped breathing as the announcer called out the number assigned to each of the top ten riders in the first class.

In a daze, I untied the number from my back and stared at the white, plastic rectangle. The bold, black number was the same one that belonged to the first-place winner.

Did I hear that right? Did they make a mistake? Or was it possible I'd won a class at WEF, beating thirty-one other riders? I was making my way to the awards table to check the results when a new announcement erased any doubt from my mind.

"First place goes to Milo," the loudspeaker blared, "owned and ridden by Lissa Bachner."

A crowd of people surrounded the table, which was piled high with rows of brightly colored ribbons. Since Milo was with me, I couldn't get close to it.

"We'll wait a few more seconds," I said, feeling guilty for keeping my horse at the show. He had to be hot and his tightly braided mane couldn't have been comfortable. As badly as I wanted my ribbon, Milo came first.

I turned around and was about to begin the long walk back to the tent when someone behind me said in a thick, southern accent, "I think this belongs to you."

It was the same voice I'd heard in the warm-up area before I showed. Stopping short and looking over my shoulder, I saw one of the bullies from Middleburg smiling at me.

Stunned, I stared at the ribbon she was holding out to me and when I failed to take it right away, she hooked it onto the side of Milo's bridle.

"Thank you," I finally managed.

She smiled again and told me the person in charge of the awards table had asked her to deliver the ribbon to me.

"I love your horse," she said, patting Milo. "And your first course was amazing. I actually thought I had a chance to win until I saw you guys go."

For the first time I noticed the yellow third-place ribbon in her hand.

Relaxing a little, I smiled back at her and, nodding toward the ribbon, said, "You must have been great. Congratulations."

This was not at all how I'd pictured my moment of vengeance. I'd been dreaming of crushing these women, flaunting my blue ribbons in front of them, and making them admit I wasn't a joke. But suddenly I knew their opinion of me didn't matter. As I stared at the young woman next to me, I realized she and her friends had done me a favor. I thought I needed to prove to them that I could ride as well as they did. I was wrong. The only person I needed to prove that to was myself.

CHAPTER TWENTY-ONE

"Something has to be done about your contact," Bob said, bringing me back to the present.

"I know." I was exasperated.

"I mean it. You could have won both classes today if you hadn't pulled up."

"I know," I said again. "I'm not doing it on purpose. What do you want me to do, Bob? I've tried everything I can think of and I'm fresh out of ideas."

"Well," Bob said as he made his way to the door, "you better think of something. You have two more classes tomorrow and my heart can't take any more of your impromptu pit stops while you're showing."

"*Your* heart," I groused. "What about *mine*?" But Bob was already walking down the aisle and didn't hear me.

On the way home, Linda and I picked up a pizza and sat in the den in our pajamas, watching TV while stuffing our faces.

"I hope you don't mind we're not out celebrating your big win," Linda said as I pulled my third slice of pizza from the box.

"Not at all. I'm not in a celebratory mood, anyway."

"Still can't think of a way to handle your contact?"

I shook my head.

"What are you going to do, show or scratch?" Linda had pushed her plate aside and channel-surfed.

I looked down at my own plate, no longer hungry. "I don't know, and I can't imagine I'll have an answer by tomorrow."

My classes were scheduled to start around noon, but I was too tired to think about my contact lens. All I could do at this point was hope for a miracle.

At least I won a class today, I reminded myself. But, as Bob had said, I could have won the other round as well, which would have given me a strong lead going into the second day of competition.

Don't go down that path. Agonizing over what could have been was a waste of time and energy. Today's classes wouldn't count for much anyway if I had to drop out tomorrow. Unless I found a way to keep my contact in place, I was done showing.

Why does everything have to be so difficult? I fell into bed and buried my face in a pillow. I wanted to scream, but the thin layer of stuffing wouldn't muffle my cries, and I didn't want to frighten Linda or Spike. Instead, I burrowed under the covers, taking my pillow with me, and cried myself to sleep.

At dawn, I woke up feeling defeated by a tiny plastic lens. I didn't bother to dress in my show clothes, but at the last minute I decided to put them in Linda's car. "You never know what can happen," I said, looking down at Spike. "Maybe today I'll get lucky and I won't have to scratch."

We got to the barn around six. Milo was enjoying himself in the paddock and I wandered the tent aisle in search of Tom or Bob. I found them both in the grooming stall.

"What," Bob asked without so much as a hello, "are we going to do about your classes today?" His abrupt tone put me on edge.

Throwing my hands up, I snapped, "You know what, I'm sick of that question, and I don't have an answer. So, I guess I should give up and scratch."

Both men were quiet. Finally in a calm voice, Bob assured me he knew I was doing everything I could to hold my contact still.

"I hate the idea of having you scratch the rest of the division. Especially after you did so well yesterday." Bob took a step forward and put his arm around me.

"Me, too." My voice cracked as I fought back tears.

"Why don't we give it until the last minute before we decide anything?" Bob said, leaving my side. "You don't show until later and I'll let you make the call. If you want to try showing and you think it's safe, then I'll keep you in the division."

"Okay," I said, feeling a little better.

Tom looked at his watch and tapped Bob on the shoulder. "We have to go."

They started to walk down the aisle toward the front of the tent, but Bob stopped and called back, "Just don't put yourself in danger, please. After all, it's just a horse show."

Maybe for you it is, but not for me. Bob probably had hundreds of competitions ahead of him and maybe I did, too. Or maybe not. The only thing I knew for sure is that one day — it could be anywhere at any time — I would go blind, and nothing could be done to stop it. Each and every show mattered deeply to me, because I never knew which one would be my last.

I caught a ride back to our stalls with Tom. He was driving Bob's golf cart and the constant flow of air in my face caused my contact lens to go haywire. Eventually, I closed my eyes and enjoyed the ride.

Tom pulled up in front of the tent and I was surprised to see Ben, our farrier, standing by his truck. I thought he wasn't supposed to shoe the horses for another two weeks.

I looked at Tom but before I could ask, he said, "Milo lost a shoe in the paddock this morning. Sorry, I forgot to let you know. He didn't do any damage to his foot, and we found the shoe, so Ben just needs to tack it back on."

"I'll hold Milo for him." I had a couple of hours before I had to decide whether I was showing. Ben was always good for a laugh or funny story, and I could use the distraction.

Milo rested his chin on my shoulder while Ben shaped his hoof with a rasp. He was Milo's favorite blacksmith, perhaps because he came with a pocket full of treats and was constantly telling Milo how handsome he was.

"How's the show going for you?" he asked after he finished filing Milo's toe.

"We won our first class yesterday," I said proudly.

Ben let Milo put his foot down and looked up at me through his safety glasses. "You won? That's amazing. Congratulations."

I described my second course and the problem with my contact while Ben began the twenty-minute process of re-attaching Milo's shoe.

"That's quite a dilemma you have there," he said when I ended my rant.

"I'm sorry," I said, realizing I'd rambled on long enough for Ben to finish. "You have better things to do than listen to me complain." I paid him and started to lead Milo back to his stall.

"Wait a second," Ben called me back. "You say you've tried glasses, right?"

"They didn't work. They helped a little but not enough."

"Your glasses block the wind from the front but not the side, correct?" he confirmed. Then he reached into his tool bag and pulled out something wrapped in cellophane.

"Give these a try." He handed me a pair of plastic safety glasses identical to the ones he'd been wearing.

The cellophane sleeve crackled as I examined the glasses. The front piece was molded into two rectangles large enough to cover most of my face. I tried them on and was surprised at how snugly they fit. Even the wide sidepieces lay flat against my cheeks. I shook my head from side to side, giving the glasses every chance to move, but they remained flush against my face.

"What do you think?" Ben asked.

"I think," I said slowly, expecting the worst but hoping for the best, "they're definitely worth trying." I must have thanked him a dozen times while he packed up his truck and climbed into the cab.

"It'll be thanks enough if they work. If they do, you and that 'Magic Milo' of yours can win a class for me."

I looked at Milo and back to Ben. "If my contact stays put, every class we win will be for you."

Leaning out the driver's window, he teased, "I'm gonna hold you to that."

I put Milo in his stall and on the way to Linda's car to get my show clothes, I ran into Tom.

"Where are you off to?" he asked.

"I have to get dressed."

"You've decided to show?"

"Yup," I said, with more confidence than I felt.

"All right then. I'll let Bob know and we'll meet you at the ring."

I didn't put the safety glasses on until I got to the warm-up area. The thick plastic frame fit even more tightly against my face when I had my riding helmet on.

"Are they comfortable?" Bob asked, staring at me.

"Not at all," I answered, rubbing the bridge of my nose where the glasses were applying the most pressure. "I'll get used to them."

"If you say so." Bob walked over to one of the jumps and adjusted the height, so I could begin with a smaller fence. "Come on. Let's see if these glasses are worth the permanent dent you're going to have on your nose."

After wearing them for five minutes, my ears, nose and cheeks were throbbing, but my contact lens hadn't budged so I ignored the pain. By the time Milo and I walked through the ingate, I'd all but forgotten about the glasses.

As we cut across the ring to begin the course, I reminded Milo, "Take care of me." His ears twitched and I was sure he understood what I was asking him to do.

My first marker was the leader board at the end of the ring. It was so big, even I could see it. When it was directly in front of me, it was time for Milo to start cantering.

This was my last chance to prove I could hold my own against sighted riders. If my contact wouldn't sit still in this round, I wasn't going to bother with the next one.

Stay focused and positive. As I rode the path to our first fence, the wind picked up and I was sure my contact was going to slip out of place. I told myself to relax, but the tension in my body grew worse and I tightened my grip on the reins. Milo, sensing something was wrong, slowed his canter. We jumped the first fence, but the loss of momentum caused Milo's hind foot to clip the top rail. When it hit the ground, I heard a hollow thump.

The rail would cost me, but there was nothing I could do about it. I had a marker to find and there was no time for me to dwell on my mistake.

"Sorry, M." We needed to pick up our pace, and I hoped his foot didn't sting.

I found my next marker and pressed my heels against Milo's side.

Gray wall, storage shed, bleachers. I followed the trail of objects that would direct me to the next fence.

Now that we were moving faster, the wind beat harder against my face.

Come on ugly glasses. Do your job.

Jumps two and three were excellent, but I still had lots of ground to cover, and my eye was already so dry it was burning.

Nine markers separated us from our next jump, and I cursed the course designer for setting the fences so far apart. The wind was relentless, and I was certain my contact wouldn't hold much longer.

I turned Milo to the right and a gust of wind pelted us.

Here we go again.

I readied myself to be cast into darkness but to my delight and relief, the lens stayed in place when we jumped the next fence.

Holy crap, they're working.

It wasn't time to celebrate yet. We had four fences left. After cantering through a cloud of dust and jumping three of them, my contact lens hadn't budged.

We landed on the backside of the final jump and despite our first fence, I was ecstatic. *Now you can celebrate.* I knew I wouldn't win the class, but I had won the battle. I felt like I'd been at war from the moment I started losing my vision. My contact lens was my latest enemy and it had almost beaten me. But now, because of Ben and his safety glasses, nothing else stood in my way.

When Milo and I left the ring, Bob was waiting at the ingate. As I knew he would, he immediately brought up my first fence.

"You look happy for someone who just had a rail."

"I am happy," I beamed. I pulled the glasses down so they rested on the tip of my nose. Tilting my head back, I squeezed a stream of saline into my eye.

"My contact didn't move once. The glasses work."

"Well, hallelujah," Bob grinned. "It's about time something went your way."

Milo and I returned to the ring and, for the first time in eight months, I felt freed from the burden of blindness. Thanks to my markers, I knew the course and where I was going probably better than anyone, and thanks to my glasses, the wind couldn't push my contact out of place.

Perhaps Milo sensed a difference in me or maybe he was feeling frisky. Whatever it was, when we began to canter, he picked up speed until we were practically at a full gallop as we advanced toward the first fence.

My upper body was loose and relaxed, and Milo and I were in unison when he leapt over the jump. Three strides after landing, we were moving swiftly, and the markers flew by.

Tall tree, short tree, bleachers, red flowers, I sang in my head like lyrics of a song.

We came to a triple lineup of fences, with four strides between the first and second jumps, and only two strides between the second and third. Riders typically misjudge the distance between the fences in a triple, but since I couldn't see, I relied on Milo's rhythm to get me down the line. Milo jumped all three fences in perfect form and adrenaline rushed through me as we neared the end of the course.

Leaderboard, judges' booth, green fence on my right. Each marker materialized as though conjured up by my thoughts.

Milo sprung from the ground, and it felt like we cleared the final jump by a foot.

"Show off," I said, patting him as we cantered a large circle before slowing down and going through the gate to an empty corner of the practice ring. Bob and Tom followed us as we walked by riders waiting to hear today's results.

Milo was breathing hard. I slid off his back and tried to loosen his tight girth, but my hands were shaking so badly I couldn't work the buckles that attached the girth to my saddle.

"I got it," Tom said, coming to my aid.

Bob opened his arms wide. "You're amazing."

Thinking I was about to receive a congratulatory hug, I reached out and leaned forward.

Bob stepped around me and put his arms around Milo's neck.

"You're the best horse ever," he crooned.

Milo's lower lip trembled as Bob gave him a well-deserved scratch under his braids. Eventually, my trainer paid some attention to me.

"I've never seen you ride that well. I'm so proud of you."

"Thank you," I said, turning my face away so Bob wouldn't see me blush.

"How'd you do that?" Tom asked. He'd taken the saddle off and was rubbing a towel over Milo's sweaty back. "I mean..." he paused, "I've seen you get lost walking from the stall to the tack room."

"That only happened once," I laughed.

Bob stepped away from Milo and leaned on the fence rail, several feet from the awards table. "They should be announcing the ribbons any second now."

Milo pushed his head against my chest while I tickled his chin. I'd put the safety glasses in my pocket and Milo sniffed them trying to decide if they were edible. My skin was puckered and painful from wearing the thick frames, but they were my salvation and could have drawn blood for all I cared.

The results for the first class were announced with no mention of Milo and me. *Stupid downed rail.* I kicked myself for making such a crucial error at jump one.

I fed Milo a mint, fussed with his bridle, and wiped dust from my coat. Anything to keep busy while I waited for the results of the second class.

"Relax," Bob said watching me.

The loudspeaker went silent, and I stopped fidgeting, but I was far from relaxed.

Several riders lined up in front of the awards table, congratulating each other as they were handed their ribbons.

"The results are in for the second class," the loudspeaker boomed.

Please. Please. Please.

I silently willed the announcer to start with my number.

"Winning the class…"

I closed my eyes and waited.

Then Milo's name and mine echoed across the show grounds.

"I knew it!" Bob crowed and thumped me on the back.

"Good job," Tom grinned at me and shook his head. "I still don't get how you do that."

I looked at Milo and brimmed with pride. "I love you, M." I kissed his white star and detected a spark of fire in his eye.

Bob pushed away from the rail and pointed to the glasses in my pocket. "You need to buy a hundred of those." Turning on his heel, he added, "I'll get your ribbon for you."

I could see that a woman in a bright red dress blocked his way. As she stepped around him, she held a blue and red ribbon out to me.

"Congratulations," she said. I thanked the woman, who was in charge of the awards, and hooked the ribbon onto Milo's bridle, just below his ear. I admired it and reminded myself to put it aside for Ben.

"We're going to head back," I said to Bob and Tom as I began to lead Milo away.

"You can't go anywhere yet," the woman called to me.

Confused, I circled back around and when I was close enough, I could see she was holding another ribbon in her hand.

"You're our Reserve Champion," she said, referring to the title given to the horse in each division with the second highest total points. She unhooked the first-place ribbon from Milo's bridle, handed it to me, and replaced it with a much larger one. The rosette was red, yellow, and white with long streamers in the same colors. We'd won two classes, but I never imagined we had enough points for a tricolor.

I stepped back and watched in awe as the bright streamers danced in the wind.

Forget the first-place ribbon, Ben. This one belongs to you.

Tom brushed Milo with renewed enthusiasm while we waited for the formal presentation. Several trainers walked over to congratulate Bob, who stood at my side.

We waited by the ingate while the horse and rider with the most points overall, the Division Champion, posed for pictures.

When they were finished, I led Milo into the ring. Our names were announced, and the photographer started snapping pictures. I moved closer to Milo until I could feel his warm body against my back. Center stage was not where I liked to be, and the photographer had to keep reminding me to smile.

Between the gauze eye patches, glasses with Coke-bottle lenses, and my prosthetic eye, I'd been stared at my whole life as if I were a circus freak. Most people enjoyed the awards presentation, but I couldn't wait to be out of the spotlight.

Finally, we were excused. Bob was waiting for us outside the ring.

"You did great," he said. "You should be so proud of yourself."

"Well," I looked up at my trainer, "I am. But I didn't do it by myself. It takes a village, and I couldn't have done this without you and Milo."

Before racing off in his golf cart to help a client at a different ring, Bob took the first-place ribbon from me for safekeeping but left the reserve champion tricolor on Milo's bridle for all to see. I held Milo's reins in one hand and cupped the top of his neck with the other, as we slowly walked side-by-side through the show grounds. When they caught sight of our impressive ribbon, some of the riders we passed smiled and nodded, others said "congratulations." I didn't know any of them, but their acknowledgement made me feel accepted.

I felt like my skin was the only thing keeping me from exploding with happiness. "I must look like the cat that ate the canary," I told Milo as we came to the dirt path to the tent. He was tired and dragged his toes wearily. "You can have a few days off before we start practicing for next weekend," I promised.

Thinking about showing again sent a wave of anticipation through me. Winning was like a drug. I loved the way it made me feel and, like an addict, I wanted more. I stared at the tricolor ribbon and suddenly I had a new goal. *Reserve is nice*, I thought, *but it's only second-best.* I knew I wouldn't be satisfied until I was the top rider and Milo was named Division Champion.

CHAPTER TWENTY-TWO

Bob, Tom, and a couple of Bob's teenage clients and their parents stood shoulder-to-shoulder in front of the tent. As soon as Milo and I came to the end of the path and headed toward them, Bob started clapping and they all joined in, with cheers and whistles punctuating the applause.

"Thank you." I blushed and took a bow.

Milo had no interest in our welcoming committee until someone came forward and offered him a handful of Fritos leftover from her lunch. While he chomped on the corn chips, his admirers encircled, patted, and praised him.

"Milo, you're so good," said one of the girls.

"He's not just good, he's magical," said another.

The horses had Monday off, riding resumed on Tuesday, and a new week of competition began on Wednesday. Once again, Milo and I were scheduled to show over the weekend.

I was now riding six horses a day instead of four, and I spent most of my time in the ring next to our tent. To ensure my day began with a smile, I always rode Milo first.

I didn't see much of Bob until Thursday morning, when he strolled into the middle of the ring, dressed in his show clothes. Milo had just started cantering alongside the rail when I recognized Bob and circled back toward him.

"Look who's come to visit us, M," I said when we reached him.

"I had a little time between classes." Bob unbuttoned his coat and swung it over his shoulder. "You need to jump a little before you show this weekend."

Normally, Bob would have smiled and said hello, but today he was oddly serious, and it made me uneasy. "Is everything okay?"

He ignored my question and walked to one of the jumps a few feet in front of us. "Jump this back and forth a few times," he said distractedly.

I adjusted my safety glasses, walked Milo back to the rail, picked up a canter, and began jumping the fence. Milo and I finished jumping what felt like six superb fences, when Bob's phone rang.

"I'm late, I have to go," he said in the same preoccupied tone he used throughout my lesson.

Something was going on, but obviously Bob didn't want to talk about it. I'd find out eventually, but for now, all I could do was yell, "Thank you," as he ran out of the ring.

I didn't see Bob again until Saturday when he met me at the show. Milo and I got to the ring early so I could go over the course a few more times. We were competing in Ring 6, a smaller ring than the Rost, which meant I had fewer markers to memorize, but they would come up faster.

Bob smiled and said some words of encouragement, but he still seemed preoccupied. At least he was friendly, and I'd take this Bob over the one who was so distant on Thursday.

Our first round was excellent. I found the close quarters of the small ring fairly easy to navigate, though I thought my approach to the first fence could have been smoother. But when I finished the course, Bob assured me, "I don't think it gets better than that."

The perfectionist in me disagreed. When I went back for my second round, I picked up the canter and said softly, "C'mon, M, let's show them how it's done."

I could hear Bob clapping and whooping as Milo and I landed from our last jump. When we left the ring, I spotted him standing on the far side of the practice area, waving me over.

"I was wrong," he said.

"About what?"

He moved to Milo's side and looked up at me. "I didn't think you could do better than your first round, but you just did. You two are on fire today."

I laughed and patted Milo. "Well, I have a secret weapon."

"Don't kid yourself." Bob tugged on my stirrup. "Milo is amazing because you ask him to be. If anyone else rode him, he would just be a good horse. You two bring out the magic in each other."

The results were in and Bob was on his way to the awards table before the announcer had time to declare Milo the winner of both classes. When Bob walked back to us, he held a bright blue ribbon in each hand. "Not bad for a horse nobody wanted and his rider who can hardly see."

"Don't listen to him, M. Everybody wants you."

Bob twirled the ribbons in his hands. "They do now, that's for sure."

I understood what Bob was getting at. The more Milo won, the more valuable he became. I assumed quite a few people were interested in buying him, but Bob kept those conversations to himself. He knew the thought of selling Milo made me ill, and there was no point in discussing it.

Bob was about to hang Milo's ribbons on his bridle, but I stopped him. "I'll carry them."

"Are you sure?"

I nodded and held my hand out to Bob. "I can see them better if I keep them with me."

Bob handed over the ribbons but first let me know he thought I was weird.

I held them up and watched the blue and red streamers unfurl. "I was told I could never ride never again, and I almost believed it. But here's proof that I can, and I like holding onto it."

Later that afternoon, I was working one of Bob's horses in the ring by the tent when I felt raindrops on the back of my neck. *Just a shower* I told myself, but when I looked up at the sky, all I saw was a mass of dark clouds.

Crap. I wheeled the big gelding around and galloped toward the ingate. I slowed down when we neared the stalls and jumped to the ground as a bolt of lightning lit up the sky. One of the grooms met me at the opening at the back of the tent and took the now skittish horse from me.

A deafening *Boom!* rattled the stalls and shook the ground. Heedless of what I could trip over, I ran down the aisle to the front of the tent where Spike's metal pen was out in the open, grabbed my dog, and raced back to Milo. I could hear the rain pounding the fabric roof and, for the first time, I wished we were stabled in an actual barn.

I threw the stall door open and burst in. "It's okay, Milo, I'm here, I'm here," I said breathlessly.

Milo was snacking on a pile of hay. He stopped eating long enough to look up at me lazily, wads of hay hanging out of his mouth, before he dropped his head and continued chewing.

"Really? That's it?" I thought a storm of this magnitude would terrify him, but apparently nothing could ruin Milo's appetite. "Aren't you the bravest boy," I said, patting his shoulder. "Thank you for being so good today," I added, but the storm swallowed my words.

I put Spike down and joined him on a cushy pile of shavings, where we stayed safe and dry until I heard Linda calling my name.

"In here!" I bellowed.

"Let's get out of here!" she yelled back.

I kissed Milo goodbye, picked up Spike, and walked out of the stall into darkness. I blinked a few times, panicking until I realized the tent flaps had been pulled down, blocking any source of light.

"This way," Linda called, and I turned to my left and saw a shadowy figure moving toward the front of the aisle. "We'll have to make a run for it to the car," she said as she pulled the tent flap back and rushed out ahead of me.

I could hardly see anything through the driving rain and had to walk carefully as I followed the sound of Linda's footsteps. By the time I flung myself and Spike into the passenger seat, we were both soaked.

The storm raged the rest of the day. After dinner, when I went to my room to get ready for bed, I could hear coconuts crashing on the patio as the wind whipped through the palm trees.

I should lay out scuba gear instead of riding clothes for tomorrow. I was scheduled to show in the Rost ring and if the rain didn't stop soon, it was going to be underwater.

By morning, the sky was clear, but the show grounds were drenched. Tom was adamant about keeping Milo in his stall while I walked around the ring.

"I'm sorry," he said sternly, "Milo stays here where it's clean and dry, while you go play in the mud."

The Rost wasn't as bad as I thought it would be. Most of the larger puddles were by the rail and would make excellent markers. I trudged through the wet sand and mud, memorizing every detail of each jump and deciding where to start my approaches. Without Milo walking next to me, I felt naked, and I cursed Tom for denying me my companion. But one look at my mud splattered clothes made me realize Tom had been right.

Usually, I roamed the ring, double- and triple-checking the fences until a show official kicked me out. But today, instead of maximizing my time, I left the ring early. My classes were the first of the day and I had less than an hour to get clean, get dressed, and get on.

Tom and Bob were standing by the fence that separated the warm-up area from the Rost when Milo and I arrived.

"Have you watched any of the rounds?" Bob asked when I rode up to him.

I heard poles fall and looked into the ring in time to see a riderless horse careen along the rail.

"That's the third one to hit the dirt," Tom whispered. The fallen rider walked past us toward the gate. She was caked in mud and her pants were soaked, but she didn't look hurt. Someone had caught her horse and was leading him out of the ring.

"Which fence are they having trouble with?" I asked.

Bob pointed to a jump in front of us. "The one with yellow flowers."

Closing my eyes, I pictured the fence and wasn't surprised that riders were falling off. A small puddle in front of it reflected the morning sun. The glare could startle a horse so badly that it would stop in its tracks and throw its rider. To make matters worse, there was a gigantic pool on the landing side of the fence. Unless a horse tested the water first, it had no way of knowing if it was shallow or deep.

I presumed that's why the previous rider fell. Once her horse noticed the water, the frightened animal either landed before he got over the fence and knocked it down, or he tried to clear the puddle and his hind legs caught the rails.

"You're sure I should ride in that mess?" I asked Bob.

"It's up to you, but I don't think Milo will care about the mud," he said.

"We know he likes rolling in it," Tom joked.

It was easy to joke about, but slogging through the mud was hard on both horse and rider, and added one more element of risk to an already dangerous sport.

I thought of all the times I'd pulled Milo out of a field, covered in filth. Then I remembered the two classes I won the day before. I was leading the division in points and I wanted that champion ribbon.

"Okay," I said, turning Milo toward the practice ring to begin our warm-up. "Let's see if my boy likes to jump over puddles as much as he likes to lie in them."

When we entered the ring for our first course, I trotted Milo through the large puddle by the second jump so he would know that it was shallow. Water splashed against his belly and sides, which could make some horses misbehave, but Milo didn't react at all.

We began to canter, and I caught a glimpse of my beige riding pants, streaked with brown water. As I looked for my first marker, I pitched forward and said, "All right, M, let's get dirty."

Heart-shaped puddle, bleachers, ingate, judges' booth. I was so focused on finding the second fence, I forgot about what was waiting for us on the other side of it.

Splash!

A wave of gritty water hit me in the face. I could taste it and feel it on my cheeks. My safety glasses were also covered in muck and wiping them with my wet gloves made it worse.

Just what I need.

I could still see out of the right corner of the right lens and, as long as we were cantering to the left, I could still find markers along the rail. Our jumps were excellent, and I knew we had a good chance of winning the class.

Then I realized the last jump was off my right lead and a splatter of mud blocked my view of the markers on my left. My heart sank a little and I wished Milo could canter in place for a few minutes while I decided what to do.

"Screw it." I yanked the plastic glasses off my face and held them in my right hand.

Come on you stupid contact. You owe me.

Milo and I made it all the way to the final fence before my contact shifted. By then, he was already leaving the ground and I didn't need to see to know we put in a winning round.

Bob and Tom, towels in hand, were waiting for us when we left the ring. They took one look at the slop covering my face and dripping off Milo and roared with laughter.

Bob grabbed his stomach and doubled over. "Fantastic," he wheezed. "I told you he liked the mud."

Their laughter was contagious and by the time Tom had cleaned my glasses and handed them back to me, all three of us were hysterical.

Another horse and rider team fell victim to the second jump, and Milo and I returned to the ring sooner than expected but ready to take on the swamp again.

A clean sweep. That's what the announcer called it when Milo and I walked into the ring to receive the division champion ribbon after winning all four classes. Judges rarely speak to riders during competition, but my judge congratulated us when she left her booth to take a break.

"You know," she said, walking over to me, "every other rider looked petrified as they went around the course. Then you two walk in and look like you're having the time of your lives."

"Thank you so much," I blurted before hugging her.

Luckily, the judge wasn't offended and hugged me back. "That's a special horse you have," she said as she reached up and patted Milo on the nose.

Bob and I decided to give Milo the next week off. After outriding everyone in my division, I thought my competitiveness would ease up during the break.

At least that's what I told myself. Two weeks later, Milo and I were Division Champion again, which sharpened my competitive edge, instead of dulling it. Now that I was the rider to beat, I worked even harder to stay on top.

By the middle of March, we were Division Champions two more times, and Milo was looking a little worn out. Like any athlete, a horse can take only so much pounding, and Bob and I agreed not to show him in the final three weeks of competition.

Almost every day I rode Milo along the canals where we could do whatever we wanted without judges and spectators scrutinizing our every move. We didn't have to be on the watch for speeding golf carts or dirt bikes. The only traffic we encountered were flocks of White Ibis that cleared the way for us as we rode by. Instead of P.A. announcements buzzing in our ears, we heard insects, birdsong, and gators splashing in the canal. After nearly eight months of non-stop training and showing, I gifted both of us with unstructured time in a wide-open space.

Since I was finished showing for the season, my list of horses to ride had grown to seven. One afternoon at the end of March, I'd been cantering for ten minutes in ninety-degree weather when Bob made a rare appearance at the ring.

"Come here!" he called out, and I was more than happy to take a break. "I need to talk to you," he said dully.

Bob was acting strangely again, and I didn't like it. He wouldn't stop me in the middle of riding unless there was a problem. I jumped off the horse and faced my trainer.

"What's going on?" If it was bad news, I wanted him to tell me now and get it over with. Rip the Band-Aid off, so to speak.

Bob sighed and patted my arm. "Give Nicky to Tom and meet me at the front of the tent."

I found Linda and Bob sitting at the little table where we often congregated to swap stories about our day. Linda's computer was in front of her, as it always was, and Bob held Spike on his lap.

"Did I do something wrong?" I asked woefully, already close to tears.

Bob chuckled, "No, not this time." When he told me, in an uncharacteristically soft voice, to "take a seat," I knew the situation was serious.

Bob cleared his throat twice and said, "I was offered a private job in January. It was very tempting, but I turned it down because they wanted me to give up all of my other customers. But we renegotiated, and I've accepted the position and can keep my current clients."

"Oh," I smiled, relieved. "Well, that's not so bad." I slid into the chair next to Linda. "Will you still have time to train me? I know I need more help than most riders, but I've gotten better. I can take fewer lessons."

Linda was shaking her head and I realized I hadn't heard the whole story.

"The job is in Richmond, Virginia," Bob said huskily. "I'll be moving there as soon as the Florida circuit is over."

CHAPTER TWENTY-THREE

For many trainers, a private job is the ideal situation. It's typically a full-time gig with salary and benefits, working for a family with several riders, their own barn, and multiple horses. I wanted to be happy for Bob. He worked hard, was a knowledgeable trainer, and deserved this opportunity and, as his friend, I supported his decision to move 150 miles away from me.

However, as his student, I counted on Bob to do what was best for Milo and me, and his announcement felt like a kick to my gut.

"You're deserting me?" I scowled and stood up so quickly, I knocked my chair over.

So much for being a supportive friend.

"What are Milo and I going to do without you?" I wailed. "I can't move to Richmond." Tears threatened to spill over as I thought about riding without Bob. "Please don't leave me."

I'd been training with Bob for five years and he'd done so much for me, most of all convince me to buy Milo. He'd been the perfect combination of supportive and demanding as I learned how to ride with low vision, and once I figured it out, he adapted his training to my unconventional technique. Milo and I were a quirky pair, and I wasn't sure I could find another trainer willing to take us on.

Bob got up, hugged me tightly, and took a step back. "You'll be fine," he said with conviction. "We'll still see each other, and I'm only a phone call away."

"It won't be the same," I said sadly, wiping tears from my cheeks. "I can't believe this is happening."

"This is not a decision I made lightly." Bob's voice was hoarse. "Try and understand. I need to do this for myself."

"I get it." I threw my hands up in defeat. "I just," I fumbled for the right words, "I'm just going to miss you."

I needed time alone to think. I righted the fallen chair and walked away.

Later that night, while moping in my bedroom, I thought of Rachel Kennedy, a rider and trainer who'd recently moved to a small town thirty miles from Baltimore. I'd heard about her new barn. It was small—only eight stalls—and quiet, on ten acres of rolling fields freshly seeded with Kentucky Blue Grass.

Rachel was known for taking exceptional care of her horses; she made sure they had the finest hay, the best fitting tack, and the cleanest bedding. I followed her career, but our paths hadn't crossed until two years ago, when we briefly stabled at the same barn. Busy as she was, Rachel always spared a few minutes to chat whenever we ran into each other. When my vision began to fail, she noticed my absence and asked Bob about me. He told me how upset she had been to hear I'd stopped riding, and I was moved by her concern.

I didn't see Rachel again until the show in Middleburg. She fully supported my decision to compete, gave me a warm hug, programmed her number into my phone, and made me pinky swear to call her if I ever needed anything.

I couldn't imagine ever using her number. Rachel was a big deal in a world where I was small potatoes, and despite her kindness, I felt inadequate around her.

The next morning, I sat on my bed in my pajamas trying to gather enough nerve to call Rachel and, if necessary, beg her to let Milo and me into her barn. Though I wouldn't be surprised if she refused to take on the responsibility and hardship of training a rider with low vision and her sensitive horse.

I could hear Linda in the kitchen making breakfast and for a second, I considered putting the call off and getting something to eat first.

No procrastinating. Get the phone call over with. Milo needs a place to live.

Wearing glasses on top of my contact and holding a magnifying glass over the phone, I scrolled through the names until I found Rachel's.

She picked up on the first ring, and her friendly "hello" and the small talk that followed helped put me at ease until she asked, "What can I do for you?"

I reminded myself to stay calm, but my voice wavered as I blurted, "Do you, by any chance, have room in your barn for another horse?"

"That depends. Would that horse be Milo?"

I explained the situation, took a deep breath, and concluded, "Milo and I need a new trainer and I really want it to be you."

Even though no more than thirty seconds went by, it felt like minutes before Rachel casually replied, "Sure." I moved the phone away from my face so Rachel couldn't hear me let go of a long, ragged sigh of relief. She was still talking when I put the phone back to my ear. "I'll be back in Maryland by the end of the month. Milo can move in any time after that."

A huge weight was lifted from my shoulders. Saying goodbye to Bob was going to be painful. He was a good friend and I'd grown very attached to him. Plus, I was comfortable with his teaching style. But just as he needed to take care of himself, I needed to do what was best for Milo and me. I was hopeful Rachel would be a good replacement. And I knew when Milo left Florida, he'd be on his way to horse paradise.

Milo was booked on a trailer headed for Maryland before dawn on April 1 and dropped him off at his new home on April 2, 2003. That next morning, Mom, Spike, and I boarded a plane destined for Baltimore.

Before we got to the airport, I'd already received two calls from Rachel. The first came at 7:00 am. Milo had just gotten off the trailer and was settling into his new stall. An hour later, Rachel was on the phone again, this time to let me know that Milo had been turned out in a paddock and was flirting with the mares in the field next to his.

Rachel wanted Milo to have a few days off to rest and get used to his new surroundings. This would give me time to find a driver to get me back and forth from Baltimore to the barn. Between traveling and her hectic schedule, my mom couldn't spare four hours a day six days a week to be my chauffeur.

My first day home, I unpacked, cleaned, organized, and decided I wanted to go back to Florida. Baltimore was cold and rainy. The trees hadn't leafed out yet and piles of dirty snow littered the sidewalks.

It was too depressing to go out and too boring to stay in. I had nothing to do but think about Milo, which was upsetting. Having never been to Rachel's barn, I had no way of picturing where he was or what he was doing.

Finally, my three days in limbo were over and Mom, Spike, and I were on the way to my new barn. Though Mom had hired a driver for me, I didn't want my first trip to Rachel's farm to be with a stranger.

It was unsettling to have no idea where I was going. We turned down roads I didn't recognize, passed buildings I didn't know, and drove through countryside I'd never seen before. Obsessively, I stared out the window, collecting markers and adding them to a new list.

Blue road sign, doughnut shop, fire station.

"It's beautiful out here," my mom said, making a left turn onto a dirt road surrounded by woods.

Unlike Baltimore, the trees out here were covered in bright green leaves that blocked the sun. The deeper into the woods we drove, the gloomier it became.

The car rumbled over a stone bridge and for the first time, I created a marker out of sound, not sight.

"According to these directions," my mom glanced at the paper in her lap, "we should be close."

We came to a hill and, as we reached its crest, the trees thinned, and the inside of the car was bathed in sunlight.

"That must be it, over there." Mom flipped her visor down and veered to the right.

She slowed the car as we drove past paddocks with brown fencing and lush blue-green grass. A large white house stood on the hill overlooking the farm and when we rounded the corner, I could see the barn and ring.

"Well, this is absolutely gorgeous," my mom said as she pulled up next to the stable.

Immediately, Rachel came out to the car to greet us. "Welcome," she said cheerfully. Her long red hair was pulled back in a braid and although she was in her forties, Rachel exuded a youthful energy that made her seem much younger.

As I was introducing her to my mom and Spike, two golden retrievers barreled out of the barn. "Let Spike run around with the other dogs while I give you a tour," Rachel suggested.

Mom and I followed her into the building, which I could now see was dark gray with white trim. Knowing I was in my comfort zone, my mom stayed close by my side but didn't hold my arm. Even so, my steps were tentative so I wouldn't trip on something and fall in front of my new trainer. Before I'd gone too far, Rachel pointed out a dip in the concrete floor that could cause me to stumble. Her thoughtful gesture made me feel safe, and I started to relax.

The barn was remarkably clean and well organized. Nothing littered the aisles; a neatly folded plaid blanket hung on each stall door; every saddle in the carpeted tack room sat on its own rack. In most barns I could smell mildew and dirt. Here, all I could smell was hay, grain, and the citrusy scent of saddle soap.

We stopped at an empty stall, and I marveled at how bright and airy it was. When he heard my voice, Milo started neighing for me. Smiling, I excused myself to go be with my horse. By the time I found him in the last stall on the left, he was banging on the door with his front foot.

Rachel and my mom caught up to me and stood at the stall door laughing at Milo, who was holding on to the front of my jacket with his teeth.

"Is that normal?" Rachel chuckled.

Milo tugged on the nylon until I was flush against his chest.

"There isn't anything normal about these two," Mom said, sounding genuinely perplexed. "I used to think they existed because of each other. Eventually, I realized they exist for each other."

"Don't mind us," I said, my voice muffled by Milo's fur.

"Good grief," Rachel said. "Meet me in the tack room when he lets you go. I want to talk about a few things before you ride."

I pushed Milo away from me and wiggled out from under his head. "Sorry, boy, I have to go, but I'll be back in a few minutes."

Mom and Rachel were already seated in the overstuffed leather chairs in the tack room when I got there and took my place in the empty chair between them. Flipping through the pages in a binder, Rachel went over the cost of board, farrier, and any vet work Milo may need. Her fees were similar to Bob's, but the numbers still made me cringe.

"Now that you know what I need from you," she said, setting the binder aside, "what is it that you need from me?"

To me, the answer seemed obvious. "Besides taking care of Milo and training me, you mean?"

"I'll rephrase." Rachel sat forward in her chair. "My job is to help you achieve your goals. I can't do that unless you tell me what they are."

I'd been thinking about something, but I was hesitant to tell Rachel or my mom about my newest ambition.

"I want to try showing in the Amateur Owner division," I said apologetically, ashamed of having to ask my mother and trainer for more and more help to take my riding to the next level.

Like the Adult Hunters I competed with in Florida, the Amateur Owners were non-professionals over the age of eighteen. But the Amateurs were nationally ranked, had to own the horses they rode, and instead of jumping up to three feet, their fences maxed out at 3'6".

There's no margin for error when jumping three-six, and I expected Rachel to shoot me down right away. Instead, she asked, "Do you see well enough to jump that big?"

"No," my mom and I answered in unison.

"The courses are more technical than what you're used to," Rachel said dismissively. "I know it's only six inches higher than what you're jumping now, but believe me, those six inches make a big difference." She leaned back in her chair and folded her arms across her chest, a clear sign that our conversation was over.

"I don't think it's a good idea," my mom piped in.

Resigned, I slumped in my chair. "Okay."

Rachel got up and asked one of the grooms to put my tack on Milo. She and Mom watched while I walked, trotted, and cantered him along the rail in the small sand ring for about twenty-five minutes. The early spring day felt chilly to me, but Milo enjoyed the cool weather and didn't need any encouragement to pick up his pace.

When we were finished, my mom went to the car to make a phone call and, while Milo was getting untacked, Rachel pulled me aside.

"I'll make a deal with you," she said. "If you and Milo are champion at Capital Challenge, then I'll consider letting you move up to the Amateurs."

"Really?" I said dubiously. "You want me to be champion at the most competitive horse show of the entire year?"

"Well, yeah, don't you want that, too?"

"Sure, but I never thought I'd be good enough to show there."

"Sorry," she smiled wickedly. "That's what it's going to take. You have to prove to me that you're ready to jump bigger. I want to help make all of your dreams come true, but I also need to keep you safe."

Granted, I'm a good rider, but to be champion at the Capital Challenge Horse Show, I needed to be better than good. Only the top riders in the country bothered to enter that show. "Where the Champions Meet" was its slogan.

I feared my Adult Hunter division would be especially competitive. It wasn't unusual for riders who regularly competed in the Amateur Owners to enter in the Adults at Capital Challenge. They wanted a tricolor so badly they were willing to compete in an easier division to get one.

My chance of making it to the Amateurs was slim, but I agreed to Rachel's terms.

"Okay, I'll give it my best shot, but if I'm not champion, don't expect me to give up on the three-six."

"Understood," Rachel said, and we shook on it.

I had nothing to lose and, perhaps, much to gain. I'd overheard Rachel teach a few lessons at my old barn and I liked her approach to training. She was a confidence booster; her critiques always ended on a positive note. She took plenty of time with her students and, from what little I'd heard, she explained herself well. Maybe by the time Capital Challenge rolled around six months from now, I'd be riding so skillfully that a champion ribbon would be within reach.

Rachel's business was smaller than Bob's, and Milo and I received lots of attention. I must say, I enjoyed it.

Two days a week, Rachel gave me jumping lessons. The other four days I hacked Milo on my own. Most trainers wouldn't even notice, but Rachel stopped whatever she was doing to watch me walk, trot, and canter on the flat, and shout out a few pointers.

"Raise your chin," she reminded me again and again, so I wouldn't lean forward and throw off my balance.

"Right rein, right rein," she called out over and over, so I wouldn't favor my left, making Milo look to the left instead of straight ahead.

I'd been riding with Rachel a little over a month when she poked her head into the tack room one morning and asked, "Is it your left or right eye that's fake?"

Shutting the lid on my tack trunk, I turned around and pointed to my prosthetic. "Left one, why?"

"I want to try something," was all she said as she backed out of the doorway.

I wasn't scheduled to have a lesson, so I took Milo for a leisurely ride. The sun was out for the first time in days and as I rode Milo down the gravel driveway to the ring, I glimpsed the meadow behind it. Compared to the small enclosure filled with sand and dirt, the sprawling hillside, thickly carpeted with grass and purple clover, looked like an oasis.

"Isn't that heavenly, M?"

I'd check with Rachel first, but I didn't think she'd mind if I rode Milo in the field. Horses need a change of scenery as much as people do and trotting up and down the grassy hill would help strengthen Milo's muscles.

Rachel was jumping one of her horses, a young mare named Winnie, and from what I could see, they were having some issues. For a better view, Milo and I walked into the ring and stood in a corner, out of the way.

Aiming for one of the fences, Rachel cantered past us but circled in front of it as though, at the last second, she changed her mind. After her second time circling, she jumped the fence, but her timing was off.

Rachel rarely made mistakes when she was on a horse. I cringed as she approached another jump at an angle instead of in a straight line. She was so off-center, her horse struggled to clear it, and she pulled up after they landed and walked toward me.

"Are you okay?" I asked.

"I don't know how you do this." Rachel sounded annoyed and Winnie didn't look particularly happy either. Her steel gray body was covered in white foam, and I could hear her teeth grinding against the bit in her mouth.

"How I do what?"

"I've got my left eye closed," Rachel said, as though that explained everything.

She stopped in front of me and loosened the reins, and Winnie stretched her neck out toward Milo to greet him. "I'm riding with only one eye."

"On purpose?" I searched Rachel's face for signs of trauma or infection. Her eyes didn't look red or swollen, but I wasn't close enough to be sure.

"Yes," she chuckled. "I've got my left eye closed, so I have a better idea of what it looks like for you when you ride."

"Oh, okay." I sat back in my saddle, amazed. No one else had ever tried to put themselves in my position. I was wowed by Rachel's compassion and her willingness to go to any length to make me a better rider.

"Well," I cocked my head and grinned, "what do you think?"

"I think it's hard," she said emphatically, "and I've never been so happy to have two good eyes in my head."

Milo turned his neck and looked back at me as I shook with laughter. "You get used to it."

I heard a tractor engine kick to life at a neighboring farm and it reminded me to ask Rachel about riding in the field. She thought it was a great idea, and we parted ways when we left the ring. Winnie's hooves crunched against the gravel on her way back to the barn, while Milo made the tall grass on the path to the meadow swish as he moved through it.

Though thrilled to be training with Rachel, I was constantly supervised, and sometimes I just wanted to goof off with my horse. I decided we should skip the hill work and simply enjoy each other's company.

Milo chose to walk along the path that ran the length of the meadow. There was nothing but open land to our right and woods to our left. The massive trees formed a silent wall of green until the breeze brought it to life. Branches swayed and creaked; leaves rustled and floated to the ground.

The tranquil setting was interrupted by a loud crack and the sound of a creature running through the foliage. Milo stopped short and sniffed the air wildly. I took a deep breath and caught a whiff of damp dirt and newly cut grass. Something was out there, and it was spooking my horse. Milo's tail went up and he arched his neck to make himself look bigger and more powerful. His slow walk turned into a fast prance, and I grabbed onto his mane in the nick of time as he took off up the hillside.

"Yah!" I yelled in his ear, pretending I was a cowgirl, and Milo charged to the end of Rachel's land where I was forced to pull him up. As soon as I did, he calmed down and the only hint of our exhilarating race across the field was my pounding heart and his heavy breathing.

"It's nice to know you still have some natural instincts left in you," I teased Milo. "Although, I'm pretty sure we just ran away from a squirrel."

Milo walked down the hill slowly, stopping every few steps to eat some grass. Occasionally he would look back at me with his soft, brown eyes, and I would smile and tell him how much I loved him.

The barn was in sight which, for me, meant we were close. Before we got any farther from the field, I twisted around so I had a fresh picture of it in my head. Like so many other images I'd committed to memory, I tucked this one away for safe keeping.

The next week, Rachel and I left for my first show with her, the Quentin Horse Show in Pennsylvania. Spike slept in the back seat the entire three-hour trip while I grilled Rachel about her early show career — competing on ponies when she was four years old — and how hard she had to work for several of her horses to become number one in the country. She'd been to all of the shows I'd only heard about, and she knew everyone in the horse business.

I was enjoying our conversation so much that before I knew it, we were pulling up to the barns at Quentin.

The facility was older and much smaller than Wellington and well-worn in comparison. There wasn't much to the show grounds, and when Spike and I finished surveying the two rings, small vendors' area, and clubhouse, we met up with Rachel as she was leaving the show office.

On our walk back to the barn, I learned that the show used to attract more entries but over the years, it had gotten smaller and smaller.

"As of right now, there are only ten other entries in your division." Rachel's tone was a touch sad as she added, "I'm not sure how much longer the show will be here."

It had been almost three months since my final performance at Wellington, and the smaller division here didn't bother me a bit. In fact, I was glad to be riding against fewer competitors. Showing takes finesse and timing that can't be practiced at home, and I was out of competing shape. I was even having a tough time memorizing the ring and keeping my markers straight. Normally, this was easy for me, but my brain must have grown lazy during my break from showing.

The number of competitors may have been low, but the competition turned out to be intense. After the first day, another rider and I were essentially tied. On the second day, a third rider upped her game and the three of us battled for champion and reserve. Thanks to a faultless course, Milo and I won the second class and eked out champion by a point.

Rachel was ecstatic and her enthusiasm was contagious. She danced up and down the aisle by our stalls waving my champion ribbon like a flag. I was bent over with laughter, but that didn't stop Rachel from grabbing my hand and dragging me to Milo's door.

"You are the best horse ever." Rachel pointed at Milo and held up the ribbon. "And you," she said turning to me, "ride better at the show than you do at home."

Milo wanted attention and pressed his nose against the steel bars on his door. I gave him a mint and took a seat on the tack trunk next to his stall.

"I know. I focus better under pressure."

Rachel sat down next to me and put an arm around my shoulders. "I'm so proud of you."

I smiled wearily. The past two days of showing had drained me mentally and physically.

Rachel got up and held out my ribbon. "You're officially on your way to the Amateurs." She let the ribbon drop into my lap. "We just need to shake the rust out of you, and you'll be in good shape for Capital Challenge."

I had plenty of time for that. Capital Challenge was three months away, and between now and then I was scheduled to show at six other venues.

CHAPTER TWENTY-FOUR

That summer, I had more fun riding and showing than ever before. Milo and I were winning consistently, which had a lot to do with it, but so did my growing friendship with Rachel.

When we were on the road, I was almost totally dependent on her and, whether she liked it or not, we were inseparable. She was my driver, social planner, and dinner companion, but never once did she make me feel like a burden. And if someone else invited her out, she always asked me to tag along. When I won, we celebrated, and if I had a bad day, we found something else to be happy about.

Not that we had many bad days. The winning streak Milo and I started in Florida continued. By the end of the summer, we'd competed in seven shows and been Division or Reserve Champion at all of them.

"Don't these count for anything?" We were leaving for Capital Challenge in two days, and Rachel and I were in the tack room repacking the trunks with everything we'd need for the show. In one hand, I held a bag full of blue and red ribbons and in the other, I held seven giant tricolors. I placed my awards on the counter that served as Rachel's desk. "Milo and I won some big classes this summer. You're really going to stick to your guns about Capital Challenge?"

Rachel barely looked up from the trunk she was organizing. "Yup."

"So, if I'm not champion there, I can't do the Amateurs?" I stared at her with my hands planted on my hips.

She added some of her own ribbons to my pile and looked over her shoulder at me. "That's correct."

"Fine." I stomped out of the tack room before she had a chance to say anything else. My legs, on autopilot, took me straight to Milo's stall where I picked shavings out of his mane and tail while quietly venting my frustration.

"We've been champion or reserve every time we showed this year." I watched a handful of shavings float to the ground. "Why can't that be enough? I don't even want to go to this show." I kicked at a pile of hay and felt badly about lying to Milo. In all honesty, I was looking forward to competing at Capital Challenge. But I was nervous, and the deal I'd made with Rachel wasn't doing anything to ease my anxiety.

I leaned my back against Milo's stomach, and he curled his neck around me, sniffing my jacket pockets for treats. "Hold on." The empty, plastic wrappers crinkled as I rifled through them in search of treasure. "Voila," I said and plucked a mint from the bottom of my pocket.

Rachel and I spent Wednesday morning cleaning out her RV. Instead of staying in a hotel near the show, we would be living out of her deluxe 5th wheel camper. Lucky for us, Capital Challenge was held at the Prince George's Equestrian Center in Upper Marlboro, MD, only thirty-five miles from Rachel's farm. I was shocked when Rachel told me that several trainers on the West Coast were flying dozens of horses east for the prestigious competition, to the tune of $6,000 per horse.

This was my first time showing at Capital Challenge and, as we drove onto the grounds, I stared out the window at the ornately decorated tents. It was the first week of October and pots of mums, bales of straw, and scarecrows adorned the entrances.

"It looks like a fall festival," I said as we pulled into the parking lot closest to our tent. Rachel had to go to the show office to pick up our numbers and, rather than stay by myself in the car, I went with her.

An old racetrack separated the stabling area and the show rings, and as we walked across the packed dirt, I caught my first glimpse of the show's crowning jewel.

The indoor ring was in an immense, fish bowl-shaped arena. When it wasn't filled with horses, I imagined rock stars, gymnasts, and basketball players in their stead.

An enclosed, concrete ramp led to the ring on the ground floor. Spike and I followed Rachel down the steep ramp on a path of thick, rubber mats, laid out to prevent the horses from slipping. Very few shows had an entrance like this, and I found it unnerving. It was claustrophobic and potentially dangerous. A single misstep and a horse could go down.

I'm glad I'm not showing in here.

My eye had trouble adjusting to the lighting and I couldn't see much until we got to the show office at the base of the ramp. While Rachel went in to take care of business, I stayed by the ring to watch a few rounds. I blinked several times and saw two perfectly groomed dark horses—a chestnut and a bay—by the white ingate. Their riders chatted easily with one another as they waited for their turn, and even though they were pros, I wondered how they could sound so calm. My stomach was filled with knots, and I wasn't even showing.

Creak! The ingate swung open and a tired looking gray horse walked out as the flashy chestnut with a white blaze and two white socks strutted in. The announcer broke into the music playing over the P.A. system to introduce the chestnut. When the music came back on, a country song, *Beer for My Horses,* was playing, and the irony of it made me smile. Nothing short of Dom Perignon would do for my steed.

Five more horses completed their rounds, and I was beginning to worry I'd missed Rachel leaving the office. I spun around to make sure I hadn't strayed too far just as she walked out the door.

"Let's go," she said happily. "The horses should be here any second and I want to get on and get going."

Two days later, I woke up at 5:00 a.m. and couldn't fall back asleep. Spike and I were snuggled together in the warm twin bed in a little room in the back of Rachel's camper. I rubbed his belly while I tried to decide what to do next. Fifteen minutes later, I heard Rachel's alarm. Smelling coffee brewing, I threw a sweatshirt over my pajama top and stumbled tiredly into the kitchen.

"What are you doing up?" Rachel asked, filling a mug for each of us.

"Couldn't sleep." I sat across from her at the small, round kitchen table.

"Why not?"

"Nerves, I guess."

Rachel put her mug down, looked at me, and tilted her head to the side. "What are you so nervous about? Is it our deal that's driving you crazy, or are you losing sleep over something else?"

"It's not about our deal. I watched the Amateur Owners yesterday, and now I'm not so sure I want to move up to the bigger jumps. I saw some of the country's best riders crash and burn, and one was taken away in an ambulance."

I got up and took my mug to the sink. "Here's my problem. Milo and I couldn't be better prepared. He's in the best shape of his life and so am I. But what if our best isn't good enough here. If I manage to win, then I'll be known as a great rider on a great horse. But if I don't, I'll just go back to being a good rider for someone who's blind. And that's the last thing I want defining me."

Rachel looked at her watch and got up from the table. "I have to get dressed," she said, climbing the steps to her bedroom. At the top, she turned around and, with her hands on her hips, asked, "Why are you so worried about the other riders in your division, when they're the ones who should be worried about you?"

I went back to my bedroom and thought about what Rachel said.

The tightness in my gut began to ease and the tension headache I'd had for days started to go away. Rachel believed in me and made me realize I should believe in myself. There was no reason I couldn't win here. The competition may be fierce, but so was I.

"I'll see you in a couple of hours," Rachel said, opening the door and stepping out into the darkness.

Feeling better, I leaned against my pillows and closed my eyes. When I opened them again, it was light out and time to get ready to show.

Normally, I would have gotten up earlier to walk from jump to jump to find my markers, but by 5:30, the small show ring was already packed with riders getting their horses used to the layout. Rachel had forbidden me to take a single step in the ring, fearing I'd be trampled.

Luckily, I had an hour before my class began, and I used that time to walk along the rail and pick out whatever markers I could from outside the ring. Mums, straw bales, and scarecrows liberally decorated the jumps, making it much easier than I expected to spot landmarks to guide me through the course.

The class before mine was almost over and I chose a sunny spot next to the practice ring where I waited for Milo and Rachel. Horses and grooms walked along the worn path directly in front of me, but only one of them caught and held my attention.

Milo was a sight to behold as he walked alongside Emilio, one of Rachel's head grooms. The braider had taken extra care to make sure each braided knot lay perfectly straight along the length of his neck. His coat was so shiny, it was almost iridescent, and I saw several people turn around to admire him.

I waited to get on until Rachel told me it was time and as I slid my boots into the stirrups, someone called my name.

My mom and her sister, Karen, were walking toward me, and I felt the last bit of anxiety melt away as I leaned down from Milo's back and hugged them the best I could.

"You made it," I smiled broadly at them.

I hadn't seen my mom in two weeks, and it had been at least a month or two since I'd spent any time with my aunt. I wanted to stay with them for a few more minutes, but Rachel was waiting for me in the warm-up area.

They wished me luck, and Aunt Karen, who wasn't that fond of horses, patted Milo's neck and told him to be a good boy.

After we jumped a few fences, Rachel said, "You're ready. Let's go."

While Milo and I waited for our turn, Emilio painted Milo's hooves with dark oil, brushed his legs, and wiped off my boots. I adjusted my safety glasses so they fit tightly against my cheeks, and listened to Rachel describe how she wanted me to approach each fence and, above all, keep my chin up.

"Remember," Rachel said softly, "you're the one they need to beat."

We entered the ring and everything went still, as if the Earth held her breath. Music played overhead but the only sound I heard as we approached the first jump was the steady three-beat rhythm of Milo's canter.

One, two, three. One, two, three.

Milo's strides were in perfect unison, their length and pace unchanging from one to the next. We cruised along the rail until we came to my first marker. Silver bleachers, at least five rows high and full of spectators, sat about fifteen feet from the ring.

My first fence is the most crucial. I think of it as the make-it-or-break-it fence. If it's a disaster, the rest tend to follow suit. But, if we nail it, I can continue with confidence knowing Milo and I are in the zone.

Inhaling deeply, I waited until I was past the bleachers, counted to three, tightened my fingers on my left rein, and steered Milo off the rail. At least fifteen strides separated us from our target, but it was too far away for me to see, so I had to rely on my horse to find it.

In between counting our steps, I reminded myself to be patient. *Let the fence come to you.* I had just counted our twelfth stride when, to my immense relief, Milo's ears angled forward, and I knew he'd sighted in on the jump.

"Hold on, M," I breathed, seconds before I, too, saw it and the fiery red and orange mums lined up in front of it.

We were dead center of the fence, and I gave myself a mental pat on the back. The rest was up to Milo. I braced my hands against his neck and shifted myself into jumping position as he propelled us into the air.

Milo jumped way up and over the fence, and as he reached the top of his arc, I was so focused on the rail ahead of us, I hardly felt our smooth landing on the other side of the jump.

We passed a scarecrow and as I asked Milo for more pace, I noticed that his canter felt stronger and more rhythmical than ever.

Milo had brought his A game today and we met our next four fences so perfectly, they took my breath away.

Back on the rail, I was looking for one of my last markers, a tower of straw bales, when a little voice in my head whispered, "You're going to win."

A shiver went through me, and I knew the voice was right. So far, every approach, fence, and landing had been superb, and we had one fence left to go.

We flew by our final marker and Milo picked up speed.

We will win this.

Then, I saw her, standing outside the ring and leaning against the rail. My mom was so close, I could have reached out and touched the top of her head. She was smiling but her hands were clasped tightly together as though she were nervous.

I wished I could tell her not to worry but, in a flash, we galloped by her.

We landed from our final fence and the world that had been so calm exploded around us.

Our exit from the ring was accompanied by applause, whoops, and whistles unlike any I'd received before. We were surrounded as soon as we were out of the ring and the next rider to compete barely had room to squeeze past us.

"Jump down," I heard Rachel say urgently and I immediately dismounted. Emilio took Milo from me and started to lead him away.

"Wait," I said, and began to follow them, but Rachel put a hand on my shoulder, stopping me.

"He needs to get cleaned up," Rachel chuckled. "You're definitely going back in for a ribbon." She threw her arms around me and hugged me tightly. "I knew you could do it."

"It was really good, wasn't it?" I started to laugh. "It felt incredible. Like we were dancing."

"That's what it looked like." My mom came toward me, her arms opened wide, and she and my aunt squeezed me in a group hug.

"I don't even know what I'm looking at and I thought it was amazing," Karen said, making us all laugh.

Emilio brought Milo back to me, his body wiped clean, his feet darkened with oil, his tail brushed out, his coat smooth and shiny. All of us, except Milo, waited anxiously for the class to finish. While I gnawed a hole into my leather glove, Milo rested his chin on top of my helmet and fell asleep.

"Sorry, M," I said, moving my head and waking him up. "I'm too nervous to stand still." I led Milo away from the ring and walked in a small circle, putting some distance between us and the other riders and horses.

The P.A. system began to crackle and a man in a red hunt coat walked to the center of the ring. I froze and held my breath. The announcer came on, "In this order, please." Riders hoping to place in the class started leading their horses to the ingate, but I couldn't move.

The numbers were called, and had I not gone weak in my knees, I probably would have jumped for joy.

Milo and I won the class.

Tears rolled down my cheeks and Rachel had to come get me because I was in shock and, for a moment, forgot how to walk.

With four sharp blasts on his trumpet, the man in the hunt costume called the top ten competitors to the ring. Rachel gently pushed me forward, and the other winners who were crowding the gate cleared a path so Milo and I could lead the way. The awards coordinator — a woman in a flowing beige dress — hooked a blue ribbon onto Milo's bridle and positioned us in the center of the ring, apart from the other nine riders. After receiving their ribbons, they filed out, leaving Milo and me alone in the spotlight. The woman joined us and draped a red, satin ribbon around my neck. I didn't notice the round medallion hanging from it until it thumped heavily against my show coat.

"And now, let me introduce you to our class winner," bellowed the announcer, the applause growing as he recited our names. The woman gave me a polite hug and had me stand by Milo's left shoulder to pose for the photographer.

In theory, a winning horse is supposed to stand still and look straight ahead, neck stretched out, ears up. But Milo had a mind of his own. He started chewing on the ribbon around my neck. When I brushed him away, he started licking the back of my show coat. When I shrugged him off, he pressed his front teeth against my shoulder, a sign of endearment between horses but a real headache for the photographer who finally gave up and told us we should go.

Our second round was almost as good as the first, but I could tell that Milo was running out of steam. He jumped slightly out of form over the last fence and the tip of his toe lightly tapped the top rail. The barely audible tick was enough to put us in second place.

We were leading in points but to clinch the championship, I needed a ribbon in the third and final class, the flat class. All I had to do was walk, trot, and canter to the left and then to the right while the judge scored us on how well Milo moved.

Milo was a good mover and we'd won our share of flat classes. But this division was full of exceptional movers, and I tried not to get my hopes up. When the class was completed, we all rode into the center of the ring and waited for the winners to be announced.

The top four horses were called, and my heart began to sink.

Please, please, please.

The rider next to me picked up fifth place and I began to feel queasy.

Oh, thank God.

My number rang out and I'd never been so happy to come in sixth.

"Thank you so much," I said, taking a green rosette from the woman who'd been handing out ribbons all morning.

"You're most welcome," she smiled up at me. "Give us a minute to clear the ring before you come back in for your champion ribbon."

I was shaking by the time I got off Milo. My mom had to help me stand while Emilio and Rachel got him ready for our biggest win ever.

When they handed Milo back to me after his makeover, we started feeding him treats. The menu featured root beer barrels and butterscotch buttons from me, baby carrots from my mom, peppermints from Emilio and Rachel, and a big Red Delicious that Aunt Karen retrieved from the car. Milo went from hand to hand, taking bites as if he were helping himself at a buffet. What he couldn't chew, he stuffed in his cheeks, and each time he took a bite, bits of his stash flew out of his mouth.

It was time for me to return to the ring and Emilio scrambled to clean up Milo again. After the woman draped a blue, red, and yellow sash around Milo's neck and another medallion around mine, I leaned forward and kissed his face above his muzzle.

"You did it, M," I said softly. I stepped back to admire the horse who made the impossible possible for me. He made me get out of bed. He made me want to ride. He made me win.

The announcer asked the crowd to join him in congratulating us, and suddenly the ring came alive. The photographer snapped pictures from every angle, the awards crew filled my arms with gifts, and the cheering swelled with every mention of Milo's name over the P.A. I felt proud of myself, proud of my horse, and so grateful to my mom and Rachel.

Remember this feeling because it may be the happiest I'm ever going to be.

When the ceremony was over, Rachel met me at the ingate and linked her arm around mine. "You are always going to be the one to beat. Never forget that, especially next year when you're jumping three-six. A deal's a deal after all, and I'd say you earned it."

CHAPTER TWENTY-FIVE

I got home from Capital Challenge the second week in October and hung Milo's champion sash on the wall in my bedroom. It was the last thing I saw before going to bed and the first thing I looked at in the morning. It made me think of everything Milo and I had accomplished and reminded me to have faith in myself.

Milo was given four days off before we resumed our riding schedule. I was looking forward to January when we'd be leaving for Florida, although instead of Wellington, Rachel preferred showing in Ocala. I'd heard Ocala was friendlier and less pretentious than Wellington, but it was farther north, and the weather could be unpredictable.

Ocala would be the backdrop for my debut in the amateur owner division and I was having mixed feelings about jumping the bigger fences. Lately Milo was jumping so high over three-foot fences that I had to struggle to hold myself in position. If my legs were going to hold me tight in the tack over three-foot-six, I'd have to whip myself into better shape.

I removed the stirrups from my saddle, took the stairs instead of the elevator to my condo, and increased the length of Spike's walks. I lost a few pounds, but I didn't feel any stronger.

I'd never used the gym in my building's basement, and the idea of fumbling with exercise equipment while my neighbors watched made me uncomfortable. But one day in early December, I got up the nerve to check it out and was relieved to have it to myself. The smallish room was furnished with a treadmill, a set of weights, and a tall piece of equipment resembling a guillotine. Vowing to avoid that one, I hopped onto the treadmill.

Every day after I got home from the barn, I changed into my workout clothes and went down to the gym. Not once did I have to share the space with another person. After two weeks, I could feel the difference in my legs, and when Milo jumped, I wasn't coming loose.

Right before Christmas, I had a lesson with Rachel. When we finished, I dropped the reins and let Milo walk where he wanted. He meandered around the ring trying to eat the fake flowers. When that didn't pan out, he found Rachel in the middle of the ring and stood next to her, begging for attention.

"Do you feel ready to start the Amateurs in a few weeks?" Rachel asked, looking up at me.

We jumped a lot of fences during the lesson, and I felt firmly rooted to my saddle the whole time. "I'm ready," I said with a triumphant smile. "I just hope I'll be able to stay on over the three-six jumps. I've felt so loose lately. The cold weather must be affecting my muscles."

Rachel put her hand to her mouth, trying to stifle a laugh.

"How big do you think these fences are?" she asked, pointing to our practice course.

I studied the fences closest to me. "I don't know," I shrugged. "Three feet, maybe a little bigger."

Rachel started to laugh so hard she had to hold onto Milo's neck for support. "I don't know how to tell you this," she wheezed, "but you've been jumping three-six for a month."

"No way." I picked up the reins and rode Milo over to one of the jumps. "Huh," I grunted. Standing this close to it, the fence did look bigger than I thought it was. I turned Milo around and walked him to another jump. There was no question, this fence was gigantic, and I looked back at Rachel dumbfounded.

"I guess that explains why I couldn't hold on over the jumps." I chuckled and walked Milo to the ingate where Rachel was now standing.

"I thought you knew," she grinned.

I shook my head and looked back at the course. "I had no idea. Unless I'm right next to them, I can't tell how high they are."

"So," Rachel started to walk to the barn with Milo close behind, "now how are you feeling about the Amateurs?"

We reached the barn entrance and I patted Milo before sliding off him. "Fantastic, now that I know I've already been jumping three-six for a month."

Rachel and the horses left for Ocala on New Year's Day. I met them a few days later after ringing in 2004 with my mom at her house in Florida.

At first, I had a hard time believing Ocala and Wellington were on the same planet, much less in the same state. The show grounds were limited to two colors, brown and dark brown. The trees, fences, and paddocks were brown. There was dirt everywhere, very little grass, and no flowers except for the fake ones in the ring.

I depended on contrasting colors to define the shape of things. With its monochrome palette, nothing at the horse show stood out to help me go anywhere. I'd have to get used to being lost until I learned how to distinguish one place from another by its sound or smell.

Spike and Milo took to Ocala much faster than I did. The only water on the property came out of a hose, so I didn't have to worry about gators and Spike was freed from his pen and leash. Milo liked the cooler weather and, when he wasn't showing, he stayed at a barn down the road that Rachel had rented, away from the commotion and confinement of the horse show.

The day before I was set to show, Spike and I hung out on a hill next to the main ring where the professionals were competing over 3'9" and 4' fences. Rachel had ordered me to watch them so when it was my turn, 3'6" wouldn't look so bad. Halfway through a class of four-footers, I shuddered when I saw a dappled gray "swim" over the last fence, his front legs paddling the air as his back legs kicked out.

"How are you doing?" Rachel was walking up the hill behind me. "Do you feel better about your fences now?"

"This has definitely been helpful, but I'm still a little nervous."

"That's okay. When you're finished, come hop on Milo. I found an empty ring for you to lesson in."

We watched a round together and compared notes about what we did and didn't like about each horse. She went back to our tent, but I stayed until the class was over, then re-traced my path to the stalls where Milo was tacked up and waiting for me.

I checked Milo's girth before accepting a leg-up from Emilio, while Rachel loaded Spike into her golf cart. "I'll drive slowly so you can follow us," she said. Following was not one of my strong points, but I trusted Rachel not to lose me.

"Come on, M!" Rachel had to shout to be heard over the cart's engine. Milo trailed her as she dodged other human and horse traffic. Our small caravan came to a halt in front of a medium-size ring surrounded by majestic oak trees dripping with wispy necklaces of Spanish moss. These trees were the best feature of the landscape and the only one I could see. When the sun hit the leaves, they turned lime green. And when the wind blew through the moss, it swayed like dark gray plumes of smoke. I took a moment to savor the oaks' elegant beauty before joining Rachel in the ring.

Milo and I warmed up as Rachel set some fences. As we began to canter, I heard someone trotting up the path toward us. Without slowing down or saying a word, the rider entered the ring and started working her horse on the flat. I cantered Milo in a small circle until Rachel told me to start jumping. By then, the other rider was cantering, and I kept looking over at her.

"Don't worry about her, she'll stay out of your way," Rachel predicted. "I'll make sure she knows where you're going."

Toward the end of the lesson, Rachel raised the jump in the middle of the ring to 3'6" and said, "Go ahead." I had plenty of room to establish a rhythm as Milo cantered down the long side of the oval ring. I rode the corner, turned Milo toward the fence, and headed for it in a straight line. I was almost able to make sense of the blurry image in front of me when I heard Rachel scream, "Watch out!"

Something large and heavy slammed into Milo's left side with a thunderous whomp. I never had a chance to get out of the way. The force of the other horse's body made Milo reel backward as my forward momentum sent me somersaulting over the side of his neck. Milo fought to recover his balance as I hit the ground on my back at the base of the jump. I forgot to let go of the reins, and I pulled Milo down. He landed with his right shoulder on top of my left leg, pinning me underneath him, and the jump rails crashed all over us.

Rachel ran to us, pushed Milo off me, and swatted at his haunches until he stood up.

"She can't see!" she screamed at the other rider, who had managed to stay on her horse.

To which she replied on her way out of the ring, "Then maybe she shouldn't ride."

I pushed myself up, wiped the dirt off my face, and took a few shaky steps toward Milo. He was breathing hard. "Is he okay?"

Rachel gave Milo a pat. "I think he just had the wind knocked out of him."

She checked Milo for abrasions but didn't find any. Then she had me hand-walk him in a small circle to make sure he wasn't limping. Though she believed Milo to be sound, I decided to lead him to the barn instead of ride him.

I asked Rachel to wait until I put my saddle in the golf cart. When I went to undo the girth, my hands shook so badly I couldn't get a grip on the strap. I told myself Milo was okay, but

I had to run my hands down his warm neck to his chest and feel his slow, strong heartbeat before I could stop shaking and slide my saddle off his back.

Milo and I started out for the stalls. We walked slowly, Milo with his head held low and pressed lightly against my back.

I had to stop whenever I heard something—a car backfiring, rails hitting the ground—that made me relive the collision: the sound of two horses smashing into each other, the sight of Milo's legs thrashing as he went down, the feel of his heart pounding against my leg as he lay on top of me. It was too much to bear and I'd start shaking again.

"I'm sorry, baby," I said, combing my fingers through Milo's mane until I felt strong enough to continue walking. But before long, something else triggered my memory, forcing me to stop until I assured myself that Milo wasn't hurt.

I felt along his spine, slid my hands up and down his legs, and lifted his feet to check his hooves. He seemed perfectly fine, but I would have picked him up and carried him if I could.

By the time we got to the barn, I was feeling the effects of my fall. My body ached from head to toe, and I was grateful when one of the grooms took Milo to bathe him and apply poultice to his legs. I felt dirt rolling around in my pants and couldn't wait to shower and change.

Rachel, with Spike seated next to her, pulled up alongside me in the golf cart. "Here," she said, holding out two aspirin and a bottle of water.

"Thanks," I gurgled as I sipped the water. "I think I'll go wash up and change in one of the bathrooms." Luckily, I had brought an extra set of clothes. "I have half of the ring down my shirt." I tugged on the front of my polo, and bits of sand and dirt scattered about me.

Rachel chuckled. "You're wearing some of it on your face, too."

"Lovely," I said, wiping my face with both hands. "Better?" I asked, sticking my cheek out for Rachel to inspect.

"Much. Now you have to brush that crash off, too. Don't give it any more thought."

"Easier said than done," I groaned.

"No." Rachel was not going to allow this to defeat me. "You have every right to be in that ring. Besides, she ran into you. The crash was her fault, not yours."

"Yes, but if I could see, it never would have happened."

"You don't know that," Rachel insisted. "Just a few days ago we watched two horses run into each other, and I know for a fact that both of their riders can see just fine. Besides, no pun intended, but I think you've lost sight of what's really important."

"How so?"

"I brought you to that ring so you could practice over bigger jumps. How well you ride is what matters, and you were riding really well."

"I was having a good time."

Rachel smiled and handed Spike to me. "Go clean yourself up. I want to check on Milo."

"I'm not showing tomorrow if he isn't one hundred percent."

"Of course not, but he's fine. I'm going to give him some aspirin, just like I gave you. By tomorrow, you'll both be as good as almost new."

"Almost new?"

"It's just aspirin. They're not magic beans."

With my confidence and humor restored, I happily left Milo in Rachel's capable hands, caught a ride to my apartment, took a long, hot shower, and fell into bed.

My alarm began beeping at 7:00 a.m. I would have done anything to sleep longer, but my neighbor was giving me a ride to the show, and I needed to hurry.

Everything hurt. Slowly, I swung my legs over the side of the bed and examined the hideous, dark purple bruise that had surfaced on my thigh overnight. "That's not pretty," I said, flinching as I pulled on my breeches, buttoned my shirt, and zipped up my boots. I grabbed Spike and my backpack and limped out the door as my neighbor was starting his truck.

When I got to our tent, Rachel and Milo were returning from their morning ride and he quickened his step as soon as he saw me.

"How is he today?" I asked, giving Milo a kiss on the nose.

"Better than you, I think," Rachel said as she dismounted. "Did I just see you limp?"

"A little bit, but the more I move, the better my leg feels. I'll be all right by the time I have to get on."

I was supposed to show in a couple of hours, which gave me time to learn my courses. Higher fences require a more precise ride, and since this was my first appearance in the Amateurs, Rachel wanted to help me plot my way around the jumps. We loaded Spike and my show gear in the golf cart and drove to the ring where I was competing.

The main hunter ring was a good size for me, with ample room to establish a canter rhythm but not so big that I'd have to memorize more than fifty markers, my usual amount.

Rachel parked by the board where the course charts were posted and read them aloud. Starting with the first course, we walked around the ring from fence to fence. She described how to approach each one and I found markers to help me execute her plan. When she was certain I knew what to do, she helped me carry my belongings, including Spike, to the bleachers, where I stayed until it was my turn to show.

After yesterday's collision, Rachel thought it would be best if she warmed up Milo. The schooling rings were small and crowded and the fewer fences I jumped in them, the better.

Eager to begin my first round in the Amateurs, I patted Milo on the neck, nudged him with my heel, and trotted into the ring.

On our way to the rail, we passed a 3'6" fence we'd be jumping later in the course. I smiled because Rachel's idea had worked. Compared to the four-footers the professionals jumped, these fences looked more doable.

"We're in the big leagues now, M," I joked as we started to canter.

Our first fence was only 3'3", but after practicing the bigger fences, Milo was jumping every fence as if it were 3'6". Pow! He gave a mighty push as we left the ground and bounded over the jump.

Overachiever.

Our next jump was every bit of 3'6"and Milo pricked his ears as he sighted in on it. Getting ready for takeoff, I pushed my heels down and held onto Milo's braids as he launched us over the fence.

The show ring had never been so much fun and as we approached our final fence, I had to fight the urge to lean over Milo's neck and yell, "Whee!" I was having such a good time, I didn't think about how we were doing until we finished the course. I couldn't remember either of us making a mistake.

The judges give a score at the end of each Amateur rider's round. Anything over 80 is considered excellent. My score for the first class was 85.

"Yes!" Rachel clapped after the announcer read my score and we discovered I led the class by five points.

"It's not over yet. Don't change a thing," she called after me as we returned to the ring.

Another score of 85 and Milo and I won both classes.

"I don't believe it!" I led Milo from the ring, two blue ribbons hanging off his bridle. I walked straight to Rachel and tackled her in a hug. "Thank you, thank you."

I held her tightly until Milo started pulling on the back of my show coat.

"Hold on, M," I said, limping to my backpack on the golf cart and getting him a few butterscotch candies. My leg was starting to throb. I got into the golf cart next to Rachel and propped up my foot on the dashboard. After five minutes, I felt well enough to walk Milo to our stalls, but not before I fed him a butterscotch and rubbed his little white star.

"We're unstoppable, M."

Rachel laughed but reminded me, "Don't start getting cocky. This is an extremely difficult division and I'd hate to think this is beginner's luck."

As she drove away, I whispered to Milo, "Don't listen to her. It's not luck, it's your magic."

The next day, I couldn't wait to get back into the ring. I rode well and Milo was super. Our scores of 83 and 81 were a bit lower, but good enough for second and third.

"Don't worry, you'll still be champion, Commander Competitive," Rachel joked as she watched me fidget while we waited for the final results.

"Are you sure?" I asked but the announcer was already calling me back into the ring.

"How do you feel?" Rachel took hold of Milo's reins as we came back out with the champion tricolor dangling from his bridle.

I let out a breath and smiled broadly. "Amazing. Who needs to see when you have a magic horse and a miracle worker for a trainer?"

Having so much success my first time out in the Amateurs, I mistakenly thought the division was going to be easy. But during the next three weeks of competition, our highest score was 79.

Frustrated and embarrassed by my bad riding, I sat under an oak tree with Rachel and begged her for help.

"I feel as if I've forgotten how to ride," I said sadly. "I'm either too fast or too slow. I can't get my canter rhythm right. I don't know what happened to me." I picked a blade of grass and twirled it between my fingers. "The harder I try, the worse I get."

Rachel patted my knee. "All riders go through a rough patch. Frankly, you're overdue for yours. You've done nothing but win for a year. Why don't you take some time off? Go on trails, find fields to gallop in, and stop worrying about being perfect all the time."

Milo and I didn't step foot on the show grounds for three weeks. When we returned to the ring, our canter was smooth and steady, and our score was 82.

"See, what did I tell you," Rachel crowed happily.

"Whew. You were right. Not that I doubted you."

Milo and I were Division Champion the final week of the Ocala circuit. I finally believed I could do anything on a horse, no matter how big the fences or how little I could see.

After three months of showing, Rachel and the horses were exhausted and I was glad she was planning on taking a break. As much as I would miss competing, my trainer and my horse needed to rest.

It would be three months before our next show, and by the time June rolled around I knew I'd be eager for the illustrious competition in Virginia to begin.

The Upperville Colt and Horse Show is the oldest horse show in the country. Famous for the sprawling oak trees that grow inside the main ring, the courses were often tricky for riders with two good eyes. On more than one occasion, I had witnessed a rider leaving the ring with the remnants of a low-hanging branch adorning his or her helmet.

On my first day of showing, I woke up early to walk around the ring with Milo and memorize the course. The longer we walked, the more upset I became. Not only were the jumps hidden between trees, but they were made of natural materials to look like the fences, gates, hedges, and brush piles in a hunt field. While charming, the jumps were all but invisible to me against the backdrop of trees and grass. I tripped over roots as I trudged from one fence to the next.

"How are we going to do this?" I asked Milo, who snorted in response.

Thirty minutes later and five more times around the ring, I still couldn't find most of the jumps. As I led Milo back to the barn, I felt as though I had been beaten before I had a chance to show.

"What's wrong?" asked Rachel, who noticed I was unusually quiet when I put Milo in his stall.

"I can't tell what I'm supposed to jump. Everything looks the same, I can't even pick out markers," I said, my frustration mounting. "Not to mention, the ground is so uneven, I doubt I'll be able to establish a rhythm."

"The other riders have to deal with that, too," Rachel reminded me.

"Yes, but they can see where they're going. I don't know how I'm going to make it around."

Rachel tugged on the sleeve of my jacket. "C'mon, let's go to the ring and come up with a plan."

Together, we studied the course and discussed in great detail how each line, every turn, and even my entrance should be ridden.

"Don't worry about the tree roots, or if you have to canter uphill or down a slope," Rachel instructed. "Just make sure you start off with a steady pace, and Milo will hold it for you."

This was all well and good but for one problem that remained. "I still have no idea where most of the fences are," I repeated for the third time.

"Do the best you can," was all she could give me.

I was next to go, and as Rachel and I stood at the ingate, I wondered if this was how soldiers felt as they approached the battlefield.

"You look like you're going to be sick." Rachel fed Milo a mint as she took note of my pallor.

We went over the course, and Rachel may as well have been giving me directions to grandma's house.

"Pass the small hill with grass and don't turn until you come to the group of trees on your right," she was saying.

The execution drum roll reverberated in my head as Milo waited for me to cue the canter.

I located the first jump easily enough. Milo gave a slight tug on the reins to remind me to loosen my hold, which was uncharacteristically tight. I was able to relax when I cantered up to the next jump and recognized its white birch poles.

Okay, maybe we can do this, I thought, and I asked Milo to open his canter a fraction more as the ground sloped slightly uphill. After ten strides, I still didn't see anything that could be a jump. I turned my head to the left, and a large branch whacked me in the face and momentarily trapped me in its leaves. Milo's ears rotated back at the commotion I was making. Finally, I saw something big and green ahead of us. I pointed Milo toward the jump and, for the first time since I began riding him, I felt him hesitate. I nudged him with the heel of my boot and he jumped the fence, but I could tell something wasn't right.

"Off-course!" a man's voice boomed over the loudspeaker before Milo had all four feet back on the ground. Automatically disqualified, I immediately brought Milo to a walk and we left the ring, his reins slack and my head bent.

"What did I do?" I asked Rachel, who was standing at the gate.

"You jumped a fence backward."

The realization that I could have injured Milo shook me. "I told you I couldn't do this."

She gave me a minute to calm down before she hooked her finger around Milo's bit and turned him to face the ring. Again, Rachel tried to map out the course using landmarks, but after her third attempt to explain my approach to a particular jump, she stopped.

"You know what?" her cheeks puffed out as she expelled her breath. "You don't have to do this."

I stared down at her. If Rachel was giving me an out, she must be truly rattled.

I shifted my gaze from Rachel to the ring. A smart person would have turned her horse around and called it a day. I was about to do just that when Rachel had another idea.

"Jump the first fence. If you're comfortable, keep going. But if at any time you don't want to continue, then pull up. That way, it'll be your decision to leave the ring. It won't be because you've gone off-course. And you won't be putting your life or Milo's in danger."

That sounded reasonable. *At least we probably won't have to jump more than one fence*, I thought as I guided Milo past Rachel and into the ring.

In the history of first fences, none was ever so perfect as the one I began my course with. Our canter was brilliant, not too fast but full of energy. Each stride was identical, and it felt as though Milo was floating. When I found the jump, it was directly in front of us. I relaxed and let Milo take us to it. He pushed off effortlessly, sailed high over the fence, landed softly, and continued to canter in the same rhythm.

What a shame that the next fence was hidden behind some trees, and I was going to have to pull up.

"Sorry, boy," I told Milo as I began to pull back on the reins.

All of a sudden, I heard someone to my left.

"Keep going, I'll let you know where to turn," came Rachel's disembodied voice as she ran along next to me on the other side of the rail.

Both Milo and I looked over at my trainer, who was charging to the end of the fence line. We met the corner at the same time, and Milo cantered three strides before Rachel shouted, "Turn now!"

I knew she was putting me on a straight path to my next jump, though I couldn't see it, and I kept Milo cantering toward two trees. I remembered from this morning that the fence — dark brown poles with a brush pile underneath — was behind the trees, but I didn't recognize it until the last second. That was all we needed. Milo cleared the fence easily, I counted six canter strides to the next fence, and we completed our first line.

Rachel had made it to the end of the ring, where she was now on my right side. I had enough time to notice her red face before she yelled, "Turn, and the jump is to the left of the tree!" This was the jump I had missed in the first course, and I held my breath as I looked for it. I craned my head to the left. *There it is.* Milo, too, zeroed in on it, and now we had four exceptional jumps behind us.

I cantered back to the rail and there was my guardian angel, doubled over and gasping for air. As soon as she saw us, she took off, sprinting along the rail to lead us to the turn that would line us up with the final four fences. Rachel couldn't keep up with us, but I heard her behind me as she managed to wheeze, "Turn...keep going... diagonal jump...by the gate."

Our last fence was as superb as the first. It was the best round I had ever ridden, but my accomplishment was nothing compared to what Rachel had done for me. I leapt off Milo and handed him to Emilio.

"Where's Rachel?" I asked, fearing she had collapsed. He pointed at the golf cart where Rachel, still panting and beet-red, was sipping water. I ran to her and hugged her. "I'm in awe of you," I said breathlessly. "You are amazing."

She couldn't speak, but I could tell she was just as proud of me, and when my score of 92 was announced, she summoned the strength to high-five me.

The entire show was talking about my second class and what Rachel did to help me win it. Even the show secretary asked me about it when I went to the office to drop off the form to officially scratch from the second day of competition.

"Are you sure you want to do this?" the secretary asked. "After all, you won a class today."

I pushed the slip toward her and smiled. "I'm sure. I don't think Rachel would survive if she had to chase me around the course two more times."

"She really did that? The whole course?"

I nodded. "From start to finish."

"Wow," she said as she put a giant X on my entry form. "You're a lucky girl."

"Yes, I am," I smiled at her. "The luckiest."

CHAPTER TWENTY-SIX

July in Maryland can be oppressive. The heat and humidity lay on you like a hot, wet blanket. While the rest of the population is indoors obeying temperature warnings, riders are donning wool coats, long breeches, and gloves. Milo, too, had a problem with the summer sun. Twice while at a show, he became overheated and had to be wrapped in a blanket soaked in ice water.

It was eight o'clock in the morning, and I was already sweating through my shirt as I threw a bag of Milo's mints into my tack trunk. In an hour we would be heading to Manchester, Vermont, for a month to compete in a cooler climate. Spike emerged from behind the trunk, bringing a dusty cobweb with him.

"Yuck," I said, wiping him off with a towel.

He urffed at me, letting me know he desired a treat.

"You saw me pack your goodies, didn't you?" I handed him a slice of jerky and he scampered out of the tack room. I followed, calling after him, "That gourmet jerky is expensive. Don't bury it somewhere."

I would have pursued him, but Milo nickered at me from his stall, requesting my attention.

"Hi, M," I said, presenting him with a piece of candy. "Are you ready for your road trip?" I looked into his buckets and was glad he'd been drinking plenty of water. The drive to Vermont would take eight hours, and I didn't want him to become overheated in the trailer.

I stood at his withers and tickled his chin and scratched his back until his lips began to twitch with pleasure. When I tried to leave, Milo swung his head back toward me and stared at me for at least a minute. I returned his gaze, and our connection grew so intense, I could feel the love flow between us. It was as though we had our own language.

When he had said all that he wanted to say, Milo broke the spell by pulling me in for a hug. I threw my arms around his neck and hugged him back.

"You're my magic horse," I told him, to which he snorted and tossed his head as if agreeing with me. "We need to be good in Vermont, M. I have a feeling we won't be showing much after this trip." I cringed, thinking about the conversation I'd overheard last night.

Mom and Howard had invited me to dinner so we could say goodbye over a home-cooked meal. Since I wasn't going to see my mom for several weeks, I decided to go up to her condo early so I could spend some extra time with her.

The door to the condo was slightly ajar and I could hear voices coming from inside. Howard was doing most of the talking and I was about to walk in when I heard my name and stopped.

"How can her bills be this much?" He wasn't yelling but he definitely sounded irritated. "I thought she won money at these things."

I usually did win enough to cover most, or all, of my entry fees, but my winnings would never come close to paying for everything else. Riding and competing at my level cost a fortune and I could understand how Howard, a non-horse person, would think Mom was crazy to support me.

I was debating the wisdom of going inside when I heard Howard tell my mom, "This is going to bankrupt you."

I gasped and quickly covered my mouth with my hand to muffle the sound. Slowly backing away from the door, I pressed the elevator's call button and slunk to my apartment.

I sat on my couch to think about what Howard had said.

I'd always hated having to ask my mom for so much, but since I started riding with Rachel, I'd been having the time of my life and tried not to think about the cost.

Disgusted with how selfish I'd become, I started to cry tears of self-loathing.

There was no way I could continue showing. My mom had already paid for Vermont, and I couldn't back out of it, but as soon as we got home, I was going to tell Rachel my showing days were over. The only thing I cared about more than Milo was my mom, and I would gladly give up everything for her.

Later, I went upstairs, and Mom and Howard were all smiles as if they hadn't been arguing about me an hour before. I kept what I heard to myself. I was already a leech and there was no need to let them know I was an eavesdropper as well.

Rachel and I had been in the car for five hours, but it felt like a week. Spike had abandoned my lap for a pile of towels in the back seat, and Rachel spent most of the time catching up on phone calls. I smiled as I recalled Bob, who also used his time in the car to contact clients and other trainers. I was so preoccupied that I didn't notice Rachel was off the phone and trying to get my attention.

"Hello," she was saying. "I was just talking to my husband who was checking the Amateur Owner standings online. Guess who's tenth in the country."

"You're kidding!" I whooped. "Milo and I are tenth?"

I couldn't wait to tell my mom, but remembered she was vacationing on Canada's west coast, and I'd have to call her later.

"Oh, and tomorrow, some reporter would like to interview you," Rachel added.

"Why would anybody want to interview me?"

"Off the top of my head," teased Rachel, "I'd have to say they're interested in you because you're the only legally blind rider winning in the Amateurs."

"In that case they should sit you and Milo down and ask the two of you questions."

"They don't want to talk to me, and Milo has a previous engagement," she said as we crossed the state line into Vermont.

The following day, while Rachel rode the horses, I holed up in an air-conditioned doublewide with a reporter from the local newspaper. She asked about my background and riding experience, but avoided questions about my vision until the end of the interview.

"You and Milo have compiled quite a winning record this year," she said smiling. "As a legally blind rider, how do you do it?"

"I get asked this question a lot," I said, leaning forward in my chair. "Basically, it took a lot of trial and error, but I finally learned the two most important things about riding are maintaining the canter rhythm and listening to what the horse is telling me. I had to lose my vision to figure that out. Now I ride in the moment, and sometimes I don't have to do anything but wait for a jump to happen."

The reporter finished scribbling in her notebook then said she had one more question.

"What's been the hardest thing for you?"

"Thinking I'd never ride again," I answered without hesitation.

Rachel read the article to me when it came out a few days later. We were sitting in her golf cart by the ring, waiting for a groom to bring down the horse she was showing. When she got up to ask the ring starter a question, another trainer walked by and stopped to talk to her. I couldn't hear their entire conversation, but I picked up a few words and I didn't like them. "Milo," "customer," "sale," and "offer" should never be used in the same sentence.

It was time for Rachel to get on and I was left alone in the golf cart. I rubbed Spike's belly, trying to untangle my feelings and thoughts, which went from outrage (*I'll never sell Milo*), to guilt (*Mom's going bankrupt because of me*), to denial (*I'm not going to think about this and it'll go away*). I decided not to mention any of this to Rachel. We'd be in Vermont for a month, and there no point in starting off with a fight.

After our first week of showing, we had accumulated so many blue ribbons, we didn't have enough room to hang all of them from the banner stretched across the front of our stalls. Rachel won her share of classes during the week. Over the weekend, Milo and I were completely in synch and won all five classes, including the flat class.

"Do you ever get tired of winning?" a friend from the barn asked after the awards ceremony.

"Nope," I smiled. "It just balances out all the times I don't win."

On Wednesday we began our second week of showing. I spent the morning watching the professionals compete and cheering for Rachel. It was Milo's first day back at work after having Monday and Tuesday off, and after lunch I took him for a light hack around the grounds. The practice rings were overrun with riders preparing to show, so I rode Milo to the open land behind the tents, where instead of working him on the flat, I let him get his fill of the sweet Vermont grass.

When I rode up to our tent, I saw Rachel talking with someone. I had an inkling it was the same trainer who'd asked about Milo the week before, but I shoved the thought out of my mind. Wanting to appear unavailable, I put Milo in his stall and hurried to retrieve Spike to go for a walk. As I was unlocking the door to his pen, Rachel called me over and introduced me to Brenda, a trainer from North Carolina.

After a brief exchange of small talk, Rachel turned to me and said, "Brenda has a client who'd like to try Milo."

Warily, I snapped, "Try him for what?"

Brenda smiled as she described her client. "Ashley just turned fourteen and has been riding with me since she was ten.

She's a timid rider and we haven't been able to find a horse that suits her. After her father read the article about you, he suggested we ask about Milo. I didn't think he would be for sale."

"Neither did I." I shot an accusatory look at Rachel.

"Would you mind excusing us for quick chat?" Rachel took me by the elbow and pulled me into the tent. I braced myself for a lecture on manners and was surprised when Rachel put a hand on my shoulder and said, "We've talked about this before. I know the thought of selling Milo is painful, but I think now is the time."

I began to cry.

"I can't do it, I just can't do it," I said, hugging myself and shaking my head.

"No one's telling you that you have to," Rachel said with a hint of impatience. "This is your decision. But remember Milo is at his peak. He will never be worth this much money again. I know you love him, but—"

"He's my world," I interrupted her.

Rachel sighed. "I know he is. You have to decide whether you want to continue winning in the Amateurs for another year or so, and then go back to jumping three feet when he can't jump three-six anymore. Or would you rather sell Milo to a caring home and buy a younger, more athletic horse that you can show over the bigger fences for years to come?"

In my head, I knew I shouldn't be upset with Rachel. She was only doing her job as my trainer and agent. Plus, everything she said was true. My heart, however, had no use for practicality.

"I'm sorry, Rachel," I sniffed. "I can't."

Wordlessly, she walked out of the tent and back to where Brenda was waiting. They spoke for less than a minute before Brenda left.

Rachel found me in Milo's stall, leaning against his neck, patting his face, and weeping. I pulled myself together enough to apologize again. Rachel simply said, "If you change your mind, I'll let Brenda know."

"Okay," I said. "By the way, how much money am I turning down?"

"A lot," she said, then told me the amount.

"You're right, that is a lot for him," I said, "and he's worth every penny."

I was cried out by the time Rachel dropped me off at my hotel, and I skipped dinner and went straight to bed. I tried to sleep, but my brain refused to turn off. It was midnight in Vermont, 9:00 p.m. in British Columbia, and I needed advice. So, I reached for my cell phone over Spike, who was sharing my pillow, and called my mom. She answered on the second ring and just the sound of her voice made me breathe a little easier. I hadn't gotten much past, "Hello," when she asked, "What's wrong?"

I avoided her question and instead tried to hold my voice steady as I described how Milo and I swept the division our first week in Vermont.

"That's tremendous! So why are you up at..." she paused to check the time, "midnight and sound like you're upset?"

"There's a trainer here who wants to try Milo for one of her students."

"Oh."

"I don't know what to do," I said, squeezing the back of my neck.

"I'm not sure I can help you," she replied guardedly.

"Yes, you can. You're my mother. You live to tell me what to do."

"Not in this case. I'm sorry, I wish I could, but only you can make this decision. All I can do is support you in whatever you decide."

I closed my eyes and rubbed my forehead. "We've had two horses before. Is there any way I could keep Milo and get a new horse?"

"If I could afford to do that for you, I would," my mom said sorrowfully.

"I know." I didn't want her to think I was ungrateful for everything she did for me. "I wish there was an obvious answer, but my head and my heart don't seem to agree with each other."

"I know this must be terrible for you," she said. "What does Rachel think?"

I propped myself up against the headboard and gave her a synopsis of my conversation with Rachel, leaving out the part where I dissolved into hysterics.

She was silent and I hoped she was going to tell me what to do. But instead, she said, "A horse can jump only so many fences in his lifetime, and I'd say Milo has given you his best ones."

I began to cry softly.

"If it's so painful, why sell him?" she asked gently. "Keep showing him until he has to retire. At least then you won't ever be apart from him."

"I'll have to stop riding, though. If there isn't any money for another horse, when Milo's done, I'm done."

"That's true."

"I don't know how to exist without riding and showing," I confessed. "It's all I have."

"Then you should consider that when you make your decision," she said tenderly. "But I should warn you, whatever you decide to do, at some point you will have made the wrong decision."

Before we hung up, she told me she loved me. I spent the rest of the night searching for an answer.

"Why do you look like something the cat coughed up?" Rachel asked in an attempt to make me smile when she picked me up the next morning.

I refused the bait and turned away from her. Rachel didn't say another word until we got to the show grounds and she parked her car in front of our tent.

"What's going on with you?" she asked. "If this is what you're going to be like without Milo, then please don't sell him because I don't like it when my friend is this sad."

"She can try him," I said opening the car door.

"I think it's going to be too rough on you," Rachel cautioned.

"I'll be fine," I lied.

"Are you sure?" She made an attempt to read my face, but I looked away.

Biting my lower lip, I managed a strangled, "Mmm hmm," before grabbing Spike and bolting from the car.

I put Spike down when I reached Milo's stall and he whinnied sweetly at me. "Hi, M. I did a bad thing. I'm sorry." I began to cry. "I'm so sorry."

Milo turned around to eat some hay. I laid my head on his shoulder and memorized the way he smelled and felt. When he moved, I moved with him. When he breathed, I breathed with him. And when he looked at me, I told him I loved him.

A groom came to get him for Brenda's client to try. I looked away and heard the snap of a lead rope on his halter. When I looked back, Milo was halfway out the door. He stopped, turned his head, and stared at me. "Go on, Milo, be a good boy," I said.

The groom pulled him forward and I watched Milo leave the stall.

I hid for the rest of the day in a storage area at the back of the tent. I heard a groom bring Milo to his stall, but I remained in my hiding place. Eventually, Rachel found me. She was still dressed in her show clothes, and I assumed she had just finished for the day. She squatted next to me and the look on her face confirmed what I already knew.

"They bought him," she said gently.

I closed my eyes against the pain and barely managed to whisper, "Okay."

"He leaves tomorrow."

I nodded my head, and Rachel left me to fall apart in private.

After my breakdown at the show, Rachel drove me to my hotel. Neither of us said a word until we were parked in front of my room. I opened the car door, but Rachel stopped me before I could get out.

"Are you going to be okay?" she asked flatly, as though I was wearing her down.

Unable to look at her, I stared, unblinking, at the walkway in front of us.

Rachel hadn't done anything wrong but the rage and sorrow inside me exploded like a geyser. I was powerless to stop the hateful words that poured out of me.

"How could you let me sell him?" I hissed. "You know better than anyone else, I can't live without him. Why did you let me go through with it?"

My breath came in ragged spurts and when I was suddenly seized by a wave of pain, I welcomed it. This was my doing and I needed to accept my punishment.

Rachel didn't answer me. She must have known it would be pointless to argue.

I snatched my bag from the floor, stuffed Spike under my arm, and snarled, "Get him back," before slamming the car door.

The next morning, I was on a plane to Baltimore. Mom picked me up at the airport and I held myself together until I was in the car.

"How could I have done this?" I moaned and erupted into gut-wrenching sobs.

Taking my hand, my mom held onto me until we were home.

My apartment was cool but offered me no comfort. Standing in the foyer, Mom cupped my chin in her palm and gently turned my face from side to side so she could see the dark circles under my swollen eyes. "You'll feel better after you get some sleep."

"I don't want to feel better." I let my purse and duffle bag fall to the floor with a clunk and staggered down the hall to my bedroom. When my mom brought my bags into my room, I was already in bed. Like a zombie, I lay on my back and stared at the ceiling.

My mom hovered over me until she realized there was nothing she could do to help me.

"Call me if you need anything," she said, plugging my phone into the cord on my bedside table. "And please answer when I call you."

I stayed in bed but couldn't sleep. I tried to talk but had nothing to say. My mom brought me food, but the thought of eating made me sick. Milo was gone and it was my fault. I was so disgusted with myself I couldn't look in the mirror. I created this nightmare and deserved to live in it.

Rachel called to check on me, but our conversation ended badly, and I didn't answer when she phoned a second and third time.

I replayed the call in my head and winced when I remembered nastily commanding, "Get him back."

"You know I can't do that," Rachel said firmly.

"Please," I started to cry. "I made a mistake. Rachel, I can't live without him."

She didn't say anything and for a second, I thought she might be considering my demand, until she said, "You're going to have to learn how," and I hung up on her.

I didn't speak to her again until twelve days later when she returned home from Vermont.

"Are you coming out to ride?" She sounded lighthearted, as if nothing had changed.

I hadn't left my condo in two weeks. I was tired of fighting with Rachel, being mad at the world, and staying in bed. This wasn't the first time I had to start over and as much as I hated it, I was going to have to learn to live without Milo.

"I guess." I sat up in bed and pulled a pillow onto my lap. "I don't have a horse, though," I reminded Rachel sourly.

Her tone was still light, if not a little forced. "Lucky for you, I have plenty of them."

You don't have the right one.

"All right, thank you." I hugged the pillow tightly to my chest.

Rachel filled me in on what I'd missed in Vermont, which of her horses won, who asked about me after I left, and who had too much to drink at the exhibitors' party. The conversation was strained on both ends and it made me feel worse.

"I'm sorry I was so awful to you," I said, hoping an apology would clear the air. "I'm just so sad, I don't know what to do."

"I know," Rachel said sympathetically. "We'll figure something out."

When I got to the barn the next day, I walked straight to Milo's stall hoping to find a trace of him, anything that would connect me to him. But the stall had been completely stripped and cleaned. Not a single bucket, shaving, or piece of hay remained. Every sign of Milo was erased. All that was left were the black rubber floor mats.

Rachel discovered me in a corner of the stall, on my knees, hunched over, my shoulders heaving, and Spike licking my salty cheeks as I choked on my sobs.

She rushed forward, put her arm around my back, and hoisted me to my feet. "You're a mess. You can't ride like this." Keeping her hold on me, she helped me walk up the hill to her house and sat me on a bar stool in her kitchen.

"When's the last time you ate?" Rachel asked.

"I'm not hungry."

But that didn't stop her from making one of her famous grilled cheese sandwiches. The aroma of frying butter made my mouth water, and I realized I hadn't eaten anything but saltine crackers the past three days.

"You need a new horse," she said, handing me a box of tissues. "It's the only way you're going to get over this."

"But," I drew in a quick breath and hiccupped, "I can't ask my mom for more money." I sniffed loudly and leaned my elbows on the counter.

"Talk to her," Rachel suggested. She flipped the sandwich onto a plate and set it in front of me. "Milo sold for plenty of money. Certainly, there's enough for you to buy a new horse. Maybe if you don't show that much and we keep the expenses to a bare minimum, she'll let me find you something."

I had a mouthful of gooey cheese and couldn't speak but I nodded in agreement. I didn't really want a new horse. I wanted Milo. But sooner or later, I was going to need a horse of my own. I knew I could ride Rachel's horses for now, but I couldn't do that forever.

I wolfed down the last few bites of sandwich. "That was exactly what I needed. Thank you."

"There's nothing food can't fix." Rachel grinned. "Feel like you can ride now?"

I did, and Rachel put her arm around my shoulders as we walked out of the house. Halfway down the hill, I turned to my friend.

"I'm really sorry for the way I acted. I wasn't fair to you and—" I stopped myself. I could feel tears welling in my eyes and I didn't want to cry in front of Rachel anymore.

She squeezed my shoulder. "I understand," she said quickly. When we reached the barn, she let go of me. "Let's get riding."

I rode three of Rachel's horses and though they couldn't compare to Milo, life always looked better to me when I was on a horse. Smiles, laughter, and even breathing came easier. I felt free and definitely stronger.

Rachel and I chatted easily as we walked our last rides of the day around the ring to cool them off. "You look much better," she said.

"I know you think your grilled cheese did it, but for me there's nothing a horse can't fix."

Rachel chuckled and gave me a thumbs up. "All the more reason for you to talk to your mom as soon as possible," she said.

On the way home, I realized I had to be honest with my mother. I'd tell her I knew about the money issues, but there must be a way for me to have a horse without breaking the bank.

While I sat at my kitchen table working up the nerve to call her, I must have crossed and uncrossed my legs three times. Finally, I took a deep breath, squared my shoulders, and dialed her number.

"Hi," she said cheerfully. "You're back. How was the barn?"

I told her about falling apart in Milo's stall and how Rachel put me back together with the help of three horses she let me ride.

"I really need a horse, Mom. I don't know who I am without one. I was hoping we could use some of the money from Milo's sale to buy a new horse for me." I wiped my clammy hands on my pants. "Would that be all right?"

"Of course," my mom said without a second of hesitation. "I've set money aside for just that purpose."

She told me the amount and I thought I heard her wrong. It was almost the full amount we got for Milo.

"How much?" I asked.

I'd heard her correctly, but the numbers made no sense. Confused, I wasn't sure what to say. I pressed my lips together.

"Hello?" my mom asked after I'd been silent for too long.

"Sorry, I'm here, but I don't understand. I thought I was bankrupting you. Why would you put that much money aside for a horse if we can't afford to keep it?"

"Who told you I was bankrupt?" Her tone was sharp and demanding.

I squirmed in my chair but knew I had to tell her the truth.

"I sort of overheard you and Howard talking one night. I didn't mean to eavesdrop, but you guys were arguing pretty loudly, and I could hear you through the door."

"Is that why you sold Milo?" She was furious now. "Please tell me that's not the reason. Howard had never seen the horse bills before that night, and it was a shock. It's an incredibly expensive sport, but I'm fine. You weren't bankrupting me. If you were, I would have said something or told you to stop showing for a while."

The room started to spin, and I tried to grab the table for support, but I slipped out of my seat and fell to my knees. The last thing I heard before I dropped the phone was my mom's livid voice: "Why didn't you ask me first?"

I'd sold my beloved Milo, ruined my life, and broken a promise all because I'd been too ashamed and guilt-ridden to find out the truth.

Bile rose in my throat, and I knew I was going to be sick.

My mom was saying something, but the carpet muffled her voice. I scooped up the phone. "I have to call you back," I whimpered and got to the bathroom just in time.

Hours later, I was back on the phone, but this time it was with Rachel. She'd already heard from my mom and knew the whole story.

"She told me to find you a new horse," Rachel said kindly, and I appreciated her attempt to make me feel better.

"It won't be the same. It will never be the same," I murmured.

"I know," my trainer said carefully. "There will never be another Milo. I'll do my best, though, I promise, to find you something close."

CHAPTER TWENTY-SEVEN

A week later, Rachel and I began our search. We traveled all over Maryland, Virginia, and Pennsylvania, but the bar was too high and not a single horse I rode held a candle to Milo.

Eventually Rachel gave up on finding a horse in the States and she, Mom, and I flew to Germany where Rachel had a horse scout line up trials at several barns. Over the next three days, Rachel and I rode at least fifteen horses each, and although we liked some of them, I couldn't find "the one."

On our last day in Germany, we were taken to a large breeding farm where I was supposed to try a five-year-old bay gelding that our German contact raved about. He was a striking animal, similar to Milo in height and coloring, but heavier and more muscular.

I watched the groom drop a saddle on the horse's back. Next came the bridle, and I noticed that the animal gnashed his teeth at the groom before opening his mouth and accepting the bit.

"Looks like he has an attitude," I remarked as the horse pawed the ground.

"Oh, this one knows exactly how good he is," the groom said. "He'll put on an act for you, but once you get on, he calms down."

The horse's arrogance didn't faze me. I didn't have to fall in love with him. All I needed was a horse that did his job well enough for us to win.

I had to ride him only once to know that he was the right choice. He had a rare combination of tremendous power and perfect balance. You're lucky if you can find a horse with one or the other, but this horse had it all. When I jumped him, he exploded off the ground, bringing his knees up so high over the fence that he almost hit himself in the face.

"Wow," echoed Rachel and my mom.

"Oh boy," I uttered after righting myself in the saddle.

My mother wired the money for the horse the following day, and two weeks later he was flown to New York. After a brief stay in quarantine, he was put on a horse transport and shipped to Rachel's. I wanted another name beginning with M, so I named him Maddox, Max for short.

Despite my longing for Milo, I had to admit I was excited about my new horse. I began riding and showing him right away.

I insisted on starting off in the Amateur Owner division and we were a disaster. It was impossible to maintain a rhythm as we jumped around a course of fences. Max would speed up for no reason, and instead of helping me in front of a fence, at times he would lunge toward it. I was frustrated and bitter. It wasn't uncommon for me to finish a course and say to anyone who'd listen, "I should never have sold Milo."

In spite of my effort to bond with Max, he remained hostile. I brushed him, spent hours in his stall talking to him, and fed him bags of carrots and apples, which he greedily seized from my hands. He never whinnied when I came near him. Instead, he would kick the door with his front hoof until he was given a treat. In trying to gentle the beast, I spoiled him and created a monster.

It took a year for me to admit defeat. One fall day in 2005 after a particularly bad round at a show in Maryland, I turned to Rachel and announced, "I hate him."

This was not the first time I shared these feelings with her, but it was the first time I followed up by ordering, "Fix it or sell it, but I'm not getting back on until something changes."

Tight-lipped, Rachel took Max from me, and I stormed off in search of a private place where I could call my mom. The show grounds bordered a park, and I found a picnic table in a secluded area.

My mood was so foul, even my mom's cheery, "Hi, how did the show go?" didn't make me feel better.

"I can't ride him," I whined. "I'm telling you, Mom, the horse hates me." The table was filthy, but I leaned my elbows on it anyway and rested my head on my hand. "Yesterday, he bit me so hard it drew blood. And today, Max took off bucking for no reason." There was silence on the other end of the line. "Are you still there?" I asked.

"Yes, I'm here." She paused. "If he's that bad, maybe we should sell him. It's weird, though. He was so good when we tried him in Germany. I really thought you two were a great match."

I closed my eyes and let out a shallow breath. "It would seem that there's only one match for me, and I sold him a year ago."

"Have you found out anything about him lately?" My mom was respectful of the fact that it still hurt me to hear Milo's name.

"I heard the girl who bought him decided she didn't want to ride anymore. But I have no idea what they're planning to do with him."

"So, do you think he's for sale?"

"I don't know." My voice cracked. "I assume he is."

"We need to find out," my mom said excitedly. "If he is, why don't we sell Max and buy back Milo?"

My heart leapt at the thought, but logically I knew it wouldn't work. "Max needs to do some winning before we can sell him for enough to get Milo back."

"Then let's give Rachel more time to work with Max," my mother suggested, "and hopefully she can make him more rideable for you."

Rachel was cleaning bridles in our tent when I found her and told her about the conversation with my mom.

"She's right," Rachel said, looking up from the piece of leather she was scrubbing. "I need more time to work with Max.

When I think you can start riding him again, I want you to show in the Adults instead of the Amateurs. I think you'll have an easier time learning how to ride him if the fences are smaller."

"But, Rachel," I sat down heavily on a wooden tack trunk, "one of the reasons I sold Milo was so I could stay in the Amateurs and keep jumping three-six. Now you're telling me I have to ride in the Adults anyway?"

"It won't be forever," Rachel smiled. "When you've won everything there is to win, then you can go back to the Amateurs."

Our start in the Adult Hunter division was slow, but by the fourth show of the 2006 season, Max and I had an epiphany and, all of a sudden, we clicked. We won class after class and the champion ribbons began to pile up.

In July, I returned to Vermont and, though it was one of my favorite venues, I couldn't help but be reminded of Milo and the day he was sold.

Our first week was a success and as I had done with Milo two years before, Max and I won every class in our division. We were again champion the second week, although we won only three classes. When our third and final week of showing began, I felt ready to make it three champions in a row.

Mine was the last division on the final day of the show. Trucks and trailers loaded down with horses had already begun pulling away from the grounds. Thirty minutes before I showed, Rachel, Spike, and I zipped down to the ring in the golf cart.

"The grooms are already packing the equipment, so as soon as you're done, we can start driving home," Rachel said happily. As much fun as it was to show in Vermont, we were ready to leave.

Rachel slowed down as we neared the practice ring and I was surprised that at this late hour, it was so crowded. A small bay caught my attention and I stared at it, unable to look away. The back of my neck tingled, and I yelled, "Stop!"

Rachel slammed on the brakes. "What's going on?"

I sprang from the cart and ran to the middle of the ring, oblivious to the horses around me, except for the bay. I never let him out of my sight. His rider turned to cut across the ring and trotted straight toward me. I didn't move and as they passed me, they were so close I could feel the heat coming off them.

"Milo," I said breathlessly and the horse halted in his tracks. The rider squeezed and kicked him, but he wouldn't budge.

"I knew it was you," I said, walking to him with my arms stretched out. "Hi, baby." I fixed my eye on his and smiled at him through my tears when he pushed his forehead into the palm of my hand.

Milo pulled against his rider's tight reins and in two steps, he was in my arms. I held him as he pressed his head against my torso and sighed deeply. When he lifted his head and put his chin on my shoulder, I began to cry harder.

"I miss you so much," I sniffed.

"Excuse me," the woman on Milo's back said impatiently.

I looked up at her. "Sorry," I said. "He used to be mine."

She nodded. "We should probably do this somewhere else."

"Do you own him now?" I asked as we left the ring.

"No, I'm just leasing him." She pulled Milo up as soon as we were safely by ourselves outside the schooling area.

Milo put his chin on my shoulder again. I closed my eyes, cherishing the sound and feel of his warm breath against the side of my face.

I asked the woman all about Milo, but she could tell me very little. The girl who owned him had, in fact, quit riding and he was for sale, but that was all she knew.

While we talked, I kept patting Milo. I stroked his cheeks and tickled the space between his ears. I was so happy; I wanted to hold onto him and never let go.

"Oh, look who's here." Rachel walked up to us leading Max. "I hate to cut this short, but you need to get on."

My hands tightened around Milo's face. "Rachel. Please."

Understanding exactly what I wanted her to do, she promised to find out what it would take to buy Milo back.

"Thank you," I said, wiping at my tears with gloved hands.

Letting go of Milo, I leaned forward and kissed his nose. I asked his rider which tent was Milo's before she turned him around. I hugged myself and watched them walk away. I couldn't breathe. I had the horrible feeling that I would never see Milo again.

"Can you try and focus on this one now?" Rachel asked, pointing at Max.

Max pinned his ears back as I moved to his side for a leg-up. Rachel helped me into the tack, and as I positioned myself in the saddle, she said, "Make it three in a row and as soon as we're done, I'll find out about Milo."

Distracted as I was, I managed to ride well enough to earn my third champion title, though by only half a point. I wanted to leave the ring immediately after the presentation, but I was waylaid by a second announcement directing us to the center of the ring for the Grand Champion award. Over three weeks, I had accumulated more points than any other rider at the show. Anyone else would have been ecstatic, but I was consumed with thoughts of Milo.

Rachel was already back at the stalls when I returned with Max. She looked at me and shook her head sadly.

"They still want a lot of money for him?" I guessed correctly.

"Yup," she replied, putting her arm around me.

"Do I have time to say goodbye to him before we leave?"

She looked away from me and pointed to an immense twelve-horse van as it rumbled by us.

"He's on that truck." Rachel hugged me tighter as Milo and I were parted for the second time.

As the weather got cooler, the jumps Rachel set for me got bigger. I was back to jumping three-six on Max, and as Rachel promised, starting over had made us a winning team.

I was on the way home from the barn the day after Thanksgiving when my cell phone rang. The caller was my friend Michele. A fellow rider, she wanted to know what was going on with Milo.

"I saw him this past summer. As far as I know, he's still in North Carolina. Why do you ask?"

"I know somebody who needs the best horse in the world and, of course, I thought of Milo."

Michele told me who her friends were, and I recognized the name. "They can afford any horse they want. Wouldn't they rather have one with less wear and tear than Milo?"

"He would be for their daughter," Michele explained. "She had a bad crash last year and hasn't ridden since. Then out of the blue, last week she announced she wants to ride again. Her parents called me, and I called you."

I gave Michele the number of the trainer in North Carolina and made her promise to let me know what happened.

I'd seen pictures in a magazine of the Virginia estate where Michele's friends lived, and I knew Milo would love the acres of fields and roomy stalls. If the family did buy Milo, he'd be less than a two-hour drive away. I didn't know Milo's potential new owners, but perhaps Michelle could convince them to let me visit him and even ride him. As I warmed to the idea, I became more and more excited.

If I can't have him, this could be the next best thing, I thought, already planning my first trip to Milo's new home.

After two weeks, I hadn't heard a word from Michelle. My mom was taking me to the grocery store when I gave up and called her.

"What happened with Milo?" I asked.

"Oh, I was going to call you," she said weakly. "I spoke to the trainer last week, and she said she sold him the day before I called."

"Sold him!" I cried. "Did she say who bought him?"

"She wouldn't say," Michele replied, her voice full of regret.

I hung up and turned to my mom. "He's gone," I said leaning my head against the window. "They sold him and I don't know who has him or where he is." Tears ran down my face and I angrily wiped them away.

"You can find out, though," my mom said hopefully. "You've kept track of him for this long. Just be patient. I'm sure he'll turn up somewhere."

"No," I said rubbing my temples. "I can't go on like this anymore. I made an unforgiveable mistake, and it has haunted me for more than two years. I have to let go of him. If I don't, I'll go crazy. I think about him so much that missing him has become a part of me."

"I know you miss him." She reached for my hand. "That's why I think you need to find him again."

"No," I said firmly. "After today, I don't want to talk about him anymore. I've lost him, and it's time I accept that."

Banishing Milo from my mind turned out to be impossible. The best I could do was refuse to speak about him. I stopped asking if anyone had seen him. I didn't tell anyone stories about Magic Milo. And if I saw something that reminded me of him, I kept it to myself.

I only slipped once, when I was in the car with my mom on the way to Rachel's for a birthday breakfast in my honor. It was unusually warm for January, the perfect day for galloping across a field on Milo. I hadn't meant to, but as I gazed out the window at the sunlit landscape, I whispered his name.

"Did you say something?" My mom took her eyes from the road long enough to give me an odd look.

"No," I lied.

Rachel outdid herself for my birthday. She decorated her kitchen with red, yellow, and blue balloons. Streamers of the same colors hung from the ceiling and in coils down the walls.

Three of my friends from the barn, wearing party hats, were sitting at the table and broke into song the minute I walked through the door. Rachel was warming bagels in the oven and when Mom and I took our places at the table, I saw platters of cucumbers, cream cheese, lox, tomatoes, and onions.

"Yummy!" I squealed. "All my favorites."

Mom and I split an everything bagel piled high with toppings. I was nearly finished when Rachel suddenly stood up.

"I almost forgot." She grinned at me, walked to the stove, and returned to the table with a plate of grilled cheese sandwiches. The one in the middle had a lit candle sticking out of it.

"Well, this is better than a cake," I smiled and blew out the candle.

"What did you wish for?" my friends asked.

Getting up from the table, my mom leaned over my shoulder and planted a kiss on my cheek. "Whatever it was, I hope it comes true."

It was such a nice morning, I was a little disappointed when Rachel announced, "I hate to break this up, but we have horses to ride." She went out for a moment, and we began to gather our things, when I heard her open the front door.

"I have a thought," she said, returning to the kitchen. "It's a shame to waste a day like this in the ring. Why don't we go for a trail ride?"

A chorus of cheers went up in response to Rachel's question.

Shoot. My mom was my ride home and she'd be stuck at the barn by herself if I went on a trail ride. I had to make sure she was okay with that, but I didn't want to interrupt the party and draw attention to my problem. My mom was standing next to me, and I gently pulled her aside so I could talk to her privately.

"Do you mind if I go?" I asked quietly. "I hate to abandon you but even if you wanted to come with us, I'm not sure there's a horse for you to ride. I'm not so sure I want to ride my horse," I added chuckling. "Max is wild out on the trails."

"Don't worry about me." She held her phone up. "I have a ton of calls to make, and I can get them all done while you're gone. Besides, Spike will keep me company."

Rachel and my barn mates went to the tack room, Mom walked to her car, and I went to Max's stall to say "hi" before I got dressed to ride.

"Uh-oh." I saw a silver horseshoe hanging on the stall door and frowned. Sometime between yesterday and today, Max's front shoe had come off.

He was kicking the stall door when I opened it and walked in. Sure enough, his right front foot was bare. Avoiding his teeth, I patted Max on the neck. "It's my birthday. Can you at least attempt to be nice?"

Rachel was still in the tack room going through a trunk but looked up when I walked in. I held Max's shoe out to her. "Looks like I'm a no-go."

"Your horse," she said shaking her head.

"Do you have an extra one I can take instead?"

I waited while Rachel went through a mental inventory of the horses in her barn.

"Normally I would, but with so many people here today, every horse is being used." Rachel took the shoe from me and frowned. "Do you want me to see if one of the girls wouldn't mind sitting this one out? It's your birthday after all."

I thanked Rachel for the offer but declined. There was nothing else for me to do but go home.

"Thank you for my party." I hugged her. "It was perfect."

On my way out the door, Rachel called me back. "Hold on, I just thought of something."

My hand still on the doorknob, I turned my head and looked at her.

"I had one come in last night, but I don't know much about him except he's an older show horse that was sent here to be sold. Why don't you bring him in from the far paddock and see what you think? Who knows, maybe you'll like him."

I didn't enjoy riding strange horses. Usually when a horse came in for Rachel to sell, she rode it before I did. I twisted the doorknob back and forth while I decided what to do.

"I guess I can give it a try. Do you care if I ride him in the ring for a few minutes first?"

"Go ahead." Rachel handed me a lead rope. "Do you mind bringing him in? All the grooms are busy."

Spike caught up with me on my way to the field. He danced around my feet, excited to be joining me on my walk.

Ignoring the heavy gate, I climbed the fence while Spike wriggled under it.

Kicking myself for forgetting to ask the horse's name, I started walking up the hill. I didn't dare take my eyes off the ground. No matter where I walked, it was wet and full of holes.

Every few feet, I stopped, looked around for the horse, then kept going. I also forgot to ask about his coloring and I hoped it wasn't gray or white. Dark colored horses were easier for me to see.

I saw what looked like tall, brown match sticks and knew I was looking at a grove of trees. They were bare now but if this weather kept up, they'd be leafing out soon.

I thought of the day Milo and I spent in this same field, galloping past the trees and up the hill all the way to the fence line. I could picture it so clearly in my head. The colors were so vivid that day, the grass was neon green. The trees had been full of leaves and Milo's little brown ears twitched back and forth whenever he heard a squirrel scampering along the branches.

The ache in my chest began. I looked at the ground ravaged by winter and blew out a deep breath. My memories of Milo were all I had left, and I looked forward to the day I could think about him without it causing me so much pain.

A warm breeze blew across my cheeks, and I continued my trek up the hill. It was getting hot, and I unzipped my jacket and fanned my face. I couldn't believe I was sweating in January.

I was nearing the top of the hill. I stopped again to see if I spotted anything horse-shaped. The breeze died down, making it possible for me to hear a faint sucking noise. The horse, I deduced, must be slogging through the mud in search of grass. I turned to the right and began walking in the direction of the sound.

The mid-morning sun was directly in front of me. I shielded my eye against its glare and looked toward the fence line, where I saw a hazy blur that suggested something big. When it moved, it glimmered as the sunlight bounced off it.

I stood very still, not wanting to spook the horse. He was snorting softly, and I assumed he'd run out of grass and was sniffing the barren ground for more.

"C'mon boy," I said impatiently. "The sooner you let me catch you, the sooner I'll feed you treats."

I was inching toward him when I heard a low whinny. I froze.

I knew that voice better than my own. Desperate to hear it again, to make sure I hadn't imagined it, I whispered, "Milo?"

Nothing.

He was looking at me. I could feel his eyes on me.

I'm losing it, I chastised myself. Logic was telling me there was no way I could be in a field with Milo. But something deep inside me defied logic. Even though I couldn't see Milo, I could sense him. My heart pounded and the tips of my fingers and toes tingled.

I said his name again and this time he answered.

The ground began to shake and a neigh that was more like a scream shattered the silence as he came galloping toward me.

"Milo!" I yelled and started running to him.

He was closer than I thought and, afraid I'd be trampled, I stopped in time for Milo to slide to a halt in front of me.

In shock, I stared at him.

He was so thin, his ribs stuck out, and his coat, once smooth and shiny, was stained from lying in his own waste. I could tell by his matted mane and the patches of dead hair covering his body that he hadn't been brushed in a long time. He smelled awful and I guessed it had been just as long since his last bath.

Nothing about this poor creature resembled my horse, but I had no doubt this was Milo.

"What are you doing here?" I asked as though he could answer me.

Milo grabbed the front of my jacket and pulled me to his chest. Then he dropped his head and hugged me. I held onto him, digging my fingers into his oily fur and pressing my face against his shoulder.

"I'm so sorry," I said over and over while my tears turned the hair on his neck black.

Spike barked at us, and I realized I should go back to the barn.

Milo stayed close to my side as we walked down the hill. When we came to the gate, I snapped the lead rope to his halter and led him to the top of the driveway where my mom and Rachel were waiting for us.

"I don't understand," I said, looking first at Mom and then at Rachel. "Milo was sent here to be sold?" My voice was rough from crying.

"No," my mom said gently, "he's here for you."

"I don't understand," I repeated. Milo put his chin on my shoulder, and I laid my cheek against his nose.

"I bought him back for you," my mom said, hugging me as best she could. "Happy Birthday."

"You mean," I raised my head and looked at my mom, "Milo's mine again?"

"Of course, he's yours." My extraordinary mother smiled through her tears. "He never stopped being your horse. He just needed to come home."

EPILOGUE

Milo came home in January 2006. He'd been gone for two-and-a-half years.

There were days I couldn't be near him without hating myself for letting him go. I spent hours in his stall apologizing, but Milo's wasted body and dull coat made it impossible for me to dismiss what I'd done to him. Upon closer inspection, I saw that his lower legs and ankles were thick with fluid and his hooves were cracked and rough. He never shied away from me, and I didn't see or feel any cuts or scabs, but there was a weariness about him that haunted me. Milo hadn't been physically abused but he'd definitely been neglected.

During the first few weeks of our reunion, I rode Milo up and down the hill in Rachel's field. The muscles in his back and hind end had started to atrophy, and Milo's stride, once strong and unwavering, felt weak and rickety. With each faltering step he took, I felt a fresh surge of guilt and shame.

Rachel claimed it was my imagination, but I was convinced that Milo was upset with me. He used to be all over me the moment I walked into his stall. Now, he ignored me as soon as I ran out of treats. I couldn't blame him, and while he stood with his back to me, I hung my head and told him how much I loved him, and that selling him was the greatest mistake of my life and I'd never leave him again.

Eventually, Milo began playing with my hair and resting his chin on my shoulder. His ears moved back and forth when I spoke to him and, even if my pockets were empty, he pulled on my clothes with his teeth until I was covered with streams of drool. It seemed Milo had forgiven me, though I doubted I would ever forgive myself.

After three months of daily exercise and grooming plus biweekly vet checks, Milo began to resemble the horse he was before I sold him. His stomach was nice and round, his neck and rump showed signs of muscle tone, and his body glowed with good health.

Even so, Milo was showing his age. X-rays revealed multiple signs of arthritis in his joints, and he no longer had enough push to safely clear a three-foot-six jump. As much as I wanted to go back to showing him in the Amateur Owner division, I knew Milo would never be able to compete at that level again.

By April, Milo was strong enough to clear a course of three-foot fences. Though we had nothing left to prove, I wanted to experience the thrill of showing him one last time. Rachel and I chose the Lexington Spring Premiere, a competition at the end of the month in Lexington, Virginia, where Milo was a hometown favorite.

Physically, Milo was ready to show, but I feared his competitive spark had been extinguished. During our daily rides, he did everything I asked without hesitation, but he never gave me anything extra.

My fears were put to rest when I led him off the trailer in Lexington. Holding his head high, he sniffed the air, arched his neck causing the muscle to bulge, sucked in his gut, and looked down at me with fire in his eye. I looked back and instead of seeing an arthritic fourteen-year-old horse ready to retire, I saw the Milo I'd always known—confident, powerful, and impossible to beat.

Rachel entered us in a division open to any competitor who wanted to jump three feet. There were four classes with eighty-seven professionals, juniors, and amateurs riding against us. The division began at 8:00 a.m. on the first day of showing. Fifty riders were ahead of me, and it would be hours before I had to get on.

I got to the ring at 7:00 to study the jumps and select the best markers. As was his custom, Milo touched each fence with his nose, sniffed the artificial flowers, then turned his head toward me and waited for his treat.

During Milo's absence, I'd walked hundreds of courses but never with another horse. Our pre-show routine was uniquely Milo's and mine. I was overjoyed but not surprised that Milo remembered his old habit, and I couldn't stop smiling.

The course was easy and, before long, I had everything memorized, but I wasn't ready to let my morning with Milo end. With my arm draped over his neck, we took a leisurely stroll around the ring until a show official asked us to leave.

Around noon, I got on Milo and rode him into the schooling ring. With his coat polished to a high shine and his mane and tail braided, Milo looked every bit the show horse, but as we warmed up, I again worried that he was no longer competitive. We jumped four practice fences and each one felt worse than the last. Milo went through the motions, but there was nothing exceptional about his performance.

I considered scratching, but instead, I gritted my teeth and steered Milo toward the show ring. Giving up went against my nature, and I still had faith in my horse and what we could accomplish together. I looked down at Rachel and recalled what she told me at Upperville: Jump the first fence, but if it doesn't feel right, you can always pull up.

I rode Milo to my first marker where I reminded him that he still had to take care of me. He pulled against the bit and shook his head as if telling me he was ready to go.

My hold on the reins relaxed and without hesitating, Milo began to canter. His pace grew stronger as we rounded the corner and started our approach to the first jump.

I expected Milo to jump the fence the way he did at home, barely missing the top rail and hardly picking his knees up once we were in the air. But my boy was full of surprises. He pushed off the ground with a mighty thrust, catching me off guard and jostling me loose in the saddle. I leaned over his neck in my jumping position as he left the ground and flew through the air.

Where did that come from?

We landed and Milo surged forward. I shoved my heels down in the stirrups and concentrated on finding my markers while I let Milo do what he did best. He sprung off the ground and cleared each fence by a foot. As we thundered down to the final jump, I dug my hands into his braids and said, "Get it, M."

Milo rocked back on his haunches, gave a tremendous push, and we soared over the fence.

Before we even hit the ground, I heard an explosion of whoops, whistles, and applause that continued until we left the ring. Flinging my arms around Milo's neck, I hugged him tightly as he slowed to a walk and looked back at me.

"Milo," I said through tears, "I missed you."

Our next three rounds were as good or better than the first. When we were finished, I leapt off Milo's back and loosened his girth, then stood in front of him to scratch his chin. He took a step forward and rested his head against my chest.

I let him stay there until one of Rachel's grooms tried to take him from me. I refused and led Milo back to the stalls where I untacked him, bathed him, and rubbed my exhausted horse with a towel until he was dry.

I was feeding Milo carrots when Rachel appeared at the stall door smiling and holding a stack of blue ribbons. We had won every class and were expected back in the ring to receive our champion ribbon.

"You did it, M," I told him as the tricolor was hung on his bridle. We posed for pictures and, although the photographer asked me twice to look at the camera, I couldn't stop staring at my miracle of a horse.

While the announcer congratulated us, I ran my finger down Milo's muzzle, following a path of hair that had become discolored by age. At that moment, I fully grasped how lucky we were to have each other. It literally took my breath away, and I was suddenly light-headed.

Our journey together—all our struggles and triumphs—was enough to fill several lifetimes. I leaned over and placed a kiss on Milo's nose.

"There will never be another horse like you," I said softly.

When Milo and I exited the ring, I could tell there was nothing left in him. His lids were half-closed, his head hung low, and I had to slow my walk to match his. I patted his neck, took the tricolor off his bridle, and realized I was wrong when I thought we didn't have anything left to prove.

On this day, Milo and I proved that neither time nor distance could weaken our bond.

I continued to compete on other horses, but never again on Milo. I still rode him at least five days a week and made sure he stayed strong and fit. Occasionally, I loaned him to a friend in need of a special horse. Milo was sent with a long list of instructions: He was never to be jumped higher than three feet, competing in more than two shows a month was out of the question, and under no circumstances could Milo go anywhere without my permission.

In 2012, I traded in my Maryland residency, and Spike, Milo, and I moved to Florida. I had two other horses that joined us later, but for the first four months it was just Milo and me. I boarded him at a barn less than ten miles from my house and visited him almost every day.

Now that Milo was retired from the show ring, there was no trainer telling us what to do. It was up to me to decide whether to ride Milo in the ring or in the fields surrounding the barn. Other times I chose not to ride him at all. Instead, I spent the day leading him around the grounds, letting him graze as I described the minutiae of my life, reminisced about our good old days in the show ring, and wondered aloud what he might like to do in the future.

At some point, I began to think of Milo as my friend more than my horse. I counted on him to be my sounding board, and although I didn't have the benefit of his opinion, I was sure he had one.

While riding Milo in late September 2013, I felt a weakness in his hind end, as if his legs were dragging a little bit. I hoped some time off would solve the problem. But a week later, the joints in Milo's front and back legs felt warm and swollen, and when he walked, his ankles were stiff.

I called his vet who made it out to the barn the following day. I watched closely as he lifted each of Milo's feet and gently flexed each joint. He seemed to know what he was doing and although he hadn't been Milo's vet for long, he came highly recommended.

I was worried that Milo had a torn ligament or an abscess in his foot. Both can be extremely painful and cause so much damage that Milo could never be ridden again.

Much to my relief, the doctor couldn't find any trauma to Milo's legs or feet. The stiffness, he said, was due to old age, but a few drops of steroid would loosen up Milo's joints and he'd feel better in no time. I let my breath out with a whoosh and sagged against Milo's chest as the tension left my neck and shoulders.

The vet promised to use half the usual dosage since medication such as steroids can have an adverse reaction in horses, especially older ones. A groom took Milo to one of the wash racks and scrubbed each of his legs with iodine. The vet gave him a shot to make him sleepy and within seconds, Milo's eyes closed and his lower lip drooped.

Twice, I had to stop myself from reaching out and patting him. The simple act could send dirt and hair flying, and the last thing I wanted to do was contaminate the injection sites. Finally, I crossed my arms and held them firmly against my chest while I told Milo how special he was.

The entire procedure took less than thirty minutes and when Milo was awake enough, I led him back to his stall.

To avoid complications such as infection, the vet instructed me to give Milo two full days of stall rest. On the third day, I could lead him around the grounds for twenty minutes. After four days, I could start riding him again, but I had to go easy on him for the rest of the week.

I did exactly as I was told. I visited Milo the next day and groomed him while he stood in his stall. I checked his bandages and took his temperature. Everything seemed fine.

Three days out, I led Milo from the stall and though my back was to him, I could tell by the sound of his hooves against the concrete that something was wrong. Instead of four even beats, I heard quick, erratic steps, as if Milo couldn't put any weight on his front feet. I whirled around and saw him take a step that looked like he was walking on shards of glass.

In a panic, I yelled for a groom to come help me. I handed him the lead rope and asked him to walk Milo up and down the aisle.

Horror overtook me and I found it hard to breathe as I watched Milo stagger toward me. His front feet could barely hold him up and each step sent a slice of fear through me. The groom was also upset and when he halted Milo in front of me, I could tell the man was shaking his head sadly.

I leaned over and didn't even have to touch Milo's hooves to feel the heat radiating from them. The groom raced to his cottage next to the barn and returned within a few minutes, lugging two buckets of ice water.

While Milo's feet soaked, I called the vet. I left two hysterical messages and waited an hour before he returned my call. Despite my insistence that he examine my horse, the vet refused, saying I should call the farrier instead because there must be something wrong with Milo's shoes.

The farrier, who had put new shoes on Milo the day before without any trouble, was surprised to hear from me, but he was in the area and agreed to come out. He said the shoes looked fine, but he removed them anyway. Milo was still lame, a clear sign of an internal problem, rather than an external one.

After the farrier left, I called the vet five or six times, but he didn't call me back. In a murderous rage, I threw my phone on the ground and collapsed on the grass next to it. Hot, angry tears filled my eyes, and I covered my face with my hands, indulging in a few seconds of hysteria before reminding myself I had a sick horse that needed me.

Now is not the time to fall apart.

I suspected Milo was foundering, which meant something had disrupted the blood flow in his feet, making them severely inflamed and putting pressure on the bone structure. If left untreated, founder will cripple a horse for life. In the worst-case scenario, the pedal bone will break through the sole of the foot causing excruciating pain, and the horse must be shot and killed immediately. Milo needed expert care and though my list of equestrian veterinarians was long, none of them lived in Florida year-round.

For four days I stayed with Milo in his stall, keeping him hydrated and his feet packed in ice. I called every vet I knew, hoping they'd refer me to someone nearby who could help Milo. I followed every lead to no avail, my panic increasing with each dead end.

Sometimes, too agitated to sit still, I paced the small area in front of Milo's stall trying to decide what to do and who to call next. I ran my hands through my hair until it fell out and I mumbled to myself in low, strained tones. I looked and felt like I was losing my mind. My stomach was in knots, and I was often doubled over by nausea.

Between phone calls, I held onto my sweet horse and sobbed. He was suffering and I couldn't make it stop.

By the fourth day, I must have called over twenty veterinary clinics. Finally, I was given the name and number of a local specialist, but a recorded voice informed me that the doctor was out of town and wouldn't be back for two weeks.

Desperate, I called Milo's vet and after pleading with him, he agreed to meet me at the barn the next day. Before Milo could hobble all the way out of his stall, the vet determined that he had a bad case of laminitis, another term for founder.

My cheeks flushed with barely contained rage. I thought of the invective I wanted to hurl at him for not coming to Milo's aid sooner, but I dug my nails into my palms and stayed quiet. I wasn't going to verbally attack the only vet in town who could take care of my horse.

While he examined Milo, he reminded me that founder is one of the risks of giving steroids to an older horse. Months later, I learned that the reason Milo foundered may have been more complicated than that.

Knowing I couldn't read Milo's medical bills and records, a friend — who was also a vet — asked to take a look at them. He discovered that Milo was vaccinated the same week he was injected with steroids. Had I known about the vaccines, I wouldn't have permitted the steroids. Injecting the two types of medication within the same week is a common cause of founder. I'll never be certain, but since the same vet administered Milo's vaccines and steroid injections, I believe he may have made a mistake.

After a month of medication and continued ice packs, the inflammation had gone down but Milo still couldn't walk. I fired the vet and replaced him with the local specialist, who had recently returned to Florida. He prescribed a different course of medication, altered Milo's diet, and warned me to watch my horse very closely because any change in his behavior could indicate that the inflammation was spiking and he was foundering again. I knew if that happened, it would be fatal.

Convinced I was going to lose Milo, I lived in a constant state of fear. When my phone rang, I panicked. If Milo sneezed, I called his vet. Soon, I was waking up in the middle of the night, drenched in sweat and hyperventilating.

When I wasn't home, I was with Milo in his stall. I wept until I choked on my own tears. I played music for him. I sang to him and never missed a chance to let him know how much I loved him.

Just before Christmas, Milo began to show signs of improvement. One morning when I got to the barn, I found him standing in his stall and he greeted me with a nicker — which he hadn't done in weeks. For the next few days, he got to his feet as soon as he saw me and stayed standing a little longer each day. During his weekly checkup, X-rays of his feet showed no inflammation and the vet seemed confident that he wasn't in pain anymore.

For the first time in months, I was happy. Milo was going to survive. I'd never be able to ride him again, but that didn't matter. All I wanted was for Milo to live free of pain and eventually be allowed to leave his stall. I promised him as soon as that day came, I'd lead him to the greenest grass I could find and once again he'd feel the warmth of the sun on his back.

Less than twenty-four hours after the vet told me Milo was getting better, I could tell by his expression that something was wrong. I took his temperature and he had a fever. I felt his feet and they were hot, and I knew he was foundering again.

The vet came out right away and confirmed that nothing could be done to save Milo. I stared at the doctor, unable or, more likely, unwilling, to comprehend what he was telling me. Each word—"bone," "pain," "destroyed"—felt like a punch in the face. All I wanted to do was escape, and I started backing away from the vet and the terrible things he was saying. But I couldn't avoid his prognosis. Milo was going to have to be put down.

"No," I repeated over and over while shaking my head violently. "Please, no." I barely got the words out before falling to my knees in front of the vet.

I looked up at him, tears pouring out of my eyes as I placed my hands over my breaking heart. "Don't make me do this," I wailed.

The vet couldn't force me to do anything, but when he described the pain Milo would be in when the bone came through his foot, I had no choice but to sign the paper giving permission to end Milo's life.

My hand shook so badly, I dropped the pen three times before I managed to scrawl my name under the vet's.

I asked if I could have one day to make arrangements and say goodbye. The vet said that was fine but not a minute longer, and before he left he injected Milo with something to dull the pain.

I called Bob, who had recently arrived in Florida, and he met me at the barn early the next morning. We got Milo up and very slowly led him from his stall to the nearest patch of grass. I kept my promise and let him eat as much grass as he wanted as the sun beamed down on us. Bob and I watched him quietly. We tried telling our favorite Milo stories, like the first time Bob showed him, or our encounter with an enormous gator on a trail ride in Wellington. But soon we were both crying too hard to finish.

When the equine clinic called around noon to let me know the vet was on the way, Bob left so I could spend my last hour with Milo in private.

I leaned against his shoulder and fought a losing battle to hold back my howls of pain. Somehow, I managed to get hold of myself. There were things I had to say to him.

I thanked Milo for making my life worth living and shakily confessed to wishing I could go with him. I told him my love for him would never end. I would love him after he was gone and even after I was gone, too.

Milo, oblivious to what was happening, continued to graze and to enjoy being out of his stall. He seemed so happy; it was hard to believe he would be dead in less than an hour.

Sickened by the thought, I whirled around, bent over, and felt my empty stomach heave. When I was able to stand up straight, I moved to Milo's side and rested my head against his warm belly.

"I don't want to live without you."

I could feel and hear Milo's heart beat, and it was strong and slow. I hated that I'd never hear it again.

Unlike Milo's, my heart was racing, and my chest ached from grief. I couldn't feel my legs and grabbed onto Milo's neck to keep from collapsing. Consumed by sorrow, I didn't know he reached around me until I felt the heavy weight of his chin on my shoulder and a stream of warm air on my face.

Milo inhaled and then sent another breath dancing across my cheek. I rested my forehead against his and stared into his golden eye, so close to my face that his long lashes tickled my nose.

We stood like that until I heard the rumble of an SUV coming up the driveway.

"You're the love of my life," were my last words to Milo before he was gone forever.

A week later, Spike was diagnosed with liver cancer, and I told him he was not allowed to leave me yet. He made it another three months before I had to say goodbye to little Spikers, too.

I carry the memory of my boys, my Milo and my Spike, wherever I go. I can only hope if they are somewhere, they are together. Maybe one day I'll be lucky enough to see them again.

I live in Wellington now and continue to ride and compete. Each year I lose more vision, but Milo taught me that it takes heart, not sight, to be a successful rider.

Every now and then, someone will tell me about a horse that is "just like Milo."

I smile and nod, but I know there will never be another Milo. He was, after all, magic.

ACKNOWLEDGEMENTS

First and foremost, I would like to thank my editor, Margo Melnicove. Margo, you forced me to dig down inside myself until we reawakened the past. Despite a river's worth of tears, a mountainous load of frustration, and a lifetime's worth of computer glitches, you helped bring my boy back to life. It's the second greatest gift I've been given, and I could fill another book with words of gratitude. In my heart, you are the only one with whom I ever want to search for synonyms.

Robert Crandall has the unique ability to see potential in horses and humans. Thank you, Bob, for finding my Milo for me and never giving up on me. You are the truest of friends.

The unstoppable R.B.K., to say you go the extra mile is an understatement. The only thing better than having you for a trainer is having you for a friend.

E.B. Castleman, this project began with you, and I will treasure the hours we spent together in Starbucks. Just the two of us, your computer, and cake pops. I couldn't ask for a better sister.

Howard Castleman, thank you for bringing love, laughter, and a sense of family into my life. I was in dire need of all of it.

Thank you, Aunt Karen, for all the red-eyes you've taken on my behalf. You have inspired me, loved me, and fiercely protected me. You are the best aunt anyone could wish for. I love you.

Wendy Fields, thank you for always picking up the phone when I called for advice or simply needed to hear my "Aunt" Wendy's voice.

To my friends at Brass Ring Farm: Amber, Tommy, and Sally. Thank you for giving Milo his final resting place.

Carolyn and Joe Sargent, this book would not exist if you hadn't put the idea in my head. Thank you for the years of support, coaching, and cheerleading.

Sonja Massie, thank you for the emails and long phone conversations.

Dr. Diane Schiereck, thank you for being you.

Ben Phillips, Jacob Pope, Kim Stewart, Lena Horowitz, Erica Quinn, Sam Scales, Susan Conoby, Molly Sewell, and Kris Livengood, it is an honor to count you all as my horse show family. Thank you.

To Lynn Price my editor, publisher, and friend. Thank you for believing in Milo and me. Your insight and kindness have been invaluable throughout this journey, and I couldn't have asked for a better champion and role model.